THE STORIES
WHITENESS
TELLS ITSELF

THE STORIES WHITENESS TELLS ITSELF

RACIAL MYTHS AND OUR
AMERICAN NARRATIVES

DAVID MURA

UNIVERSITY OF MINNESOTA PRESS
MINNEAPOLIS
LONDON

A different version of "How We Think—or Don't Think—about It" was published in *About Place Journal* 6, no. 3. Portions of "The Contemporary White Literary Imagination" and "Racial Absence and Racial Presence in Jonathan Franzen and ZZ Packer" were published in *AWP Chronicle* and *A Stranger's Journey: Race, Identity, and Narrative Craft in Writing*; reprinted with the permission of the University of Georgia Press. A version of "White Memory and the Psychic Sherpa" was published in *Brevity*, issue 67 (May 2021). A version of "Black Lives Matter and the Social Contract" was published in *Gulf Coast Literary Journal*.

Published by the University of Minnesota Press
111 Third Avenue South, Suite 290
Minneapolis, MN 55401-2520
http://www.upress.umn.edu

ISBN 978-1-5179-1454-7 (pb)

A Cataloging-in-Publication record for this book is available from the Library of Congress.

Printed in the United States of America on acid-free paper

The University of Minnesota is an equal-opportunity educator and employer.

30 29 28 27 26 25 24 23 22   10 9 8 7 6 5 4 3 2 1

For Tadashi, Tomo, Nikko, Samantha, Lance, and Susie.
And for Alexs Pate.

Not every problem can be solved. But no problem can be solved unless it is faced.

—James Baldwin

The subject of drama is The Lie. At the end of the drama THE TRUTH—which has been overlooked, disregarded, scorned, and denied—prevails. And that is how we know the Drama is done.

—David Mamet

Contents

PART III. WHERE DO WE GO FROM HERE?

APPENDIX: A BRIEF GUIDE TO STRUCTURAL RACISM

Introduction

I

Race in America has long been framed as a Black–white dialogue and struggle. That dialogue and struggle are the subject of this book.

Yet I come to race as a Sansei, a third-generation Japanese American. That term places me within a specific ethnic and racial history. During World War II, as a result of Executive Order 9066, my parents and grandparents were imprisoned by the U.S. government in Jerome, Arkansas, and Minidoka, Idaho, two of the internment camps placed throughout desolate areas of the American West and South. Born in Seattle and Los Angeles, my parents were citizens, and they were just eleven and fifteen when incarcerated behind barbed wire fences and rifle towers with armed guards. My immigrant grandparents were barred by racist laws from becoming citizens or owning land. No Japanese American was ever convicted of espionage, and there's evidence that the FBI determined the Japanese American community was not a military threat. And yet 120,000 mainland Japanese Americans were imprisoned without a trial or a writ of habus corpus and denied their basic Constitutional rights.

In 1988, President Ronald Reagan and the U.S. Congress apologized to the Japanese American community for their unjust imprisonment. Both Reagan and the Congress admitted that the real cause for the camps was not military necessity but "racism, wartime hysteria, and a failure of leadership."[1] Unfortunately, in our current Trumpian America, the

---

1. In 2016, candidate Donald Trump was asked about the internment camps; displaying his vast ignorance of American history in general and of this apology in specific, he replied, "I don't know. You would have had to be there at the time." In 1981, legal researcher Peter Irons uncovered evidence that the government had information refuting a War Department claim that the Japanese community was disloyal and that government attorneys suppressed this evidence from the Supreme Court. This led to the overturning of the conviction of Fred

lessons of that apology have again been forgotten. The internment of Japanese Americans and the racism that caused it are now mirrored by present-day anti-immigrant sentiment, xenophobia, and religious bigotry, and the internment is cited by certain conservatives as a precedent for any number of anti-immigrant and anti-Muslim measures.

Despite this history—or, rather, paradoxically because of it—I grew up wanting to be thought of as white. For mine was a family that fervently believed in an assimilation into Whiteness. The internment camps criminalized my parents' race and ethnicity (nothing similar was done to German or Italian Americans). The implied message, which my parents took in both consciously and unconsciously, was that you must try to shed your Japanese cultural roots, don't make waves, imitate a white middle-class identity you will never quite achieve. Growing up in a white, mainly Jewish suburb of Chicago, I, like my father, diligently worked to blend in with the white majority, to erase my difference. When one of my white friends said to me, "I think of you, David, just like a white person," I felt embraced, like I had achieved something.

One implication of such a personal history: I know intimately how it is to think like a white person. A white person is what I wanted to be, what I studied to be. I lived in a white community; all my friends were white with the exception of a few Japanese and Chinese Americans. I learned and eagerly believed in the stories Whiteness tells itself—about our history, about who we are as a country, about what it means to be a white American. When I write here of Whiteness, I am in part referencing my younger self and what America taught me about the practices and beliefs concerning white identity.

As a child of the baby boomer generation, I imbibed the films and television shows that portrayed American history as a paean to unblemished patriarchal white heroes, from Charlton Heston's Andrew Jackson to the various hagiographies of Lincoln to Errol Flynn's Custer and John Wayne fighting the savage Indians. I looked up to these white heroes, saw myself in them, and felt their terror at darker-skinned human beings (including the Japanese in *Sands of Iwo Jima*), just as I felt the terror of

Korematsu in 1983 where Judge Marilyn Hall Patel proclaimed, "I would like to see the government admit they were wrong and do something about it so this will never happen again to any American citizen of any race, creed, or color."

white colonists facing the Mau Mau revolutionaries in some film I don't recall the name of, but only their terror of Blackness. The only childhood picture I have of America's chattel slavery comes from *Gone with the Wind,* a clear product of the myth of the Lost Cause. I thought of Robert E. Lee as a noble and honorable American, who fought for the South only because of his love for his fellow Southerners and not to defend slavery; indeed, I did not even think of him as a slave owner but as a military genius. I had the suburban white child's fear of the inner city, its "ghettos" and "Negro" inhabitants. Watching *West Side Story,* I identified with the white Jets, not the Puerto Rican Sharks. Even after reading *The Autobiography of Malcolm X* as a sophomore in high school, I still thought of him as a dangerous radical and the Nation of Islam as a frightening entity. As I grew older, and especially in college, I began to question our society's portraits of American history and race relations and came to see the legitimacy of Malcolm's positions on race. Yet I still continued to identify with Whiteness and white people and to desire to be "just like a white person."

Late in my twenties, as a result of reading Black writers like Frantz Fanon, James Baldwin, and Toni Morrison, I finally admitted to myself that I was not white and would never be white. I began then to question and investigate my own racial and ethnic identity. I had to discover who I actually was. This meant reexamining my own racial experiences, the history of my family, and the ways I had been taught by Whiteness to think about race. I had to reexamine my own understanding of American and world history, of who I thought white people were, and who I thought Black people and other people of color were. I had to begin constructing a new story about myself, my family, and what our history as a country has been. This led me to understand that the stories I had been told by Whiteness about Whiteness were filled with lies, distortions, and denials. I began to live a very different life, becoming part of the local community of artists and activists of color, teaching courses and giving talks on race, teaching creative writing at VONA (Voices of Our Nations Arts), a national organization for writers of color, writing books that explored my identity and racial issues.

Looking over what I've written in this book, I am taken aback by how far my understanding of race in America has traveled from when I was a third-generation Japanese American kid growing up in a Jewish suburb of Chicago, wanting to be considered white. Unlike most Black writers, very little of my understanding of race derives from my family and the racial/ethnic culture I was brought up in. Since my late twenties (I am in my sixties now) I have been working, writing, studying, and living to educate myself about race both in our history and in our present.

Yet even when I was young and did not want to be considered a person of color, some part of me fervently believed in the promise of America, in equality and democracy, in Lincoln the great Emancipator, in the words written on the Statue of Liberty and her accompanying torch of freedom. I still believe in these things. This book is part of my efforts to bring us closer to that promise.

But a promise is not reality.

———

For my entire adult life I have lived in the Twin Cities, moving here to attend English graduate school and staying in part because of the strong local support for artists. When I first arrived in 1974, the cities were mainly white, with a large portion of Scandinavians. There was a Native American neighborhood in which I lived as a student and near where I live now; there were some Black neighborhoods, initially the product of the Great Migration north. But as the years passed, the Twin Cities became more and more diverse, with influxes of various immigrant populations—Vietnamese, Laotian, Hmong, Cambodian, Karen, Mexican, Somali, Ethiopian, Eritrean, Tibetan, Liberian, Bosnian, South Asian Indian, and many others.

Because of this history, in many areas of the Twin Cities different ethnicities and races mingle together; in certain areas, there aren't the rigid geographical boundaries that one finds in many other American cities, particularly on the East Coast. Unlike the almost all-white suburban high school I attended, my children went to a high school that was 20 percent Native American, 20 percent African American and African immigrants (Somali, Eritrean, Ethiopian), 10 percent Asian (Hmong, Vietnamese), and 30 percent white (with some Bosnian immigrants). I've coached my sons' park and school basketball teams with Black, Somali, Eritrean, Tibetan, Mexican, Native, and white kids.

The artistic community here is equally diverse and very politically active. Certainly, there are ethnic and racial tensions here, as in any American city, but this intermingling and the fact that this is not a huge metropolitan area mean that there are also connections among communities. Once while I was attending Hmong Day at the Minnesota State Fair, the Hmong emcee Tou Xer Xiong shouted from the stage, "How many of you have a Black person in your family?" and after cheers of positive responses, Xiong added, "Yeah, we all do. And we all have a white person in our families, too." In other words, our lives in the Twin Cities, our connections, are close. When something happens to someone here, we may know that someone or know someone who knows that someone.

I start this book with an essay on the death in 2016 of an African American man, Philando Castile, who was shot and killed by a police officer in a routine traffic stop in a near suburb of St. Paul. The site of this shooting is not more than a couple of miles from my home and it's a notorious speed trap. I have driven down that stretch of Larpenteur Avenue hundreds of times and even gotten a couple of tickets for speeding. But I don't think I have ever been in danger there in the ways Castile was obviously in danger. Because of my proximity to the site of Castile's murder and because I know people who knew him and know members of the Black community in St. Paul, his life and death felt particularly close to me. But the implications of his death are more than local, and the reasons why he was killed stem back to the beginnings of this country. His murder can be seen as a direct result of the ways that whites have enforced and interpreted the dictates of race, the ways whites have tried to script not only their own lives but the lives of people of color.

As I began to examine the implications of Castile's murder and the killings of Michael Brown in Ferguson, Freddie Gray in Baltimore, and other killings that sparked the Black Lives Matter movement, it confirmed my belief that our inability to deal with our racial disparities and injustice stems in part from the inadequacy of the language we use to examine and define racism. I reread the essays of James Baldwin and taught a course on his writings, tracing the development of his thinking and his incisive dissections not just of contemporary America but of America's depictions of its past. That in turn led me back into our racial history, from slavery onward, and the ways that history still structures and inhabits our present racial realities and narratives on race. And though I had been reading about race in literature all my adult life and had taught creative writing workshops on writing about race, I found myself now poring over recent studies in the history of race, the philosophy of race, psychology and race, political science and race, linguistics and race, economics and race—all the while moving deeper and deeper into the origins and lineage of Whiteness.

What is Whiteness? It is far more multifaceted than many recognize. In part, it consists of prescriptions and prohibitions for white behavior and thought, a set of dos and don'ts and beliefs about our society. These behaviors and beliefs have served to protect and preserve the racial status quo from the very beginning of America—the ways power is distributed unequally and undemocratically in our society through the categories of race. Here our history and our stories of the past come to have a greater effect on contemporary America than is generally acknowledged: how we narrate and interpret our racial past structures how we narrate and interpret our racial present.

In the process of creating their histories, white people certainly excluded the lives and consciousness of Black people; they came to record a history from which Black people were rendered almost invisible or only in negative stereotypes. At the same time, as recorded by white people, this history not only distorts the actions of whites in the past and the depth of white historical racism, but it now distorts white perceptions and judgments of our present moment. In conducting a historical racial excavation, in this book I examine the ideological origins of Whiteness through accounts of our past—Jefferson's defense of slavery, Lincoln's racism, the backlash of Reconstruction, and the attempts to re-create slavery in the post–Civil War era. I then link these accounts to modern and contemporary depictions both of this past and our racial present (including Trump's call to "Make America Great Again").

Everywhere we look in contemporary America, there is the white story of what has happened and the stories witnessed and created by BIPOC America. A key example is the recent spate of controversial racial incidents involving the police and the justice system, such as the murder of Philando Castile. The reason there is now controversy regarding such killings is less because white America has started to believe the stories, the knowledge, and the words of Black America, but because technology (mainly in the form of cell phone videos and police dash and body cams) has caught up with American racism. Black Americans have been telling of abuses and injustices, of the murders of Blacks by the police since the end of the Civil War, but that did not matter to white America; white America saw no reason to listen to or to take seriously the words of these witnesses. It's not so much the conscience of white America but the technology of visual recordings that has forced white America to begin to confront the truths, stories, and epistemology of Black America.

———

There is now a Philando Castile Memorial near the spot where he was killed, a large wooden plaque with the dates of his birth and death and a message from his mother, Valerie Castile: "Son, you never talked much here. But you're making a lot of noise now, baby!" That noise is certainly the senseless waste of his death and the grief and anger of his loved ones and his community, but that noise also highlights a white story and a Black story about his death: those stories stem from two very different epistemologies and ontologies, two very different ways of witnessing and interpreting not just what happened on Larpenteur Avenue on July 6, 2016, but our entire history and who we are as a nation.

When I started this book, I did not envision how it would end: I finished most of this manuscript before the 2020 Memorial Day murder of George Floyd by veteran police officer Derek Chauvin and three Minneapolis police officers outside a mini market, Cup Foods. The ensuing protests of police killings gathered into an unprecedented movement not just to reform our justice system but to address racism in all areas of American society.

Again, this killing felt very close to me—and to my family. George Floyd was murdered three miles from my home, in the neighborhood where my daughter lives and works with young people. The Third Precinct where many of the protests focused is six blocks from her home. My son works in a high school half a mile from Cup Foods, and he knows Darnella Frazier, the brave seventeen-year-old who took the central video of the murder. Both my sons went to school with the fire department EMT who tried to intervene to save George. The hospital where my wife works is a mile down the street from Cup Foods. I've danced with her at the Latin club where George Floyd worked as a bouncer, perhaps even on a night he was there.

That my book now begins and ends with essays on the killing of two black men by police just a few miles from my home is a tragic, cruel, and telling irony. Their lives and their deaths are now part of the American story, and as an American I regard their stories as part of me. These men were fellow citizens, members of my community; this entire book is in part a response to Philando Castile's murder and my desire to understand the roots of the police killings of George Floyd and others in my community. At the intersection where Floyd was murdered, there is now a memorial, echoing that of Philando Castile: "George, you changed the world." We are still a long way from racial equality and justice in this country, but maybe, just maybe, the recent activism and shifts in public opinion on race signal a change, and we are now perhaps beginning to work toward the next stage of that fight.

II

From its very beginnings America had two irreconcilable goals. One was to seek equality, freedom, and democracy. The other was to maintain white supremacy and the domination by white people over any people of color.[2] White America is fine with telling our tale through the lens of the first goal. But it is still decidedly not fine with telling the second story of America's treatment of people of color and America's desire to maintain white supremacy. All the recent ridiculous distorting, disparaging, and damning of Critical Race Theory are just the latest manifestation of this repression.

Instead, this second tale, the tale of BIPOC America, is regarded as un-American, unpatriotic, a smear on the past, an abomination to the present—or at best, a minor element. According to some, this story can

---

2. The enslavement of Blacks, the genocide of Native Americans, and the taking of their land started more than a century before the Declaration of Independence and the writing of the Constitution: white supremacy might arguably be said to be America's first goal. Certainly, the structuring of white identity through the categories of Whiteness and Blackness took place long before the colonists thought of breaking from Great Britain or formulating the principles of equality and democracy as a basis for our country.

never be integrated with the story of America's noble pursuit of its ideal goals. And this is an essential way white America has lied to itself: it has denied the voices of people of color as an essential and defining part of America's tale; it has denied their validity as Americans; it has denied that their history is also the history of white America—however white America wants to deny that fact. For the story of white America cannot be understood without comprehending how inextricably and intrinsically that story is intertwined and united with the story of Black America, of Indigenous America, of Americans of color.

Arkansas Senator Tom Cotton can describe slavery as a "necessary evil" that is safely in our past and needs no further reference. Cotton was in part responding to a curriculum based on "The 1619 Project: A New Origin Story" of the *New York Times,* which placed the initiation of slavery and its aftereffects as central to the telling of the American story. In a revealing example of how systemic racism works, Senator Cotton concocted a bill, the Saving American History Act, whose purpose was to "prohibit federal funds from being made available to teach the 1619 Project curriculum in elementary schools and secondary schools, and for other purposes." According to Cotton, the project "threatens the integrity of the Union by denying the true principles on which it was founded."

In arguing this, Cotton illustrates a common racist trope: Whiteness makes itself the victim of its own crimes and then tells that tale to itself. Cotton transforms any statement of the fact that white people have been abusing Black people since 1619 into a threat to white people, not to Black people; after all, it is not Black people who think the 1619 Project is a threat to our Union. Frankly, as my verb suggests, this is an abuser's psychology on a group level. The problem isn't what white people have done to Black people, but that Black people keep remembering what white people have done—and somehow that harms white people and victimizes them. To which Black people might reply, "If we can remember and live with the past and what your ancestors have done to our ancestors, why is it you can't remember and live with that same past? Are you that fragile?"[3]

---

3. Some white people might then say, "Well, that was our ancestors, not us." To which Blacks might reply, "If that's the case, why should it bother you that we are telling what your ancestors did if they don't have anything to do with you or the present?" But then someone like Cotton does want to remember his ancestors: he wants to remember the Founding Fathers or

Unfortunately, the tales of white victimhood go back to slavery—slavery is not an act of terror, only the slave rebellion is—and then on to the myth of the Lost Cause (but of course we can see this rush to white victimhood in any account of police killings of unarmed Black Americans).

Specifically, Cotton objected to the project's assertion that the introduction of slavery could be seen as the creation of America's racial categories and thus the definition of Whiteness, and that this could then be viewed as the origin of America. He also objected to the assertion by many historians that part of the reason the colonists declared their independence from Britain was to ensure the preservation of slavery. In other words, Cotton is perfectly fine with telling the story of America through the lens of the principles of equality, freedom, and democracy and white heroism, but he cannot countenance the story of America where white supremacy is initiated and maintained and plays a central and *inextricable* role in our history; he wants to wish away—or legislate away—the fact that this activity was supported by many of those whites whom he regards as heroes.

In viewing slavery as a "necessary evil," Cotton can assert this without really examining whether slavery was truly necessary, or how deeply evil it was and what that evil entailed—in particular, how it helped formulate white identity. Historian David Eltis argues that it would have been far cheaper to take slaves out of European prisons and poorhouses. But as Frank Wilderson III, citing Eltis, points out in *Red, White & Black: Cinema and the Structure of U.S. Antagonisms,* "what Whites would have gained in economic value, they would have lost in symbolic value, and it is the latter which structures the libidinal economy of civil society." In other words, if whites had been made slaves, the value of Whiteness, its force as an

---

perhaps Robert E. Lee, but he doesn't want to remember they had slaves, and he doesn't want Black people to remember that either or say that out loud. So the past is important to Cotton but only his definition of the past, his white version of the past. When white people say to people of color, "Why can't you let the past go?" the reply might be, "Why can't *you* let the past go?" The current outcry against Critical Race Theory and the 1691 Project can be seen in part as a recurrence of white backlash, which is one of the themes of this book—in this case, a white backlash against how protests over George Floyd's murder moved the country to confront and address racial inequities and police brutality. Invoking this aspect of American history, Nikole Hannah-Jones, creator of the 1619 Project, said to the *Los Angeles Times,* "This idea that racial reckoning has gone too far and now white people are the ones suffering is the most predictable thing in the world if you understand American history."

instrument of social and group cohesion, its ability to Other and oppress those of different races, would have been lost or severely diminished.

Certainly in blithely proclaiming the necessity of slavery Cotton is not regarding as primary or utterly abhorrent the destruction of Black lives and bodies and families. He doesn't want to think about those Black lives, and that is why he objects to the *New York Times*'s 1619 Project, which tells the tale of Blacks in America since its inception. Of course, all this denial of history bears a direct connection to his lack of concern for Black lives in the present, to his belief that the mere phrase *Black Lives Matter* is blasphemous and an attack on America—and in actuality, it *is* an attack on his version, his white story of America. Certainly, he does not see the story of Black Americans as his story, too. And if you cannot face clearly the more obvious and egregious racism of the past and the way it destroyed Black lives, how can you see and face the damage and destruction of Black lives in what Cotton believes is a less racist present?

But then, if Cotton is not interested in the destruction of Black lives in the present or the past, neither is he interested in the destruction of white souls and their moral compass. For this destruction was intrinsic to slavery, since slavery demanded an acceptance of evil that challenged and defeated the moral compasses of our Founding Fathers. Nor is Cotton open to acknowledging that slavery was essential to the wealth and building of America and to America's transition into a modern superpower; he can still maintain that the story of 1619 doesn't need to be central to the telling of the American story. And of course Cotton just knows that any questions or problems concerning race in America have long ago been solved, and he, like many Americans, probably still believes that slavery ended with the Emancipation Proclamation, or that segregation, racial violence, systemic discrimination, and hatred against Blacks ended with the passing of civil rights laws.

Beyond all this, what Cotton surely cannot acknowledge is our divided struggle toward the goals of equality, freedom, and democracy, and our true past where white supremacy reigned.

––––––

Throughout our history, a portion of white America, much larger than we can admit even now, fiercely fought to maintain white supremacy, its institutions and practices—slavery, genocide, white-settler colonialism, racial violence against Blacks, Jim Crow, racial profiling and brutality in policing, racial redlining, the invention of myriad forms of discrimination. This white America sincerely and deeply desired to maintain the benefits of an unjust, undemocratic, and racist America; it fervently and devoutly (after all, such beliefs were sanctioned by their religion) desired to maintain a system of white supremacy, and it concocted defense after defense of its beliefs and practices. This white America has structured all our major political institutions, starting with our Constitution, almost all the mainstream tellings and depictions of our history, and it has fought any racial progress in each period of our history—and continues to do so.[4]

There is also a progressive white America, but this America has never been as prevalent or powerful or prescient as many would believe; it has never constituted the majority of white Americans, even in the present. Just as important, its actions have been limited in scope, more often than not. Fitfully and after long periods of relative silence and inactivity, and more often half-heartedly and with great reluctance, a portion of white America comes to recognize that some part of our white supremacist practice and ideology might be wrong, might need to be identified and abolished. True, this progressive America fought the bloodiest war in American history supposedly to end slavery, but it was not until 1864 that Lincoln signed the Emancipation Proclamation, and even after that many aspects of slavery were reestablished in the postwar South. And of

---

4. The effort to separate conservatism from racism runs against the evidence of history, and the roots of our contemporary Trumpian, openly racist Republican Party is a product both of the party's modern intellectual roots and the resentments of its base. In the *New Republic*, in "How the GOP Became the Party of Resentment," Patrick Iber writes: "To this it might be added that the high- and lowbrow versions of the conservative movement were driven by impulses more similar than is usually acknowledged. The painters of graffiti in Charleston, South Carolina, who expressed their feelings about school textbooks containing a picture of a white girl giving flowers to a black boy with 'get the n***** books out' were not intellectuals. But after New York City's blackout of 1977, it was Midge Decter in the pages of *Commentary* who described looters as 'urban insect life.' *National Review* published pieces defending segregation and apartheid, and one of its writers speculated at a conference on the 'innate inferiority in the Negro race.' There were more and less erudite-sounding ways of deciding who deserved to be seen as fully human, but both the vigilantes and the intellectuals tended to reach the same conclusions. If what we want from our histories of conservatism is an explanation for Trump, we have the evidence that we need."

course the right to vote was quickly taken away from African Americans. Thus there is a pattern with the progressive side of America: this portion of white America has always wanted to believe that whatever small or large step it has taken, that step was certainly the last needed, and the task of ridding America of the evil of racism was now over, and no further steps were required.[5]

But in fact, throughout our history any move toward racial progress has been followed by a matching and vigorous effort to return as much as possible to the racist status quo, only by more devious and less overtly stated means and by skirting recent legal measures toward greater equality. The seemingly official and legal moves toward racial equality were always subsequently undermined, restricted, or rendered moot and lacked necessary enforcement or power.

The question for those who opposed racial progress was how to accomplish their backlash under each new seemingly progressive legal dispensation. Resistant whites understood that they could not acknowledge their true racist intentions—or at least could not declare them openly (when it comes to racism, hypocrisy is a deliberate strategy, historian David Blight has observed). A basic premise throughout our history is that racism will defend itself through often hard-to-detect intellectual sleights of hand: through camouflaging its workings and creating concepts and premises designed to make racism difficult or impossible to prove.[6] Just as important, until very recently this history of racial backlash has been thoroughly occluded from the histories students are taught in school or from popular fictional or cinematic versions of the past. Part of the objection to the 1619 Project is that it argues that a true accounting of our history must include the origins and practice of slavery and all that resulted from that, including the backlash of the Reconstruction.

---

5. The myth of racial progress is more contemporary, different in origin from the myth of the Lost Cause, which others have written about in detail (e.g., David Blight, *Race and Reunion: The Civil War in American Memory*).

6. This practice continues into the present, as in recent voting restriction laws. "We're not trying to keep Blacks and other minorities from voting," claim Republicans. "We're just trying to prevent voter fraud." In other words, you can always discriminate as long as you maintain your motive or reason for the action is anything other than racial bias. This is part of how systemic racism works—as a shell game in which it's impossible to prove racism is there.

As Audre Lorde famously observed, the tools of the master will not dismantle the master's house. And this includes the master's stories.

III

In this book, I will make complex analyses regarding the epistemology and ontology of race and how they are tied to Whiteness and white identity. I was not very acquainted with these philosophical terms when I began the first essays here, but I have come to see their necessity in understanding how racism has functioned and acted in our history and in our present. While some readers may be put off by the difficulty of these terms or deem them unnecessary, such objections miss the point: the crudeness of our usual and traditional thinking about race and our inability to critically examine our racial epistemology and ontology serve a common purpose—to obfuscate and maintain the racial status quo.

At the same time I would propose that the themes of this book are fairly straightforward and readily understandable. In the history of America's racial ontology, white people have created the categories of Whiteness and Blackness, and those categories continue to structure white identity. That identity is in part based on a belief in the myths, false histories, and racially segregated fictional stories white people tell themselves about themselves—that is, the stories Whiteness tells itself, especially about our history, are not an accurate portrait of our history and yet they continue to structure white identity (white psychology) in the present. That identity is a psychological distortion based on a denial of what white people have done in our past and what they continue to do in the present.

Part of that distortion involves the creation of unblemished white heroes and a version of our history that ameliorates, downplays, or excludes the depths of white racism and white supremacy in our history. But that distortion also involves the ways in which white history diminishes or excises Blackness from our history. In other words, that identity distorts and occludes the actual lives and consciousness of Black people in our history, what Black people have done and accomplished, what they have suffered and continue to suffer, how they tell their stories. This occurs not just through the content of the stories Whiteness tells itself, but through the *structures* of these stories, structures that often function more at an unconscious rather than conscious level. In both conscious and unconscious ways, white identity and the stories it tells segregate and separate, wall off white people from the reality of Black people, their history and experiences, the truths Black people have to tell about who we have been as a country and who we are now. White identity thus denies, excludes, and attacks the validity of Black knowledge and the stories Blacks tell themselves: it deems Black epistemology as secondary, minor, extraneous, or invalid, as subjective and always open to an objective white judgment and dismissal. Whiteness must always be epistemologically superior to Blackness, and that is one of the basic principles or rules of white identity.[7]

In this book and its analysis of Whiteness, I'm intertwining the historical, theoretical, literary, psychological, ethical, personal, and contemporary in ways I haven't quite seen before but that certainly follow in the tradition and writings of James Baldwin. I include two essays on his work. A substantial portion of this book explores two visions or versions of our history—one white, one black. But since I am a creative writer and literary critic, a portion of this book also examines Whiteness through white works of fiction and film in comparison with fiction and films by African Americans. I compare the film *Amistad,* created by the liberal white director Steven Spielberg and two white screenwriters, with the novelization of that same script by the African American novelist Alexs Pate. Similarly, I contrast portraits of slavery in the fiction of William Faulkner and Toni Morrison and the fictional social worlds of two contemporary fiction writers, Jonathan Franzen and ZZ Packer.

Our history is written not just in history books but also in the artistic works created by and about this history. In this realm, the "unofficial history," the history told from the viewpoint of Blacks and by Black creators, not only provides a more complex and fuller sense of our American history, but, just as important, that alternative history corrects the

---

7. Though part of me is reluctant to point out the obvious, I want to make this clear: I am arguing that the ways in which whites in America tend to think about themselves follow the prescriptions and beliefs of a historically constructed white identity. Whiteness, as I am using it here, is an ideology and practice. It is not intrinsic to those who are racially white, and white Americans can—and I believe must—deconstruct the Whiteness that shapes their identities and formulate a new white identity that critiques Whiteness and opens itself to the truths, knowledge, and stories of BIPOC America.

denials, repressions, and obfuscations in the white versions of our past. This is true even when those versions are created by liberal and seemingly well-intentioned white fiction writers, or as Toni Morrison demonstrates in *Playing in the Dark: Whiteness and the Literary Imagination*, by canonical white American authors such as Willa Cather, Mark Twain, Ernest Hemingway, and William Faulkner.

In my book *A Stranger's Journey: Race, Identity, and Narrative Craft in Writing*, I examine how the issues of race and identity are fundamental to the teaching and practice of creative writing in a contemporary America that is only becoming more and more diverse. I also explore the basic techniques and principles of Western narrative construction. In this book I'm using what I know of narrative construction to examine race in terms of story. In my teaching of creative writing, I am often trying to discern not just technical flaws in a student's work but psychological blocks and denials within the student that lead to or are behind these technical flaws. I try to get the student to recognize these blocks and/or denials, and if they are writing fiction or memoir, to help them to reenvision and restructure their work. I am trying to help the student to see places where their characterizations are two-dimensional or less than fully complex.

At first the student may insist that there is only one way to tell their tale, whether in fiction or memoir, and my task is to help the student to understand that there are other ways of telling the story, other forms of narrative construction, of formulating who the narrator of the tale might be, of depicting character, of envisioning the world of the story. Just as important I try to get the student to understand that their insistence on only one way of telling or on only one narrative construction often represents a refusal to acknowledge buried or uncomfortable truths about themselves or their past or their understanding of the world. I'm trying to get them to recognize their own blind spots, whether about themselves or others or their fictional characters.

There's obviously a psychological process in this creating of a new narrative. As the psychologist Arabella Kurtz has observed, constructing a revised narrative that acknowledges a repressed truth or insight into the past is an integral part of the therapeutic process. This new narrative enables the patient to stop repeating the past—in part because a portion of that past no longer remains unconscious and repressed—and to move to a new psychic space and a new identity. As Kurtz's dialogue with the South African novelist J. M. Coetzee demonstrates, the creation of a new narrative can take place on an individual level and on a national level—in the group story of a nation.

In *The Stories Whiteness Tells Itself*, I am proposing that many of the essential truths about our past and present are already embodied in the ways Black Americans view and tell the stories of our past and present. To me, it is clear that white America and white Americans need to construct a whole new tale about themselves and our past and present; moreover, they can do this only by listening to the narratives that the white versions of our history and our present leave out, the stories told by and centering Blacks, Native Americans, and other people of color about our past and present. Only then will we be able to possibly heal and move toward a future based on equity, true democracy, and an adherence to the ideals that this country has promised but has yet failed to deliver to so many of its citizens.

————

Back in late 1988, I wrote one of my first essays on race, "Strangers in the Village," responding in part to a critique of James Baldwin by Stanley Crouch. Today I'm a bit chagrined at the way my thirty-six-year-old self took on both Crouch and Baldwin. (Yes, Baldwin composed some of his most brilliant essays when he was quite young, but then he was a genius.) I see now that I misunderstood or misread Baldwin and perhaps took too much at face value Crouch's picture of the elder Baldwin as more rageful and militant. For one thing, there is a passage in the essay where I am critiquing Baldwin's rage in a way that echoes what he wrote in his essay "Notes of a Native Son." Still I do think what I wrote back then applies to this present moment; currently, there is both an increasing clarity of analysis of systemic racism and also a tendency of wokeness to stifle debate—allowing self-righteousness to lead to a rigid moral posturing that does not move us forward in the ways we all need to move. Years later, I read this passage I wrote as both a somewhat misguided critique of Baldwin and a warning to myself:

> [A]fter years of feeling inferior, after years of hating oneself, it is so comforting to use this rage not just to feel equal to the oppressor, but

superior, and not just superior, but simply blameless and blessed, one of the prophetic and holy ones. It is what one imagines a god feels like, and in this state one does feel like a god of history, a fate; one knows that history is on one's side, because one is helping to break open, to re-create history. And how much better it is to feel like a god after years of worshipping the oppressor as one.

But once one can clearly describe all this, one realizes that such a stance represents a new form of hubris, an intoxicating blindness: human beings are not gods, are not superior to other human beings. Human beings are fallible, cannot foresee the future, cannot demand or receive freely the worship of others. In aligning one's rage with a sense of superiority, one fails to recognize how this rage is actually fueled by a sense of inferiority: one's own version of history and views on equality need, on some level, the approval, the assent, the defeat of the oppressor. The wish for superiority is simply the reverse side of feeling inferior, not its cure. It focuses all the victim's problems on the other, the oppressor. Yet until one has recognized how one has contributed to this victimhood, the chains are still there, inside, are part of the psyche. Conversely, liberation occurs only when one is sure enough of oneself, feels good enough, to admit fault, admit their portion of blame.

Given the difficulty of this process, it's no wonder so many stumble in the process or stop midway through. And it is made much more difficult if the oppressor is especially recalcitrant, is implacable towards the change. When this happens, fresh wound after fresh wound is inflicted, causing bundle after bundle of rage: bitterness then becomes too tempting, too much energy is required to heal.

I now realize that my words here actually echo the spiritual journey Baldwin took to overcome the rage and bitterness he felt as a young man, which he saw deform and defeat his father. I see now: I did not know back then what I did not know.

Certainly, my own debt to Baldwin is great, and greater in retrospect. At the time I wrote "Strangers in the Village," I had recently read *The Devil Finds Work*, in which Baldwin interweaves the story of his own incipient racial consciousness with his immersion in films when a young white teacher took him under her tutelage and recognized something of the boy's genius. The book evolves into an extended critique of films on race during the 1950s and '60s, among them *The Defiant Ones, In the Heat of the Night,* and *Guess Who's Coming to Dinner,* and these critiques led Baldwin to larger pronouncements about white identity and the racial myths embodied in our official and unofficial histories. In many ways, my start on this book began with my reading of *The Devil Finds Work* and how Baldwin opened my eyes to the existence of a very different Black vision of America and its history.

It's my hope that this book will help others on a similar journey.

Author's Note

The appendix provides a further explication of how current white identity employs circular and falsely tautological arguments to dismiss almost any charge of racism, and it examines the way whites are often ignorant of or discount their group membership; instead, whites frequently insist on looking at race and their identity solely through the lens of the individual, not through the group lens. In contrast, Blacks are aware of their membership in a group; their lives often depend on such knowledge, such as in encounters with police, and Blacks are constantly forced to be aware of their group by the ways racism—which is a group practice on another group—affects their lives and living conditions. The reader can refer to this appendix after reading the book, or the appendix can be used in classrooms as a launching point for the book.

As the reader has observed in this Introduction, I've placed footnotes at the bottom of these pages. This book makes many complex analyses and arguments concerning race (some influenced by difficult academic theories), and I want the reader to be able to follow these analyses and arguments in a straightforward way. But these rely on and are supported by evidence, both historical and contemporary, and by further elaboration. In the footnotes I often offer a concrete reference or evidence or witness or expert to support my own analysis and argument. These provide proof to skeptical readers and concrete illustrations of the more abstract train of my thinking. Readers should feel free to refer to these footnotes or ignore them as they prefer.

PART I

THE PRESENT MOMENT

The Killing of Philando Castile and the Negation of Black Innocence

FALCON HEIGHTS IS A SUBURB OF 5,300 AT THE SOUTHWEST BORDER OF St. Paul, Minnesota. Because of its small population, it's patrolled by the police from the neighboring suburb of St. Anthony. Falcon Heights is so small it contains only a couple of main roads. One, Larpenteur Avenue, is about two miles from my house. The stretch of Larpenteur Avenue that police patrol is about two miles long and runs past the University of Minnesota golf course and driving range, the university's agricultural school fields, and a handful of small apartment buildings and houses. The road is not one of high-density population or a lot of traffic or accidents. Police patrol it mainly because it provides them with revenue and traffic points: the empty spaces surrounding the road make it seem like a highway and motorists are prone to drive slightly faster than the speed limit, which changes in the middle of this stretch, adding to motorists' confusion. In short, this stretch of Larpenteur Avenue is notorious only for being a speeding trap—that is, until the evening of July 6, 2016.

On that evening St. Anthony policeman Jeronimo Yanez spotted a car on Larpenteur Avenue in Falcon Heights. Officer Yanez had been aware that two black males with dreadlocks had robbed a nearby convenience store three days before. Yanez radioed a nearby squad. "The two occupants just look like people that were involved in a robbery. The driver looks more like one of our suspects, just because of the wide-set nose. I couldn't get a good look at the passenger." (Note: the two suspects in the robbery were both men, as opposed to the man, woman, and child who were actually in the vehicle Yanez saw.) Yanez then told the squad he was going to stop the car and check the IDs of its occupants.

What happened next is disputed. The accounts of officer Yanez and Diamond Reynolds, one of the occupants of the car, clearly differ.

What is certain is what resulted: Yanez fired five shots at Reynolds's boyfriend, Philando Castile, the driver of the car. Castile later died from the wounds after being taken to a nearby medical facility.

Yanez's attorney, Thomas Kelly, maintained that "this is a tragic incident brought about by the officer having to react to the actions taken by Mr. Castile. . . . This had nothing to do with race. This had everything to do with the presence of a gun . . . and the display of a gun." Kelly said that Yanez, who had been put on administrative leave, is a "sensitive man" and had been distressed by what had happened and was "deeply saddened" for Castile's family.

Diamond Reynolds's account differs significantly from Yanez's. "The gun never came out, it could never be a threat. He [Yanez] didn't ask about it, he didn't know it was on his person," Reynolds said in an exclusive interview with George Stephanopoulos on ABC's *Good Morning America*. "He came to the car, he said it was a traffic stop for a taillight. He asked for license and registration. That was it, that was all. The officer never mentioned anything other than a taillight, and we later discovered there was no broken taillight."

Reynolds said Castile had not touched his gun but was reaching for his ID, as Yanez had instructed, when Yanez opened fire. After Yanez shot Castile, Reynolds started recording from her phone: "I knew they wouldn't see me as being the person telling the truth," she told *Good Morning America*. "I knew by recording I would be able to have my side brought to the table." Reynolds knew as a black woman in America her words and story would not be believed by white Americans or the justice system; her knowledge and thus her epistemology would automatically be deemed invalid, hostile, untrue.

At this point, given what had just transpired, given the shooting of her boyfriend, Castile, Reynolds was obviously aware of the premise that guides so many of the justice system's encounters with Black civilians: Black people are presumed to be guilty until proven innocent. Since they are presumed guilty, their word cannot be trusted—and this is especially true in encounters with the police, who, whatever their race, become representatives of a justice system that practices systemic racism and protects the white majority; police, as are white people in general, are regarded as innocent until proven guilty. This means that the words of the police officer are always assumed to be more truthful than those of the Black civilian. Not only was Yanez's shooting of Castile an enactment of a previously written script; Yanez being declared innocent of Castile's killing was also already scripted—even before his trial for the murder of Castile began.

On the video Reynolds states in a remarkably calm voice, "Stay with me. We got pulled over for a busted taillight in the back and he's covered. . . . they killed my boyfriend. He's licensed to carry. He was trying to get out his ID and his wallet out his pocket, and he let the officer know that he had a firearm, and he was reaching for his wallet, and the officer just shot him in his arm."

While Reynolds records her testimony, Yanez can be heard frantically shouting, "I told him not to reach for it! I told him to get his hand out . . ."

"You told him to get his ID, sir, his driver's license," Reynolds responds, again with a calm that seems remarkable in the circumstances.

Reynolds is told to get out of the car and is handcuffed. After she says, "I can't believe they just did this!" there's a voice saying, "It's okay, I'm here with you."

The voice is Reynolds's four-year-old daughter, Dae'Anna. Dae'Anna was sitting in the back seat when officer Yanez opened fire and shot Philando Castile five times in the front seat of the car.

———

From these facts and statements we can assume that Officer Yanez approached the car he had stopped with trepidation. He had surmised that the car's occupants could be the two black males with dreadlocks, one with a wide nose, who had robbed a nearby convenience store. The two black males could be armed, as they were in the robbery.

What are we to make of Yanez's agitated emotional state after the shooting? What are we to make of the fact that Reynolds appears to be calm and far more emotionally restrained than Yanez—this despite the fact that her boyfriend, Philando, is bleeding to death in the seat next to her? And her four-year-old daughter in the back seat has just witnessed this shooting.

In that moment where the video starts, Officer Yanez knows his life and his career will forever be changed. After the shooting, his body is still coursing with adrenaline. He is safe physically, but he does not appear to feel safe.

Diamond Reynolds has just witnessed her boyfriend being shot. She worries he might be dying, and her worries prove correct. She is recording the rest of the encounter in order to help validate the testimony she knows she will eventually give about the event. She knows she is in the presence of an officer who has just shot someone whom she knows was not a threat to the officer and who did not reach for his gun. She can surmise that her being without a gun will not make her safe, especially in the presence of this officer, who is clearly still agitated.

She also knows her four-year-old daughter is in the back seat, that her daughter's life and her own life depend on her doing what the officer instructs. She suspects that the officer will most likely be upset that she is recording from her phone. Perhaps she also believes that the phone recording might prevent the officer from shooting her. It is a calculated risk she is taking. She knows that if she reacts too emotionally, she might upset the officer. She knows also that the validity of her testimony depends in large part on her ability to remain calm and in control.

In short, Reynolds knows that staying calm and in control will make her daughter less endangered. But she also knows that neither she nor her daughter *is* safe.

What we are faced with here is not just two different stories, but two different interpretations of the same reality. Two different epistemologies.

But even in this brief exchange it seems clear: Diamond Reynolds understands how Officer Yanez is thinking. She is still aware that Officer Yanez could turn and shoot her if she does something that causes him to further fear for his safety. She knows she must remain calm. She is enacting and relying on the double consciousness that W. E. B. Du Bois spoke about, a consciousness whose roots go back to slavery.[1]

---

1. Du Bois maintained that Blacks had to understand and know how white people thought about both themselves and Black people; at the same time, Black people knew that they thought about themselves differently from how white people did. Since white people believed

Yanez is clearly not thinking about what Diamond Reynolds is thinking or feeling. His mind is focused on the shooting. On his justification for the shooting. He is not thinking about how Diamond Reynolds is perceiving this event, or how her four-year-old daughter is perceiving the event. Nor does he seem to be thinking, *I need to do what I can to save the life of this man I have just shot.* Nor does he appear to be thinking, *Who is this man I have just shot?*

Yanez entered the encounter picturing the possibility of confronting two male robbery suspects. But the car obviously did not contain two males. Again, it contained a male, a female, and a four-year-old girl.

Questions arise. At what point did Yanez recognize that the occupants in the car were not the robbery suspects? Was it before or after the shooting that he saw there was a woman and not a man in the front seat beside Philando Castile? At what point did Yanez see the four-year-old girl in the back seat? Even after the shooting, it is not clear that Yanez knew there was a four-year-old girl in the back seat—that he actually sees her.

But then we may also question: did Officer Yanez actually see Philando Castile? To answer this question, we must understand that the verb *see* has two quite different meanings in this tragic encounter.

———

Let me be clear: even if the occupant of the car had been one of the robbery suspects, that does not mean that Officer Yanez would have been justified in shooting him.

But Philando Castile was not a robber of convenience stores.

Under the headline "'He Knew the Kids and They Loved Him': Minn. Shooting Victim Was an Adored School Cafeteria Manager," here is how the *Washington Post* article described Castile:

> Before he was fatally shot Wednesday by a police officer in Minnesota, before his name became a hashtag, Philando Castile was known

---

in their picture of Black people as lesser human beings, white people didn't believe Black people had their own complex consciousness or that Black people thought about white people differently from how white people thought about themselves. Also since white people had power over Black people, they didn't need to bother with how Black people thought about themselves or white people.

as a warm and gentle presence at J. J. Hill Montessori Magnet School, where he managed the cafeteria.

He was there when children streamed into school for breakfast in the morning, playing music and bantering. He was there when they returned for lunch: Laughing with kids, urging them to eat more vegetables, helping keep order in his easygoing way. . . .

"We're just devastated," said Anna Garnaas, who teachers first-, second- and third-graders at the school, located in St. Paul, Minnesota. "He just loved the kids, and he always made sure that they had what they needed. He knew their names, he knew what they liked, he knew who had allergies. And they loved him." . . .

[A parent of a student] said that one of her children has a sensory processing disorder that makes it hard for him to make eye contact and show affection. But with Castile? Her child would fist-bump him, she said, and hug his legs. Her son felt safe with Castile, she said.

Another white mother of a student—one of my writing students—called him "Mr. Rogers with dreadlocks."

But over the past fourteen years or so, this Mr. Rogers with dreadlocks had been pulled over and stopped by the police fifty-two times. He'd been given citations for speeding, driving without a muffler, not wearing a seatbelt. He accrued $6,588 in fines and fees. Half of his eighty-six violations were dismissed by the court.

Most Blacks and people of color would argue that Castile's record shows clear evidence that he had been a victim of racial profiling. Many Blacks believe that what happened to Castile could just as easily have happened to them. Many whites believe that the police do not act with any racial bias. Or that if there is bias on police forces, that bias stems from only a few "bad cops." But even these whites cannot dispute this: Philando Castile was not the robbery suspect Officer Yanez suspected him to be.

No, that is not quite true. To many whites, Philando Castile was a permanent suspect by virtue of his being Black.

––––––

Psychological studies have shown that racial bias can be expressed in two ways. One way is conscious or explicit bias. The other is unconscious or implicit bias. Until recently, discussions of racism have focused on explicit bias (as dictionary definitions of racism still do).

In "Faces of Black Children as Young as Five Evoke Negative Biases" from the Association for Psychological Science website, the article reports on research published in *Psychological Science*:

> Previous research has shown that people are quicker at categorizing threatening stimuli after seeing Black faces than after seeing White faces, which can result in the misidentification of harmless objects as weapons. [Lead study author Andrew] Todd and colleagues wanted to find out whether the negative implicit associations often observed in relation to Black men would also extend to Black children.
>
> The researchers presented 64 White college students with two images that flashed on a monitor in quick succession. The students saw the first image—a photograph of a child's face—which they were told to ignore because it purportedly just signaled that the second image was about to appear. When the second image popped up, participants were supposed to indicate whether it showed a gun or a toy, such as a rattle. The photographs of children's faces included six images of Black five-year-old boys and six images of White five-year-old boys.
>
> The data revealed that the student participants tended to be quicker at categorizing guns after seeing a Black child's face than after seeing a White child's face. Participants also mistakenly categorized toys as weapons more often after seeing images of Black boys than after seeing images of White boys.

The problem with implicit bias is that by definition the person is unaware that they hold such a bias. This bias acts beyond the person's conscious control. It is conditioned or created by the ways our society depicts whites as different from Blacks. This difference can show up anywhere—in news, in films or television, in books, in education, in social media, in everyday conversations, and so on. Just as important, because this bias is unconscious in many whites, it is difficult to prove to them that such a bias exists inside them—unless they themselves have taken a test for implicit bias or have come upon the psychological research on implicit bias.

Blacks and other people of color have little trouble believing that implicit or unconscious bias exists. We are aware when white people treat us or other people of color differently from fellow whites even if the white people who do this are unaware they are doing so. Most Blacks and people of color believe racial bias in policing stems from an explicit bias that is far greater in police forces than is acknowledged *and* from an implicit bias that many police and whites do not even recognize or know about.

In other words, Blacks believe many police do not see Blacks as they actually are but instead see Blacks through a number of racial biases or filters.

————

How do we root out implicit bias? As Destiny Peery, assistant professor of law and psychology at Northwestern University, writes in the *Huffington Post*:

Many researchers who study implicit bias for a living, including the creators of the primary implicit bias measure, the Implicit Association Test (IAT), caution against seeing implicit bias as the newest one-size-fits-all approach to solving issues of bias and diversity. These researchers argue that implicit bias is helpful to the extent that it adds to our toolkit for understanding how bias operates, but research has not progressed to the point of suggesting concrete, long-term ways to eradicate these biases. In other words, we must remember that implicit bias training is not able to de-bias participants, no matter how well-meaning they are. After decades of research, we still don't really know how to get rid of these biases, especially biases like implicit racial and gender biases, given that they, and the stereotypes that maintain them, are so pervasive.

While not much is known about how to de-bias people, a lot more is known about how to protect against bias. Here awareness matters, so teaching people about implicit bias can help, but what matters more is creating policies and procedures where decision-makers can check their biases and insulate against them.

In other words, police can be tested for implicit bias; training to combat implicit bias can be instituted. But such measures will not solve the problem of implicit bias. *Implicit bias is rooted too deeply in our culture.* This bias stems from and is created by the society around us, its beliefs and practices, the ways it depicts whites and Blacks and other people of color. It is difficult for police training to dismantle their implicit bias if the minute they step outside the door of the training sessions they are bombarded with messages confirming or reinforcing their implicit bias.

Moreover, the cultures of most police departments have not been open to such training. While we should continue to try different ways to combat implicit racial bias on the part of police, we should also take measures to mitigate the effects of that bias. This means we need to focus not just on the individual police officer and his or her racial attitudes and beliefs but on the entire practice of policing in this country.

———

Rather than focusing on police reform, I keep going back to Philando Castile, and how conservative websites trumpet headlines about him like this: "Confirmed: Philando Castile Was an Armed Robbery Suspect—False Media Narrative Now Driving Cop Killings."[2] To such conservatives, the fact that Philando Castile did not rob the convenience store is, as one commentator put it, a "moot point." So, presumably, is the fact that he was a beloved cafeteria manager at the J. J. Hill School. To such conservatives, he was always a "robbery suspect" and not "Mr. Rogers with dreadlocks."

What's important to note here is that in the conservative narrative, there is no room for Philando Castile to be considered "innocent." The fact that Officer Yanez suspected Castile of being a robbery suspect is sufficient and renders all other considerations "moot." Such a mindset, unfortunately, is part of America's legacy, and its historical roots go back

---

2. Conservative Treehouse website on July 8, 2016.

much further than most contemporary Americans, particularly white Americans, are aware of.

Since 1619, Blacks in America, as slaves, were regarded as less than human or inferior human beings. They required discipline and punishment, literal shackles; they were seen as property, as instruments, more in the category of an ox or other farm animal. They were feared and seen as constant threats to the master's safety and control. They were to be policed and pursued when they tried to obtain their freedom, but by their very definition they could not be free. When slave patrols and enslavers hunted them, there was no question of the slave being guilty or innocent, since the slave was not a citizen and did not have rights; the pursuit of them was more like hunting escaped farm animals. If we think about this situation, its contradictions are confounding: Blacks were property, so if they tried to free themselves, they were essentially seen as stealing property. But they were not criminals, since only human citizens can break the law and Blacks were considered neither legal citzens nor humans. But with the Emancipation Proclamation, Southerners and indeed the rest of the country had to deal with the possibility of Black citizenship and thus the possibility of Black crime. After the Civil War, the place of Blacks in society had to be redefined—and recircumscribed—so that they would not occupy the same position and possess the same rights as white citizens.

In *The Condemnation of Blackness: Race, Crime, and the Making of Modern Urban America*, Khalil Gibran Muhammad explains that the end of slavery brought a "paradigm shift in the terms to discuss, debate, and deal with them [Blacks]. The slavery problem became the Negro problem." In 1868, in *The Negroes in Negroland; The Negroes in America; and Negroes Generally*, Hinton Rowan Helper wrote that the "crime-stained blackness" of Negroes meant that they could not rise to a plane higher than "base and beastlike savagery."

In 1884, Nathaniel Southgate Shaler, a Harvard scientist, wrote the first in a series of articles where he expounded on the threat of the presence of Blacks in America, a threat far greater than any posed by immigrants from Europe, a threat to civilization itself: "There can be no sort of doubt that, judged by the light of all experience, these people are a danger to America greater and more insuperable than any of those that menace the other great civilized states of the world." Shaler maintained that the development of Black brains stopped early, which left Black people with an animal nature unchanged by the "fruits of civilization." Shaler was part of a slew of white supremacist scientists and social scientists intent on proving the inferiority of the Black race, including their inherent criminality.

In making these claims, writers like Shaler framed the crimes of Blacks in a completely different context and method from that of white crimes. This pseudoscience purported to prove that Black criminals were not simply individuals but proof of the criminality of the entire Black race. In contrast, white criminals were seen as individuals rather than as indicative of any racial characteristics for whites. Muhammad writes:

> The idea of black criminality was crucial to the making of modern urban America. In nearly every sphere of life it impacted how people defined fundamental differences between native whites, immigrants, and blacks. . . . Moreover, the various ways in which writers and reformers imagined black people as inferior to and fundamentally different from native whites and immigrants in the early twentieth centuries had a direct impact on allocation of social resources for preventing crime in all communities. . . . Thoughtful, well funded crime prevention and politically accountable crime fighting secured immigrants' whiteness, in contrast to the experiences of blacks, who were often brutalized or left unprotected and were repeatedly told to conquer their own crime before others would help them.

While sentiment against white immigrants such as the Irish was also characteristic of this period, there were efforts to attribute the crimes of white immigrants to socioeconomic or demographic reasons and not to any inherent ethnic or racial traits. The case of Black criminality, though, was entirely different. As Muhammad continues:

> In one of the first academic textbooks on crime, Charles R. Henderson, a pioneering University of Chicago social scientist, declared that "the evil [of immigrant crime] is not so great as statistics carelessly interpreted might prove." He explained that age and sex ratios—too

many young males—skewed the data. But where the "negro factor" is concerned, Henderson continued, "racial inheritance, physical and mental inferiority, barbarian and slave ancestry and culture" were among the "most serious factors in crime statistics."

Of course, Henderson was echoing the beliefs common throughout the culture. What is important to note is this: academics and researchers added to and reinforced these beliefs through their purported use of scientific and "objective" methods. In such assessments there was no presumption of innocence regarding Black people; indeed, there was not even a judicial approach of guilty until proven innocent. Instead, Black people were inherently and permanently guilty.

According to the science, the stereotypes, and the legal system, there needed to be no evidence of crime: being Black was the crime. In the period after the Civil War, vagrancy laws, which continued well into the twentieth century and continue de facto to the present, asserted that Blacks could be arrested or detained for no reason other than they were not working or appeared suspicious. The spirit of those laws lives on in the assumptions of the justice system and the police: to be Black is always to be under suspicion.

What bears repeating here is that in such an ideology when a white person commits a crime, it is seen as the act of one individual and not as proof of anything inherent to the white race. Whites are viewed as individuals. When Blacks commit a crime, they are always viewed as members of and evidence of their entire race.

————

In so many ways, the stereotypes and ideology of this nineteenth-century and early-twentieth-century racial science are still present today. So is the overwhelming tendency of whites to view crimes or misdeeds by whites as individual acts and those by Blacks as proof of the characteristics of their entire race—and thus by this illogic any Black person is always potentially a criminal. Our racist history, which so many conservatives want to relegate to the past, lives on in the beliefs and psychology of white people, the roots of which go back to slavery and Jim Crow. We have still not severed the roots of that poisonous tree, in part because we will not acknowledge the source of and existence of those roots. Whatever legal measures this country may have taken toward racial progress, such as the Thirteenth, Fourteenth, and Fifteenth Amendments of the post–Civil War era or the civil rights laws in the modern era, no law has outlawed racial bias in people's psyches and the persistence of racial ontology in the ways whites conceive of their identities.

In the modern era, the ideology of Black criminality has been used by conservative politicians to formulate policies specifically aimed at criminalizing and decimating the Black community. Take, for instance, the law and order campaign of the Nixon administration. In researching a book on drug prohibition, journalist Dan Baum interviewed John Ehrlichman, Nixon's chief domestic advisor when Nixon launched the so-called war on drugs. While the administration cited the fatalities and negative social effects of drugs to argue for an expansion of federal drug control agencies, Ehrlichman admitted that the real motives for this policy were political and racial:

> You want to know what this was really all about? The Nixon campaign in 1968, and the Nixon White House after that, had two enemies: the antiwar left and black people. You understand what I'm saying? We knew we couldn't make it illegal to be either against the war or black, but by getting the public to associate the hippies with marijuana and blacks with heroin, and then criminalizing both heavily, we could disrupt those communities. We could arrest their leaders, raid their homes, break up their meetings, and vilify them night after night on the evening news. Did we know we were lying about the drugs? Of course we did.[3]

We cannot understand what happened to Philando Castile on Larpenteur Avenue in St. Paul without understanding how our history lives inside the present, both in our system of justice and in the minds of the individuals who work in that system.

----

3. See http://www.cnn.com/2016/03/23/politics/john-ehrlichman-richard-nixon-drug-war-blacks-hippie.

Explicit and implicit bias have deep roots in our history.

Explicit and implicit bias both produce blindness and blinders, false filters and lenses—not clear or true sight. Every Black adult in America knows that this blindness can come into play anytime they encounter a police officer. Every Black adult knows that in that encounter, their life may be held in the balance by someone who does not see them, someone who, because of history and the presence of that history in the present, might see them not just as guilty or a criminal but as a threat to that officer's very existence. And no matter how they behave, that Black person has no control ultimately over how that police officer views them. It is a terrifying situation to find oneself caught up in. And it occurs daily in America.

Or in the life of this one thirty-two-year-old Black man, it had occurred some fifty-two times. The fifty-third time proved fatal. It was as if the odds had finally caught up with Philando Castile.

Yet despite being the victim of racial profiling by the police, Castile had greeted the white children and white parents of St. Paul's J. J. Hill School with a smile, with the natural warmth of his personality. He tried to see each of the students as an individual, remembered who had allergies, and remembered the parents of the kids who had allergies. According to Rebecca Penfold Murray, a parent of two five-year-old children at the J. J. Hill School, Castile appeared to know every student's name: "When you see 400 kids a day and you can remember those details about them, I think that you really care about how those kids are doing. It's preposterous for anyone to die violently, but I am still unable to wrap my head around the fact that this happened to a person like him." Hill parent Angie Checco de Souza reports that her six-year-old said, "Mom, can you tell the police that they were wrong? This is our guy, who served us lunch at J. J. Hill Montessori School."

Think of how Castile woke up each day and greeted those kids, the majority of whom were white. Think about how he woke up each day and got into his car to go to work, knowing he might be stopped by the police for any number of reasons, some perhaps seemingly legal but others dismissed by the courts, courts that would not be inclined to necessarily take his word against the police who stopped him. But Castile was not bitter about this. Though his mother states that she thinks he was constantly stopped for "driving while Black," he did not take up her advice to make an official complaint about such bias.

Personally, part of me doesn't quite understand how Castile coped with this contradiction. He seems to be one of those people who tried to make the best of things, to treat others with respect and care, with openness and warmth, even if the world around him did not always treat him the same way. This is not, I would argue, the picture the general public would have if they were simply given the information that this Black man had been stopped fifty-two times by the police in fourteen years (Castile's mother maintains it was more like eighty).[4]

Beyond this, Castile is an example of how far we are from being able to act on Martin Luther King Jr.'s admonition that a man be judged by the content of his character and not his skin. Of course, King was stating an ideal to strive for, but stating such an ideal does not mean it is easily achieved. Barriers and conditions prevent the average white person from judging the character of the average Black person, even if the white person desires to do so without racial prejudice. We cannot judge a person's character unless we know what their life has been like, what they have gone through, what burdens they have carried, what they have suffered, what support they have had—the thousand thousand outside forces and incidents that create the circumstances of a person's life and thus affect the choices and actions that person takes that determine their character.

By all accounts, the white people at the school thought Castile to be a warm, kind, and friendly man, a man who went all out to know each child's name and to treat them as an individual, who cared for the students. Yes, these white people saw this aspect of Castile. But what the white people who knew Philando Castile at work did not see, or most likely did not consider, was not just the fact that he'd been stopped fifty-two times by the police in fourteen years, but the fact that each of those times brought him in contact with a justice system that did not see him as innocent until proven guilty but guilty until otherwise proven. Fifty-two times where he could have been imprisoned or beaten or shot.

---

4. When I speak on race, I often ask audience members how many times they have been stopped by police during the past ten years. I'm pretty sure there's not a white person in America who had been stopped half as many times by the police as Castile was.

Fifty-two times when the terror of being a Black man in America entered his life as a real and potentially deadly force. And of course that terror was there in his life whether he was stopped on any particular day or not.

So I would argue that these same white people, who were positively disposed to Castile, could not judge what strength, what resilience, what spiritual depth were required for him to treat them and their children with kindness and warmth and friendliness, what was required for him to see the children and other whites as individuals and not as symbols or representatives of a system of racism that had clearly harassed and oppressed him. This is because they, as white people, did not know and did not think about the world Castile lived in—a world that pursued him, denigrated him, constantly criminalized him, constantly threatened to imprison him, or as it eventually did, kill him.

In other words, I would argue that the white people who encountered him at the school where he worked, even if they liked or even loved him, did not understand what he had faced in his life. As a result, contrary to King's ideal, they were *not* qualified to judge his character, however kindly they might have been disposed to him. Given all that he faced, Castile was not just a friendly person but a truly remarkable human being.

––––––––

Officer Yanez wasn't trained to recognize or combat any racial bias he might have had—and certainly not any implicit or unconscious bias. Instead, Yanez had gone through a police training course called "The Bulletproof Warrior." There he was instructed to shoot whenever he felt his life was threatened; videos of bloody shootouts between police and civilians emphasized to the participants that hesitation can kill you. Yanez learned not to question whether his feelings might be inaccurate, might be conditioned by explicit or implicit racial bias. Instead, in this training, he was taught the first and foremost thing he as an officer must do was to make sure he remained alive, no matter what. The Bulletproof Warrior was modeled after military training—more specifically, a military occupying a *foreign* or *enemy* country. The Bulletproof Warrior conditioned Yanez to regard his fellow citizens from the point of an occupying force and certainly not under the rubric of "innocent until proven guilty." Force, physical and/or deadly, was emphasized rather than negotiation or the risks of interrogation, of ascertaining who the suspect actually is and whether the suspect should actually be a suspect.

I don't believe Yanez consciously wanted to kill Philando Castile. But that Yanez did so was not an accident. It was preordained by America's failure to deal with its racial problems and their history. It was preordained by the blindness that resided in Yanez, perhaps in his unconscious rather than his conscious mind, but still just as problematic and fatal for Philando Castile. It was preordained by a racist culture where the stereotypes of Blacks as criminals infect not just individual psyches but our entire system of justice. It was preordained by the increasing tendency to frame the job of police as military practice, as confronting potential *enemy foreign combatants*—not fellow citizens.

Philando Castile was innocent. Tragically, the society around him is still guilty of not seeing that fact.

In the end, we can view Philando Castile, Diamond Reynolds, her daughter, and Officer Yanez as actors in a script, a script that was conceived, constructed, refined, and adopted to the circumstances of each period of American history. It is a script that can override individual impulses to alter or ignore it, which overpowers any wishes to pretend it isn't there constantly waiting to be invoked and enacted. It is a script that began to be written when the first slaves came to America in 1619. Subsequently, the various iterations of that script have been in so many ways hidden from and kept from our understanding of our history and how we came to become the nation that we are—a nation with vast racial disparities and inequities in all areas of our society.

This is a script that frightens many (particular African Americans and other people of color) and comforts many (those whites who believe in the necessity and fairness of the justice system and those who work within it). It is a script that is read and interpreted differently depending on who is doing the reading. And certainly, on July 16, 2013, the adults—Castile, Reynolds, and Yanez—understood the roles they were assigned, and they understood where the script might lead them. As in any tragedy, none of them wished consciously for the outcome, and none would say they benefited from the script's conclusion.

But mostly I think of Philando Castile, how he understood probably from the time he was a teenager that the script might catch up with him—what happens when you are a Black man and the police pull you over. Of course, such a pulling over happens with way more frequency to Black men than to white men; that is part of the script. But Castile knew that not only could the script lead to a ticket or jail time but also to death. Therefore he understood that there were only a few ways he could avoid the worst tragic outcome of that script for him: be polite, keep your hands on the wheel, don't make sudden moves, and keep your permit with you at all times if you possess a gun. He understood that his only chance of survival was to somehow keep Officer Yanez from jumping to any conclusions about who Castile might be, what he might be capable of, how much danger Castile represented to Yanez. And Castile knew that his life depended on his preventing Yanez from reaching for, from asserting the script that had already been implanted within Yanez—by his training as a cop, by his identity as someone who was not African American, by the Bulletproof Warrior seminar, by whatever in Yanez's background that led him to become a policeman and thus the enforcer rather than the victim of the ultimate script of death. For even before he was stopped, Castile was already placed in the role of the suspect—not just for a traffic charge but for an armed robbery. Therefore, Castile was cast already as the criminal, as a danger to Yanez's life, and Castile's role was clearly generic, typecast, stereotyped: for no matter how hard Castile tried, how conscious he was of the danger of that script, he was already caught within it even before he noticed the flashing lights of Yanez's squad car.

But of course, it was not just the report of the armed robbery floating in the consciousness of Yanez that determined the script, but all that came before that moment in the history of America—from the time the first slave tried to run away or rebel against his master, from the first moment some action of a slave frightened the master and threatened the master's authority. The connection between those first moments of slavery in this new world and what happened to Philando Castile nearly four hundred years later is, for most white Americans, nonexistent or at best decidedly remote or insignificant. And yet most African Americans understand and acknowledge that lineage, how the scripts that govern their lives came to be. They may not understand or know all the historical details of that genealogy, but they feel them, they experience them, and they know 1619 still lives within the scripts they are trying to write about their lives—or in this case, the script that Philando Castile, friendly school kitchen worker with a smile and greeting for all, was trying to write for his life, despite being stopped by the police fifty-two times in fourteen years.

In the end, Castile could not rewrite that script, no matter how hard he worked at such rewriting in his own life, because that script was also written into Yanez's life and career, into the ways Yanez was trained to do his job, into the ways Yanez was trained both by his fellow police and the society around him to regard Black men and the roles they are to play in the realm of the justice system.

On newscasts all over the country, Diamond Reynolds's cell phone recording was broadcast, and we all witnessed this theatrical repetition, this tragedy replayed. Yet we as a country still do not understand how deeply rooted this script is within the psyche of this nation, how deeply the roles assigned by race are ingrained within the practices, beliefs, and actions of our society, how far we have to go to actually alter the script and therefore the ultimate fate of a man like Philando Castile. But let his death, and the death of so many African Americans under similar circumstances, tell us what we already know: we are all caught within certain roles in the theater of race in America, and we had better begin to understand how those roles and how the scripts that they create came to be. Only then are we ever going to change those roles and scripts so that another Philando Castile does not meet a similar fate.

———

For the Black community, and especially for Black men, the death of Philando Castile and other Black men at the hands of the police is not surprising but a constant and ever-present fear—for themselves, for their loved ones, for their sons and their daughters. The Black community has always known that their lives are not valued in the ways the white community values their own lives; the Black community knows that the very presence of Black people in America, from the time they were brought here, has been seen by the white population as a threat, as a source of fear and danger, as needing to be overseen, shackled, and *policed*.

The white community does not and to a certain extent cannot

contemplate the presence of this existential threat in Black life—for to contemplate such a condition would force them to acknowledge its evil. But in a world beyond white acknowledgment, the Black community knows that the State at any moment can take a Black life without a trial, without any assertation of guilt or innocence, can instead assume that the Black person is already guilty no matter how that individual has lived their life.

In this way, Black life, the Black body, cannot in the eyes of white America ever possess itself; it must always be subject to the judgment and suspicion of the white gaze, the white State, the white privilege to be the final arbiter of Black guilt and innocence. This power of the white State goes back to when enslaved Africans were brought to America in 1619, and in so many ways it continues to this day in ways that white America still cannot admit, much less rectify.

Philando Castile is now part of that history. So are the scripts that dictated his killing.

Black Lives Matter and the Social Contract

AT WHAT POINT DOES THE SOCIAL CONTRACT END?

If violence can be wreaked upon you without cause?

If your life can be taken from you while you are unarmed and your murderer goes unpunished?

If your rights as a citizen have been taken away simply because you were walking on the street?

If the skin on your body becomes the marker for your criminality and you become a source of profit for those who run the prisons?

Isn't all this the definition of a slave? You are not a citizen; violence can be done to you without need of justification or provocation; you are deemed to be property; you are not regarded as a human.

If the society you live in has failed to recognize and protect your humanity, what is your obligation to that society?

To put it more bluntly, how deeply does that ontology of the slave still operate within the American psyche? How does our racial ontology relate to the fact that almost always police are not convicted and punished for shooting unarmed Black people?

———

April 4, 2015: Walter Scott, a fifty-year-old black forklift operator who was studying massage therapy, is being stopped by the police. The police dash cam video shows Scott pulling his car into the parking lot of an auto parts store in North Charleston, South Carolina.[1] Later, when inter-

---

1. Later, the *New York Times* reported that local residents had been complaining of racial profiling and excessive use of Tasers by the police for years. While whites make up 37 percent of the population of North Charleston, the police force is 80 percent white. The details of this

viewed about this incident, the white police officer, Michael Slager, will say he stopped Scott because of a broken taillight.

Slager gets out of his car and approaches Scott and speaks with him. Slager goes back to his patrol car and Scotts exits his car and starts to flee.

Slager begins to chase him. They are both now out of the view of the dash cam.

If Officer Slager had had his way, no one would know what happened after this—other than Officer Slager.

But wait. There is a third person nearby with a cell phone. That person's video starts with Scott and Slager tussling in an open grassy area behind a fence.

Slager later claimed that he feared for his life and that Scott was reaching for his Taser.

Scott wrestles free of Slager. Slager shoots his Taser. Scott keeps running. His pace isn't quite a sprint but more like a jog. At a point where Scott is about fifteen to twenty feet away, Slager takes out his gun and shoots Scott in the back eight times. The coroner's report indicates Scott was struck by five of the shots, three in the back, one in his buttocks, and one in the ear.

Scott then says into his police mic: "Shots fired and the subject is down. He grabbed my Taser."

He then shouts at Scott: "Get your hands behind your back now! . . . Put your hands behind your back." Slager handcuffs Scott.

Slager goes back to where he and Scott were tussling and picks up an unidentified object. As he does so, a second officer, who is Black, approaches. Slager then takes the object over to where Scott is lying on the ground and drops the object next to Scott. The second officer puts on latex gloves but does not appear to administer CPR as he later claimed. The second officer pulls Scott's shirt back as if to look where Scott is shot.

Slager checks for a pulse.

Scott dies at the scene.

———

incident shared here are taken from an NBC news video clip.

Initially, the person who shot the video, Feidin Santana, did not tell anyone about it for fear the police might retaliate against him: "I felt that my life, with this information, might be in danger. I thought about erasing the video and just getting out of the community, you know Charleston, and living someplace else."

But Santana became angered when he learned how widely the police report differed from what he had seen. After contacting an activist of Black Lives Matter, he shared the video with Scott's family and then with the news media. In a *Today Show* interview, Santana maintained that Scott "never grabbed the Taser of the police. He never got the Taser."

After an initial mistrial in state court, Officer Michael Slager pleaded guilty and was convicted in federal court for violating Scott's civil rights and was sentenced to twenty years in prison.

Without Santana's video, Slager would most likely never have been charged with Scott's murder. Certainly, it is most likely that Slager's account of the incident would have prevailed in court and that Slager would never have been forced to plead guilty. For absent Santana's video, the court would have had to decide between the account of a police officer and the silence of a dead Black man.

————

Statistically, in cases without video proof convictions of the police almost never occur. Even partial videos will not do.

Take the example of Freddie Gray, a twenty-five-year-old Black man who was walking down a street near Baltimore's Gilmor Homes housing project on April 12, 2015. Three police officers on bikes approached Gray and one made "eye contact" with him. Gray started to run. The police officers pursued and apprehended him "without the use of force or incident," but according to Officer Garrett Miller, he "noticed a knife clipped to the inside of [Gray's] right front pocket." For possessing an illegal weapon, Gray was arrested and a struggle ensued.

Videos by bystanders show him screaming and the officers "folding" Gray, bending his legs backward while one pressed a knee to his neck. Bystanders claimed that Gray "couldn't walk" or "use his legs" and that "his leg looked broke." Gray was handcuffed and hauled away in a police van. His calls for his inhaler were ignored.

By the time Gray arrived at the police station, he had fallen into a coma with injuries to his spinal cord. He died seven days later.

Many in the Black community suspected that Gray's injuries were the result either of the violence at his arrest or from having a "rough ride" where the handcuffed occupant is tossed about like a rag doll in the police van as the driver swerves and speeds around corners. The officers involved pleaded innocent and claimed they had nothing to do with Gray's death. In the end, no officer was ever convicted of being responsible for his death.

In April 2015, in Baltimore and across the United States, Black Lives Matter held protests over the death of Freddie Gray. In the same month, in North Charleston, South Carolina, Black Lives Matter held protests for the killing of Water Scott.[2]

————

If one looks at the video of Walter Scott running away from the gun of policeman Michael Slager or Freddie Gray being handcuffed and hauled into the Baltimore police van, the history of America haunts the viewer with its reincarnation of violence against African Americans. At some level, both of these African American men understood that not just their freedom could be taken away at any moment but also their lives. They understood that living in a Black body in America is vastly different from living in a white body. And for many of their fellow African Americans, Scott's and Gray's encounters with the police invoked the practices and

---

2. As for those who respond to Black Lives Matter with the inane "All Lives Matter," given America's history, there is no reason to believe that when "All lives" or "All people" is used in terms of rights or justice or privilege, such expressions include Black people (or Native Americans or Asian Americans or Latinx Americans). When the Founding Fathers wrote, "All men are created equal" in the Declaration of Independence, we know that did not include Black people—or women. Similarly, given the state of our justice system and its myriad practices of racial bias, America does not truly want equal rights and justice for Black people; otherwise, we would have equal rights and justice for Black people. "All Americans" should have the right to a fair trial, but that is not the case in our current justice system. (Nor was it the case when my parents, who were U.S. citizens, and my grandparents, who were forbidden by racist laws from becoming citizens, were imprisoned for their race and ethnicity in World War II.) Unarmed Black Americans are twice as likely to be shot by police than unarmed whites. If all lives did matter, this would not be the case. So when whites say "all," is it any wonder that Blacks think, "You mean yourselves, not us."

images of slavery. (Indeed, the first acts of policing in the South in the early 1700s were slave patrols.)

But there is also a philosophical element to what the deaths of Scott and Gray echoed. Within the formal institution of slavery, any violence done to the Black slave never needed a justification or legal precedent: the slave was not simply a noncitizen; the slave was not human. The slave was not protected by the state or the law.

The anger and demonstrations in Baltimore after the death of Freddie Gray, as well as similar demonstrations elsewhere, contain a recognition that the social contract can end. In other words, the social contract can be deemed null and void by those who believe their humanity is not recognized and protected by the state and the society in which they live.

———————

In his book-length essay "The Devil Finds Work," James Baldwin discusses—and skewers—liberal films on race from the 1950s and '60s, including *In the Heat of the Night, Guess Who's Coming to Dinner,* and *The Defiant Ones.* This last film involves two escaped convicts, played by Tony Curtis and Sidney Poitier, who are handcuffed together. The film attempts to show how a bond develops between the two men despite their racial differences. Baldwin investigates the psychology of race and this film in ways that white society still has not yet processed:

> It is impossible to accept the premise of the story, a premise based on the profound American misunderstanding of the nature of the hatred between black and white. There is a hatred—certainly: though I am now using this word with great caution, and only in the light of the effects, or the results, of hatred. But the hatred is not equal on both sides, for it does not have the same roots. . . . black men do not have the same reason to hate white men as white men have to hate blacks. The root of the white man's hatred is terror, a bottomless and nameless terror, which focuses on the black, surfacing, and concentrating on this dread figure, an entity which lives only in his mind. But the root of the black man's hatred is rage, and he does not so much hate white men as simply want them out of his way, and more than that, out of his children's way. . . . Liberal white audiences

applauded when Sidney, at the end of the film, jumped off the train in order not to abandon his white buddy. The Harlem audience was outraged, and yelled, *Get back on the train, you fool!*

The whole film is based on a premise of an equal and similarly motivated racial hatred: whites hate Blacks and Blacks hate whites. So if both sides stop hating, we can end racial strife. That myth, with its easy solution, is what the white liberal audiences are applauding, Baldwin implies.

Because of that myth, the film never investigates, much less acknowledges, the nature of white projection, their terror of Blacks and Blackness, or the fact that Blacks have long understood the falseness of that projection. That is what makes Poitier's action—his jettisoning the chances for his own freedom for his white "buddy"—ridiculously absurd to the Harlem audience. They don't believe in the film's proffering of racial solidarity because they know how white people act in real life and how far their actions are from any practice of racial equality. They know that white people do not see themselves as they actually are and that the film is another absurd example of that. They know they should not trust white people and they believe Sidney's character ought to know that too. They know that no white convict would risk all for Sidney, so why should Sidney do the same for a white convict? And the Black audience knows Sidney must do this in this film because white people have written this absurd scenario and script for their own psychic and political purposes, even as these filmmakers, most likely white liberals, believed they were doing the opposite, that they were fighting racism rather than reaffirming it.

But there is a deeper current within this film and its final scene. As Baldwin implies, we can never understand how whites think about Blacks if we do not investigate the "terror, a bottomless and nameless terror, which focuses on the black, surfacing, and concentrating on this dread figure, an entity which lives only in his mind." For this terror is completely a white creation and was created in conjunction with and in defense of the practice of slavery—and then on into Reconstruction, the Jim Crow era, and policing practices in contemporary America.

———

Why has white America so oppressed and terrorized Black America? Baldwin argues that the source of this hatred and oppression lies within the psyche of white America; it is a form of madness, of psychic displacement and denial. And if white America does not investigate and deal with the weaknesses and terror in their own psyches over race, there is no hope for Blacks, or white Americans either.

In contrast, in order to survive, Blacks have had to combat the white fantasy of a racial difference for four hundred years. This white fantasy is something Blacks are all too aware of, and they understand that its roots lie in slavery and terror—the terror white slave masters inflicted on their slaves; the terror of the inhuman that white slave masters projected on their slaves; the terror of the white masters at any potential retaliation by their slaves.

To understand the cause and nature of this terror Baldwin speaks of, it's necessary to examine the ontology of the master/slave dichotomy and use it to contextualize how whites perceive Blacks, and in particular how the police perceive Blacks. In order for slavery to be instituted, whites had to think of Black people in an entirely different way from how they thought of themselves. Some of this is familiar racist stereotyping. Blacks were inferior, less intelligent, bestial. As man mastered and tamed the beasts of the earth, so whites mastered and tamed the Black slave.

But the distinction between master and slave required other delineations. Whiteness became the definition of human, Blackness of the nonhuman. Whites were citizens; as nonhumans, Blacks could not become citizens. Violence to whites could only be done with legal justification or through declarations of war. Violence toward Blacks could be instituted without legal justification or declaration of war. Whites could own property; Blacks were property that whites could own and sell. The human whites could retain parentage over their progeny; the Black slave could not; they were natally alienated—without rights to their offspring.

When one group, whites, held such domination over another, Blacks, these ontological definitions were always in play in the master-slave relationship. This relationship could be established only through great violence and the threat of violence. But here the ontology of the

White/Human and Black/Slave faced a contradiction. It could not accommodate the omnipresent threat of retaliatory violence and the desire of Blacks, as human beings, to retain or regain their freedom. In this ontology of Whiteness, the slavery of Blacks was supposedly part of the natural order, and so Blacks were expected to succumb to this natural order. In this ontology of Whiteness, Blacks were nonhuman and so their violence could never be regarded as a human response. It was animalistic, the violence of a beast. The violence of the Black/Slave could never be regarded as human and rational, as possessing logic; this violence could not be considered as an understandable human response to enslavement, and thus it could never be considered as moral, for of course morality exists only in the realm of the human, and Blacks were not considered as part of the human realm. Only the White/Master was moral and could rule on morality.

Instead, the violence of Blacks and the threat of their violence had to be regarded as nonhuman, irrational, animalistic, completely outside the boundaries of White/Human understanding. There could be no thought behind it, no knowledge of human rights. This is the origin of White/Human terror of the Black/Slave.

Of course, the ones actually doing violence, the actual terrorists, were the white slave owners. They projected onto Blacks all of the violence and violent emotions they had enacted on the Black/Slave. This projection continues into the present; we see it in the belief by the Tea Party and many far-right Republicans that when in office President Barack Obama was going to violently repress them, take away their rights, and establish a communist-socialist-anticolonial-antiwhite-Black power-Mau Mau–like dictatorship.

———

In 1991, in the incident that helped ignite the violence in Los Angeles, one of the policemen who beat Rodney King with his baton claimed that King's strength was "Hulk-like." Darren Wilson, the Ferguson, Missouri, policeman who shot the unarmed eighteen-year-old Michael Brown in 2014, claimed he saw a "demon," then added, "When I grabbed him, the only way I can describe it is that I felt like a five-year-old holding onto Hulk Hogan." Implicit in these reactions is an attribution to Black men and boys of inhuman strength and capacity for violence and an inhuman capacity to ignore or feel pain. This is what a psychologist would call "projection," the casting of something inside one's own psyche onto another without recognition that one is doing so.

Obviously, Wilson's implicit bias and racism factored into his shooting of Michael Brown; there was never a possibility of Wilson seeing Brown as a teenager or a "good boy," as young white defendants are so often portrayed in courts by their family-financed lawyer and by judges who let them off with probation or lesser sentences. Every Black person in Ferguson understood that Wilson viewed not just Michael Brown as a "demon" or a "hulk." No, that image—that phantasmagorical projection—characterized the way Wilson viewed all their sons, indeed all the Black residents of Ferguson.

And what are the origins of this phantasmagorical projection but slavery? The slave was a beast, and so are the slave's descendants. White America has concocted this projection, and white America continues to allow this stereotype residence in its psyche.

It is not just within the justice system that these projections affect the ways Blacks are treated in our society. How is the stereotype of inhuman strength and incapacity for pain related to the fact that in emergency rooms Blacks wait longer for pain medication and receive smaller doses than whites *for the same injuries and conditions*? This discrepancy is true even comparing Black children and white children.

In this country, the racial stereotyping of Blacks starts automatically at birth.

———

As scholars such as Khalil Gibran Muhammad have demonstrated, the ideology of Blacks as criminals did not become a dominant stereotype until after the Civil War. Before that time, Blacks were not citizens but property and thus were incapable of stealing property—unless they ran away. But the myth of the violent nature of Blacks stems from the beginning of slavery; that myth yoked itself to the myth of Black criminality in the period following the Civil War. Both mythologies inform Whiteness and the thoughts and feelings of individual whites toward Blacks. White projection of their own violence and fear onto Blacks has never stopped in this country.

In his famous concept of the double consciousness from *The Souls of Black Folks*, W. E. B. Du Bois posited that Blacks had to be aware both of how they thought about themselves and how whites thought about them; their survival depended on not just understanding their own consciousness but also the consciousness of whites. But when contemplating this Black double consciousness, many do not ask what would seem to be a logical follow-up question: why is it that whites do not possess double consciousness? Why is it that whites have such a very different epistemology—such a different processing in their knowledge of their racial other—from that of Blacks?

For whites to gain double consciousness, they must abandon and deconstruct the ways their relationship with and thinking about Blacks still connect with the origins of slavery. They must critique the myriad ways they refuse, demean, and denigrate Black consciousness, the ways whites are still bound by white definitions of what it means to be human. They must understand why Blacks and other people of color think about themselves and whites differently from the way whites think about themselves or Blacks. And whites must then be able to articulate those views with accuracy and empathy as if their lives depended on such understanding, for this is how and why Blacks have always known what whites think, since their very survival depended on this knowledge. In short, whites must listen to Blacks and other people of color, listen without editing or critiquing but with compassionate imagination and empathy and a willingness to confront the lies Whiteness has told about itself and Black people.

But to do all this, whites must lose their sense of innocence. This is because their sense of innocence depends on a lack of connection with their history and the ways that history informs how whites think about themselves and Blacks. This means that whites must understand how their identity and the current realities of race in America are still connected to the origins of American slavery, genocide, and the stealing of Native land.

This of course runs against the premise of American exceptionality—America as the new Eden, the white American as existing within and claiming the garden of innocence.

The shadow side of white identity involves the darkness and fear, the racial stereotypes that still undergird our culture, society, and politics. It involves the ways white society projects on Blacks and other people of color an aspect of whites' own psyche about which they are still in denial.

For many people of color, the presence and workings of this white shadow side within our society are everywhere present and obvious. But in the conscious mind of many whites, their own shadow side does not exist. They are innocent of all charges or responsibilities concerning race and are enraged when such charges and responsibilities are brought up.[3]

———

The civil unrest in Baltimore, the fate of Freddie Gray and Walter Scott, Black Lives Matter, the violence of the police on unarmed Black bodies, and the mass incarceration of Black bodies[4]—these are connected to our history, and we will only begin to prevent their recurrence if we understand and explore that history rather than deny its connection to our present.

In order to do this work, in order to properly understand our present and our past, we need a new definition of racism, one that explains racism as a system of beliefs, practices, and laws and not just a matter of individual bias. We need to understand why our society still clings to an inadequate and outmoded definition of racism, why so many whites reject any systemic description of the ways race works in our society. The dictionary, the terms we use concerning race—these too are racial battlegrounds.

---

3. The effects of this shadow side on our politics involve both conservative and liberal whites. As Eddie S. Glaude Jr. writes in *Time* magazine, September 6, 2018: "Our narrow focus on explicit racists misses a development that explains our current moment: that much of our struggle with race today is bound up in the false innocence of white suburban bliss and the manic effort to protect it, no matter the costs. In the late 1960s and early '70s, for example, millions of white homeowners in the nation's suburbs—for the most part, racially segregated communities subsidized by state policies—rejected efforts to desegregate schools through busing and vehemently defended the demographic makeup of their neighborhoods. These were not people shouting slurs at the top of their lungs (although some did). They were courageous defenders of their quality of life—segregated life, that is. These were the people of the so-called 'silent majority,' who insisted on free-market meritocracy and embraced a color-blind ideology to maintain their racially exclusive enclaves. Their antibusing crusades, taxpayer revolts, and insistence on neighborhood schools cut across party lines and helped shape national politics. Democrats and Republicans appealed to the interests of these voters, and many turned their backs on the agenda of the civil rights movement. These [white] Americans, it was argued, were the true victims."

4. See Michelle Alexander, *The New Jim Crow: Mass Incarceration in the Age of Colorblindness.*

Our current definitions of racism still center on individual conscious actions and beliefs, on conscious discrimination, animus, and violence. They do not take into account the existence of unconscious or implicit bias. They do not take into account the system of beliefs, practices, laws, cultural productions that have produced and continue to produce racial inequalities in all areas of society—in politics, in the justice system, in economics (Black unemployment has traditionally been twice that of white unemployment), in education, in health care, in culture (Oscars so white), in religion (the most segregated day of the week in America is still Sunday), and so forth.

———

The traditional definition of racism that focuses mainly or solely on individuals and individual acts and on conscious stated bias and blatant animus is vastly incomplete; it thoroughly misleads us as to the extent and depth of racism in either America's past or present. Yes, there were despicable acts of violence toward Blacks in the South after the Civil War, but substantial work also went into the political, legal, economic, philosophic, and cultural productions by white Southerners to reinstitute the trappings of slavery after the Emancipation Proclamation and to nullify Black citizenship and rights granted by the Thirteenth, Fourteenth, and Fifteenth Amendments. The retrenchment and regression were not just the work of "a few bad apples" or individual acts of violence and discrimination. They were created through a system of racism and history (particularly the myth of the Lost Cause, the distorted Southern account of the Civil War that drastically minimized the effects and evils of slavery and pictured Southern whites as a noble and oppressed people merely fighting for their freedom), and this system led to the establishment of Jim Crow. Similarly, the vast racial inequalities in our country today do not stem from a few renegade police or one's racist uncle. To insist that racism is not systemic in this country is a key instrument of systemic racism, for racism in this country has always attempted to disguise, camouflage, obfuscate, and deny any investigations into its systemic nature.

The structural components of racism, which go beyond the acts of any one individual, can be broken down like this:

1. **Accumulated acts of conscious (explicit) and unconscious (implicit) bias**

Most conservatives, and even many liberals, want to view racism simply through the lens of the individual, singling out "a few bad apples" who express explicit bias. But racist acts of discrimination and hatred are far more prevalent and frequent than most whites will admit, and this is even more the case when one adds acts of unconscious or implicit bias. Blacks are shot or stopped by police at a higher frequency than whites, and this occurs with openly racist (consciously biased) police as well as unconsciously biased police. When one totals up these acts, one must see them not simply as acts by individuals but as a system. Only a systemic lens can help us understand the following disparities:

> Blacks are four times more likely to be arrested for marijuana possession though whites use marijuana at the same rate as Blacks do.

> Limb amputations are 4.7 times as likely among Black patients than white patients.

> Black patients in hospital emergency rooms receive less pain medication than white patients for similar conditions.

> Black preschool boys represent 18 percent of enrollment but 41 percent of suspensions; Black preschool girls make up 19 percent of enrollment but 53 percent of female suspensions.

These disparities are programmed into our society, and the system acts through the biased beliefs and actions of separate individuals.

2. **Allocation of resources**

Throughout American history, more financial resources have been made available to whites in comparison with Blacks.

Again, these disparities are manifestations of a system of inequality. Enslaved African Americans were not paid for their labor and so their descendants never benefited from that labor; in contrast, white slave owners achieved wealth that they then handed down to their descendants. Here are some obvious examples:

> In education, there is the imbalance between the resources going to white suburban schools and urban schools with a majority of students of color.

> In the medical field, we can compare the amount of research dollars allocated to sickle cell anemia, a disease affecting mostly Blacks, as opposed to much greater dollars allocated to cystic fibrosis, a disease of similar severity affecting whites.

> Black unemployment rates have always been significantly higher than white unemployment rates, in recent years often twice that of whites.

> Discriminatory lending and real estate practices have severely limited Black ownership of land and homes. Overall, housing is a vehicle through which whites have accumulated generational wealth, which has been denied unequally to Black families in the past and present. In the twentieth century, white soldiers received GI benefits after World War II while Black soldiers were denied the same benefits: the ability to go to college, purchase homes, and build family wealth.

3. Policies/practices/rules/laws

There are rules and laws—often seemingly neutral—that in fact enable racism and racial inequities to be practiced. Here are a few examples:

> Stop-and-frisk policies more frequently target Black and other citizens of color than white citizens.

The lack of a special prosecutor against police: ordinary government prosecutors rely on the police to prosecute their cases and thus are reluctant to charge police, thereby jeopardizing that relationship.

Proof of racism or racist intent: in *McCleskey v. Kemp*, the Supreme Court ruled that absent any explicit avowal of discriminatory intent, statistical racial disparities in death-penalty rulings are not sufficient to prove bias.

Voter ID laws affect people of color at a greater rate than white Americans, often because non-white Americans do not necessarily have official government IDs.

It takes complex analysis to explain why seemingly neutral or objective criteria or practices produce such racial inequities.

4. **Beliefs/concepts/systems of thought**

America's system of racism relies on beliefs that then manifest in discriminatory actions or prevent prejudicial actions from being identified as such. These beliefs and concepts program individuals to act with racial bias. Such beliefs often denigrate and demean people of color or promote white supremacy. This is certainly true of persisting racist stereotypes.

Other beliefs deny the existence of racism in contemporary America: "Racism is a thing of the past"; "I don't see race." We know there are racial disparities in employment, for example, and these are enforced and supported by biased subjective standards or perceptions believed to be objective or racially neutral.

More generally, these systemic beliefs are based on a perspective of American history common to most white people. The maintenance and defense of a white version of history have gone into high gear in recent years. There is now an effort to severely limit the teaching of the history of race in America: for example, the banning of ethnic studies in Arizona schools; and the dismantling of Advanced Placement history in Oklahoma due to "overemphasis" on slavery and genocide practiced on Native Americans.

The above four components have all been practiced since the inception of America and thus, their effects have accumulated and been perpetuated over time. Contrary to what many conservatives believe, this history continues to have a lasting impact on the present—as do the distortions and myths in our white version of our history.

————

Here then would be a new definition of racism:

1. Racism is a system through which the power and resources of a society are distributed unequally and undemocratically by race. This system functions in all areas of society— politics, economics, law enforcement and the judiciary, education, culture, social relations, religion, and so on.

2. Actions, practices, and beliefs that support the status quo workings of this system and produce inequities are racist. There are actions, practices, and beliefs that purport to be racially neutral—sometimes to disguise their racist intent and sometimes because people consciously believe them to be racially neutral—and yet still produce systemic inequalities.

3. Thus racism can be supported both by individuals with conscious or explicit racial bias or by individuals with unconscious or implicit racial bias. Conscious and openly expressed views of racial supremacy need not be present for a person or an organization or business to act in a racially biased manner and thus contribute to racial inequities.

————

Much of this book is an analysis of historical and fictional racial narratives and how the structure and content of white racial narratives ignore, silence, or mitigate the racism of the past and contribute to the failure to acknowledge, speak of, and address the racism of the present. The way we tell stories is also part of systemic racism. Yet, insidiously, the myths, biases, and racist assumptions of these stories are often acting more at an unconscious rather than a conscious level, and so their effects on us often remain unrecognized.

James Baldwin once wrote, "Not every problem can solved. But no problem can be solved unless it is faced." The problem of race can be solved only when the nature and construction of that problem are made conscious rather than allowed to remain hidden.

James Baldwin and the Repetitions of History

From the Harlem Riots to Ferguson, Baltimore, and BLM

IN THE ERA OF BLACK LIVES MATTER, THE WRITINGS OF JAMES BALDWIN have gained a renewed prominence and mark him as *the* essential American essayist of the past century. Long before the recent scholarship on the justice system or on discriminatory financial practices such as redlining, Baldwin understood that racism in America is systemic and far vaster than any particular individual or locale. Therefore, any particular racial event cannot be viewed in isolation or as a singular incident, examined solely for its particulars. Such a narrow focus loses any chance of seeing that incident as representative of a system of power that runs throughout the body of our society—for that incident is only one manifestation of this system.

But seeing and deciphering the workings of this system create a difficult task, made only more so by white obfuscation. This obfuscation can take place, say, within the realm of the legal system and public policy; it can lie beneath the surface of events that do not seem inherently racial; certainly, it takes place within the psyches of individual whites and their inability to see their own racism or systematic racism.[1] But Baldwin was

---

1. Take the example of Ferguson. The people of this Missouri town outside St. Louis were enraged by Michael Brown's death; obviously his death represents, in its particulars, a horrible injustice and should be recognized as such. But focusing solely on that death and the rage it engendered will not help us to see the ultimate causes of his death or the ultimate sources of the rage of the Black residents of Ferguson. Instead, such a narrow perspective will lead us

not fooled or stymied by such white attempts to camouflage or ameliorate the impact of race and racism. Instead, he relied on what he saw before his eyes, on the realities of Black life in America, on the voices of his community to tell him the real truth behind the sheen of myth and mystification through which American racism has traditionally disguised itself.

When it comes to race in America, Baldwin knew that profession is not achievement, intent is not result. He understood that there is a spiritual price the oppressor must pay, and he understood how oppression affects the spirit and soul of the oppressed. His essays explore why actual equality, which entails the recognition of Black Americans as equals, is so difficult for white Americans to even begin to address.

Examine, for instance, the way Baldwin describes the purported cause of the Harlem riots of 1943, a description of particular relevance to the protests of the Black Lives Matter movement in places like Baltimore and Ferguson, Missouri:

> After the funeral, while I was downtown desperately celebrating my birthday, a Negro soldier, in the lobby of the Hotel Braddock, got into a fight with a white policeman over a Negro girl. Negro girls, white policemen, in or out of uniform, and Negro males—in or out of uniform—were part of the furniture of the lobby of the Hotel Braddock, and this was certainly not the first time such an incident had occurred. It was destined, however, to receive an unprecedented publicity, for the fight between the policeman and the soldier ended with the shooting of the soldier. Rumor, flowing immediately to the streets outside, stated the soldier had been shot in the back, an instantaneous and revealing invention, and that the soldier had died protecting a Negro woman. The facts were somewhat different—for example, the soldier had not been shot in the back, and was not dead, and the girl seems to have been as dubious a symbol of womanhood as her white counterpart in Georgia usually is, but no one was interested in the facts. They preferred the invention because this invention expressed and corroborated their hates

---

to mischaracterize and misunderstand the causes and nature of that rage, which ultimately involves the particulars of the life of every Black—and white—person in America (as well as those, like me, who are neither), and, just as important, the entire moral history of this country.

and fears so perfectly. It is just as well to remember that people are always doing this. Perhaps many of these legends, including Christianity, to which the world clings began their conquest of the world with just some such concerted surrender to distortion. The effect, in Harlem, of this particular legend was like the effect of a lit match in a tin of gasoline. The mob gathered before the doors of the Hotel Braddock simply began to swell and to spread in every direction, and Harlem exploded.

Baldwin relates both the rumor that seemingly sparked the riots and the truth behind the rumors. But he is not an investigative reporter, nor in the end is he interested in the particular details of the incident in question. He knows the particulars will not explain what happened in Harlem and are, indeed, in many ways tangential to the actual riots.

Instead, Baldwin focuses on the emotions behind the riots, their exact and true cause—which is the white oppression of the residents of Harlem and the emotional reaction of those residents to their oppression. Those emotions are rooted in the conditions under which the residents of Harlem live, and thus they cannot be reduced to the specifics of any given incident on any given day. Baldwin wants the reader to be aware of why this psychological state exists. If the riots started because of a rumor, part of which was false, the real causes of the riots were not false; instead, those causes involved years of police abuse and governmental oppression and neglect, and various forms of economic oppression, as well as the general antipathy of the white population toward Blacks.

More than seventy years after the Harlem riots, when Michael Brown was killed and Ferguson erupted, or when Freddie Gray was killed and Baltimore erupted, the particulars of their killings were gone over in detail and yet remain disputed. But what got lost in such arguments was this: the pain that those who loved these men or those who were part of their community was not in dispute, nor was the rage that followed. Instead, the rage of the Black residents of Ferguson possessed a deeper, more permanent cause. Yes, in part this involved the long history of police brutality in that town, but it also involved a police department that systemically extorted the Black population of Ferguson in order to finance the police department and city government.[2] It involved a wide-ranging machine of oppression. The excessive ticketing and arresting of the Black population, and subsequent court costs and fines—where failure to pay tickets and fines led to jail time and further fines—constituted a systematized form of highway robbery. Rather than serving and protecting the Black citizens of Ferguson, the police were exploiting Black residents in order to maintain the police department: the police department was not financed mainly by taxes, as it is in other municipalities, but was financed primarily by tickets and fines paid by Black citizens. The police were incentivized to stop, ticket, and arrest Black residents not for public safety issues but for their own salaries.[3] In this, they were more like a government-sanctioned marauding gang.

2. *St. Louis Post-Dispatch*, March 5, 2015, "DOJ Finds Ferguson Targeted African Americans, Used Courts Mainly to Increase Revenue": "In the aftermath of a scathing report showing Ferguson unfairly targeted African-Americans and preyed on its most vulnerable citizens, the Justice Department is asking the city to make more than two dozen changes to the city's police department and municipal courts—or face a costly lawsuit.

The 102-page report on the patterns and practices of the Ferguson Police Department released on Wednesday describes an out-of-control police department whose officers target African-Americans, stop and search people without reasonable suspicion, arrest people without probable cause, abuse their authority to quash protests, routinely ignore civil rights and use excessive force by unnecessarily using dogs, batons and Tasers. It describes a city government that uses its police and courts as an ATM, tolerating a culture of police brutality while pressuring the police chief and court officials to increase traffic enforcement and fees without regard to public safety. It exposes a court run by the police department that routinely violates due process and intentionally inflicts pain on the most vulnerable residents and whose supervisors circulated racially insensitive emails, one of which in 2011 depicted President Barack Obama as a chimpanzee."

3. Ferguson is not alone in depending on revenue from police stops and ticketing. In a 2021 *New York Times* article, "Across America, Many Towns' Thirst for Money Sends Patrol Cars Hunting for Any Possible Violations," Mike McIntire and Michael H. Keller write: "A hidden scaffolding of financial incentives underpins the policing of motorists in the United States, encouraging some communities to essentially repurpose armed officers as revenue agents searching infractions largely unrelated to public safety. As a result, driving is one of the most common daily routines during which people have been shot, Tased, beaten or arrested after minor offenses. . . . Many municipalities across the country rely heavily on ticket revenue and court fees to pay for government services, and some maintain outsize police departments to help generate that money, according to a review of hundreds of municipal audit reports, town budgets, court files and state highway records. This is, for the most part, not a big-city phenomenon. . . . Mayors of predominantly white suburbs in Ohio, for example, defended the ticket-blitzing of Black drivers from Cleveland as an acceptable, if unfortunate, side effect of vigorously patrolling brief sections of interstates within their borders." Excessive ticketing of Black drivers is not by chance or because of a few "bad apples"; it is systemic and purposeful.

But beyond all this, that Ferguson police system was only part of a larger-scale system of oppression and discrimination that runs through every area of our society, in economics, politics, education, culture: a segregated and inferior public school system; practices like redlining and discriminatory real estate transactions and inequities in lending patterns, which have led to the creation of a segregated town like Ferguson; a jobless rate that has always been twice that of whites; vast health disparities and unequal treatment in the health care system; and so forth. Added to all these are the experiences of Blacks in Ferguson who lived with the day-to-day manifestations of these systems, from microaggressions to personal exclusions and denials of opportunity to the pain and anguish of family members and ancestors who have dealt with the same oppression to the number of members of the community incarcerated through the justice system.

Thus, to view the anger and rage in Ferguson as caused by the tragic killing of one teenager named Michael Brown—tragic and appalling as his death was—is to mistake how deep-seated and long-standing are the sources of the rage of Ferguson's Black residents. That rage is caused not by one particular incident or even a series of police-related incidents but is the result of the sum of the whole community's experience with racism in our society. And that experience, the totality of the Black community's experience of racism—which dates back to the beginning of this country—is something that white America has never understood or admitted, that white America still cannot countenance.

Moreover, as Baldwin has observed, "People who treat other people as less than human must not be surprised when the bread they have cast on the waters comes floating back to them, poisoned." In other words, when the oppressed finally find or seize the opportunity to voice their anger over injustice, it is unfair and certainly a denial of human nature to expect that every such expression of that anger will always be well-tempered, politically strategic, accommodating, and forgiving. It is unfair and unreasonable to expect that the expression of such long-suppressed anger will always burst out in reasoned argument, into absolutely exact articulations of its causes, into perfectly organized absolutely nonviolent protest.

That Black protests have so often been nonviolent and well articulated is rarely appreciated by white America. That such protests are only occasionally out of control or destructive is a tribute to the strength, character, and spirituality of Black people and their leaders. America had no right to expect the saintliness of Dr. Martin Luther King Jr., or his followers, and yet a pronounced majority of white America, during his lifetime, still disapproved of him and the tactics of his followers.[4] At the same time, the miracle of King and his life, which Baldwin witnessed and wanted to understand, should not be used as a tool to belittle, judge, and deny the efforts of a later generation of Blacks still asking for their rights as Americans and basic human decency. Colin Kaepernick or Reverend Jeremiah Wright, Michael Brown or Sandra Bland may not be Martin Luther King Jr. (who is?), but their cause is still the same.

This brings up one of the rules of America's racism: *while white America has sometimes admitted some legitimacy to the Black struggle for equality in the past, that legitimacy no longer holds and/or is rarely valid in the present.* Any NFL player who takes a knee is, as Donald Trump disparaged, "a son of a bitch" (a dog, less than human), and Black Lives Matter activists are unpatriotic ingrates, thugs, criminals, and even terrorists. Never mind that these contemporary protesters are being critiqued in a manner similar to the ways Martin Luther King Jr. and the civil rights movement were critiqued and labeled un-American.[5] There can be no contemporary equivalent to Sojourner Truth (remember candidate Clinton's excoriating of Sister Souljah) just as there can be no contemporary equivalent of Harriet Tubman or Rosa Parks or Frederick Douglass. In the white historical imagination, these Black figures who challenged the racial status quo in the past are mere empty figureheads that serve as proof that there need to be no challenges to the present racial status quo. Indeed, the more praise and citing of these historical figures by whites, the more whites feel able to diminish Black protestors in the present. These Black historical figures were so great, whites contend, we no longer need similar figures in present-day America, and so their equivalents cannot

---

4. Martin Luther King Jr.: "A riot is the language of the unheard."

5. Five days before King was murdered, editorial writers of the *Chicago Tribune* wrote: "We think the time has arrived when the country must ask itself how much more it is going to put up with from this incendiarist." King is now considered a saint; in his own time, whites considered him dangerous, a sower of civil unrest and violence—un-American.

possibly exist in the present. Thus, those Blacks who make contemporary charges of racism can never be heroes similar to the icons of our racial past; instead, contemporary Blacks who call out present-day racial injustices are charlatans, whiners, snowflakes, thugs, criminals, and reverse racists, pulling the race card in a time when there is no racism.

In such arguments between whites and Blacks over race in the past or present, whites play a shell game where racism is always hidden. With every shell Blacks may point to, whites have made sure there's nothing there. The shell is hidden in their pocket and their pocket is not part of the game.

———

Rather than focusing on temporal details or the overtly political questions of policy, Baldwin starts with the premise that the ways oppression functions in any society are markedly similar. So too are the effects of that oppression both on the oppressor and the oppressed.

It is here that his allegorical depictions of sociopolitical conditions allow him to get at the spiritual and psychological mechanisms and effects of racial inequities in ways a more reportorial or sociological approach would prevent. Examine, for instance, his descriptions of the response of Blacks to their living conditions and to the existence of Black ghettos and spaces of poverty, in "Fifth Avenue, Uptown":

> Harlem got its first private project, Riverton—which is now, naturally, a slum—about twelve years ago because at that time Negroes were not allowed to live in Stuyvesant Town. Harlem watched Riverton go up, therefore, in the most violent bitterness of spirit, and hated it long before the builders arrived. They began hating it at about the time people began moving out of their condemned houses to make room for this additional proof of how thoroughly the white world despised them. And they had scarcely moved in, naturally, before they began smashing windows, defacing walls, urinating in the elevators, and fornicating in the playgrounds. Liberals, both white and black, were appalled at the spectacle. I was appalled by the liberal innocence—or cynicism, which comes out in practice as much the same thing. . . . The people in Harlem know they are living

there because white people do not think they are good enough to live anywhere else. No amount of "improvement" can sweeten this fact. Whatever money is now being earmarked to improve this, or any other ghetto, might as well be burnt. A ghetto can be improved in one way only, out of existence.

If a society allows racial ghettos to exist, argues Baldwin, no words or promises, no laws or political gestures can deny the truth of that existence and what it says to those who live in such ghettos: this is all you'll get, this is all you deserve. You will never live as neighbors of white people or share equally the political, economic, or educational advantages that whites enjoy and expect as a right.

How such a racial status quo is achieved is complicated. Certainly, investigations into such practices as redlining and the creation of segregated urban blocks of poverty are necessary and can lead to changes in policies and laws. We need work like Richard Rothstein's *The Color of Law: A Forgotten History of How Our Government Segregated America* or Ta-Nehisi Coates's investigation in *The Atlantic* of how de facto segregation, redlining, and predatory loan and housing practices kept Blacks on Chicago's South Side mired in poverty and unable to live elsewhere in the city. Such studies about financing and housing do much more to explain Black poverty in America—a great portion of the disparity between Black and white wealth stems from home ownership—than harangues about Black character and work habits.

However, on a day-to-day level, on an individual level, Black people feel the effects of these discriminatory practices even if they don't understand or know about all their workings. To Baldwin, then, our primary focus should start with the question, does white America want such Black poverty and segregation to exist or not? Black people know the honest answer is a resounding "Yes."

Thus, more frequently than not, talk about policy or laws by the white powers that be is not really proposed as an honest solution; instead, such talk is used to obscure the deep, painful, and difficult truth of this answer: *the conditions Black Americans live under are exactly the way white America wants them to be.*

A similar truth exists in the policing of ghettos, says Baldwin:

. . . the only way to police a ghetto is to be oppressive. None of the Police Commissioner's men, even with the best will in the world, have any way of understanding the lives led by the people they swagger about in twos and threes controlling. Their very presence is an insult, and it would be, even if they spent their entire day feeding gumdrops to children. They represent the force of the white world, and that world's real intentions are, simply, for that world's criminal profit and ease, to keep the black man corralled up here, in his place. The badge, the gun in holster, and the swinging club make vivid what will happen should this rebellion become overt. Rare, indeed, is the Harlem citizen, from the most circumspect church member to the most shiftless adolescent, who does not have a long tale to tell of police incompetence, injustice, or brutality.

It is hard, on the other hand, to blame the policeman, blank, good-natured, thoughtless, and insuperably innocent, for being such a perfect representative of the people he serves. He, too, believes in good intentions and is astounded and offended when they are not taken for the deed. He has never, himself, done anything for which to be hated—which of us has?—and yet he is facing, daily and nightly, people who would gladly see him dead, and he knows it. There is no way for him not to know it: there are few things under heaven more unnerving than the silent, accumulating contempt and hatred of a people. He moves through Harlem, therefore, like an occupying soldier in a bitterly hostile country; which is, precisely what, and where, he is, and is the reason he walks in twos and threes. And he is not the only one who knows why he is always in company: the people who are watching him know why, too. Any street meeting, sacred or secular, which he and his colleagues uneasily cover has as its explicit or implicit burden the cruelty and injustice of the white domination.

In the ghetto, the policeman is "like an occupying soldier in a bitterly hostile country," and the people of that country react accordingly—moving from unease to hatred to hostility—and the policeman reacts accordingly—moving from callousness to anxiety to hatred to hostility. As long as the policeman is a representative of an occupying force from another country that does not include the Black population, this will be the state of the relations between the police and the Black community.[6] And the fact that in so many metropolitan police departments the majority of the police do not live in the city they patrol is merely an extension of this.

The Harlem riot of 1943 that Baldwin alludes to in "Notes of a Native Son" stems from the same racial inequities that sparked the demonstrations in Ferguson in 2014 after the killing of Michael Brown, or in Baltimore in 2015 after the killing of Freddie Gray. Baldwin's truths about the Harlem riot are still true today, and they question how far we have actually come in dealing with the problems of race.

Or as the expression goes, same ol' same ol'.

———

If Baldwin speaks to us from that time as a prophet, it is because he understood certain moral and spiritual principles: obviously, oppression requires force, in myriad forms. But oppression also requires lies, and when the oppressor believes his own lies, spiritually he is lost. He is lost because he has lost touch with reality, with his own mortal fallibility; he has distorted reality in his own mind, and he can no longer see the world clearly. More specifically, he cannot see either himself or the oppressed clearly. The oppressor thus lies to himself both about himself and about those he oppresses.

If white Americans do not believe that Black Americans are equal and human, Baldwin says, then none of our racial problems can be solved. And by any reasonable assessment, or more generally by the assessment of the lives Black people are forced to live in this country, this is still clearly the case.

It is not Black people, says Baldwin, who have created the ghetto and housing segregation; nor is it Black people who have made the police an occupying force that treats Black Americans not as citizens but as a colonized people, as a foreign enemy; nor is it Black people who have ensured that Black unemployment has always been historically double

---

6. Officer Jeronimo Yanez, who killed Philando Castile, attended a Bulletproof Warrior training, which instructed officers to regard themselves as soldiers occupying a hostile territory—a positioning that replicates the attitude of the police described in Baldwin's essay a half-century earlier.

or nearly double that of white unemployment; nor is it Black people who have created the conditions that make Black poverty considerably more pervasive and greater than white poverty in America.

Both white conservatives and liberals are so fond of quoting Martin Luther King Jr.'s wish that Blacks be judged by the content of their character and not the color of their skin. But white America is—and always has been—blind to the contexts that would make the character of any individual Black person fully human and comprehensible, that could understand and contextualize an individual Black person within the community and conditions of their fellow Blacks. And yet, white America has created that context, has created and enforced with violence the parameters and strictures it places upon Black Americans. As philosopher Charles Mills has observed, the insistence on white innocence has made whites "unable to understand the world they themselves have made." This innocence, as Cathy Park Hong has pointed out, depends on not just a lack of knowledge but "an active state of repelling knowledge."

We are left with this paradox: white America enacts and refuses to see what it enacts; it purports to believe in equality and refuses to see the ways its actions prove otherwise. That is why white Americans, even white liberals, are so often baffled by Black responses to injustice—by Black rage or by Black distrust or even Black culture as a whole. That is why white characterizations of Philando Castile, Michael Brown (*New York Times*: "not exactly an angel"), Freddie Gray, Trayvon Martin, or Sandra Bland ultimately cannot provide a context to judge these individuals in light of the experiences of Black America. To repeat: *white people cannot see Black people because white people cannot let themselves see what they have done to Black people—and thus to see who they, white people, actually are.*

PART II

HOW WE NARRATE THE PAST

White Memory
and the Psychic Sherpa

OFTEN IN AN ALCOHOLIC OR ABUSIVE FAMILY, THERE IS ONE MEMBER who first acknowledges the problem, who remembers the painful and harmful acts of the past and the damage caused by those actions, who chooses to break the zones of silence the family enforces about their past, who points to the craziness and denial at the heart of the family system. One who breaks the taboo of silence. But to the rest of the family, this breaker of the family system is the mad one, the difficult one, the one who refuses to just go along, the problematic one. And this, ironically, may be especially true if the one who breaches the zone of silence is the one who has been most abused.

Race in the family of America functions within a systemic denial of our mutual past, the injustices and damage done by racism, the harmful acts of individuals and institutions and groups. Those who were damaged most by racism remember that history and speak of it. Many whites who are still caught in this dysfunctional system still maintain their repression, their denial, in order to support a system they continue to benefit from.

There is what may be called Black memory and white memory. The two are mutually intertwined and compete and conflict within the arena of the present. In the world of white memory, Black memory does not exist, or it is a lie, a distortion. It breaks the rules of what is proper racial discourse. To speak of it is to play the so-called race card. Similarly, there is a Native American/Indigenous memory and a (white) Settler memory. In the worldview of Settler memory, the Native American/Indigenous memory does not exist (in part because white America no longer believes Native Americans exist), and America's acts of genocide and land plunder must never ever be at the forefront of how America remembers its past.

In America, racism doesn't distribute the painful memories of our racist past equally in the psyches of people of color and white people. No, it is people of color who carry and hold an unequal portion of these painful memories. In contrast, white memory is designated as the realm of the ideal, a mythic and mainly blemish-free version of our past where the racial scars and injustices are covered over by declamations of racial progress—or where so many of the details of these injustices are relegated to the footnotes. As a result, people of color are constantly placed in a position of trying to hand white America their portion of this country's painful past, the white psychic burden, in order to force white Americans to deal with their true legacy. But white America refuses to hold these memories, their past. *You go on holding it,* says white America to people of color. *You keep carrying it. We had nothing to do with it. It was long ago.*

———

What does it mean to serve as a psychic sherpa? To carry the unpleasant emotions and memories of another, for another? For one person or group to be weighed down by darkness, depression, anger, madness, so the other may be lighter, happier, and seemingly sane?

Do people of color carry in our psyches the memories and burdens of our history so that whites can live in amnesia—without the burdens such memories entail?

Do we take in realities whites do not have to see and thus take up?

How does all this affect the mental energies we must put out in order to function in our lives?

When will white America take up and address their true and proper portion of our country's difficult and painful past? And what keeps white America from doing so?

How We Think—
or Don't Think—about It

Racial Epistemologies and Ontologies

"If I Knew It Was Going to Be This Much Trouble"

Once, while driving with my wife in her home state of Georgia, I passed a car with this bumper sticker: "If I knew it was going to be this much trouble, I'd have picked my own damned cotton."

For my wife, who is white and whose parents came from the North, this sighting again confirmed her high school decision to leave the South for college in the North and never come back. But for me, I began to think of the mindset of the people who would display or approve of this bumper sticker and what it said about them. Ostensibly, the bumper sticker proclaimed that our problems with race in the present weren't worth whatever gains whites obtained from slave labor. The deeper implication? The owner of this bumper sticker really seemed to wish they could live in a world where Blacks were not part of America.

Aside from its obvious racist overtones, such a bumper sticker represents a common misconception about the impact of slavery and the cotton industry on America, both in the past and present. In *Empire of Cotton: A Global History*, Sven Beckert makes a cogent and well-researched argument that slavery was instrumental not just to the cotton industry; no, that is too narrow a lens. Instead, Beckert argues that the wealth created by slavery and the cotton industry was essential to the creation of wealth in all of nineteenth-century America, both in the South and the North. In other words, the economic progress of America, both before and after the Civil War, depended vitally on slave labor and the oppression of Blacks. We as a country would not be where we are to-day economically without slavery. Our current wealth is a direct result of our racist history. Even while conservatives complain of government handouts to Blacks and other minorities, they never want to confront the myriad ways slavery acted as a free handout to the white population, from which the white population is still benefiting.

Books like *Empire of Cotton* or Edward E. Baptist's *The Half Has Never Been Told: Slavery and the Making of American Capitalism* are beginning to revise our understanding of the economic impact of slavery on America. Here is Baptist's summation of the slavery's immense contribution not just to pre–Civil War American economies but to the production of the modern American economy:

> Entrepreneurial enslavers moved more than one million enslaved people, by force, from the communities that survivors of the slave trade had built in the South and in the West to vast territories that were seized—also by force—from their Native American inhabi-tants. From 1783 at the end of the American Revolution to 1861, the number of slaves in the United States increased five times over, and all this expansion produced a powerful nation. For white en-slavers were able to force enslaved African American migrants to pick cotton faster and more efficiently than free people. . . . The returns from the cotton monopoly powered the modernization of the rest of the American economy, and by the time of the Civil War, the United States had become the second nation to undergo large-scale industrialization. . . . The idea that the commodification and suffering and forced labor of African Americans is what made the United States powerful and rich is not an idea that people nec-essarily are happy to hear. Yet it is the truth. . . . Enslaved African Americans built the modern United States, and indeed the entire modern world, in ways both obvious and hidden.

The economic effects of slavery represent a portion of history that involves business practices, facts, and figures. But when I first saw this Southern bumper sticker I was struck by its amnesia not about the eco-nomics of slavery but its psychology—the bumper sticker demonstrated an absence of any real attempt to come to grips with how slavery affected the thinking and psychology of whites. Slavery shaped the ways whites thought not just about Blacks but also about themselves; in the process it formed and constituted their identity, including their sense of morality and psychology.

The bumper sticker posits slavery as simply a phenomenon of physical labor, as merely a choice concerning who would pick the "damned cotton," whites or Blacks. What the bumper sticker does not imagine is the enormous mental effort, the practical and conceptual thinking that was necessary to maintain and justify slavery, the psychological strains and distortions that enabled white owners to enforce and believe in their superiority, sovereignty, and mastery over their fellow human beings.

For make no mistake: to hold absolute power over another human being and at the same time to believe in one's own moral righteousness while doing so was not a simple task. For one thing, it required one to live in constant fear, fear that was both conscious and unconscious. Beyond that, it required constant mental gymnastics, a constant fending off of contrary or resistant observations or feelings; it involved an insistent willingness not to see the humanity of the human beings one ruled over. It required a deep psychological, spiritual, and philosophical blindness—that is, almost pathological powers of denial.

In other words, the establishment and enforcement of slavery required obvious physical labor—torture and other punishments; organizing, overseeing, and policing slaves; going after runaways, and so on. But it also required an enormous mental labor, which manufactured its own products, products that continue to live on in our society and in the minds of many Americans today. Thus the sheer difficulty, unwieldiness, and complications of enforcing and maintaining slavery are vastly underestimated by many in the present. Slave owners were caught within both mental and practical contradictions that they struggled and failed to resolve, since those contradictions stemmed from their denial of reality: the slave was as fully human as the master.

———

In all this, then, the system of slavery rested on the obliteration of this truth—the slave's humanity—and the creation of lies. The master was supposedly the natural and God-appointed ruler of the slave. The slave was not quite human, was not as intelligent as the master, did not have the same moral, emotional, and psychological capacities. In this natural God-given order, supposedly the slave willingly and openly accepted the master's superiority and rule.

But if all these assumptions undergirding slavery were truly the case, in theory the master's dominion over the slave should have been easily enforced. But of course, in practice it was not. In *Honor and Violence in the Old South,* Bertram Wyatt-Brown writes:

> Black and white struggles over slave autonomy never ceased. Masters often wearied of trying to impose their will on every occasion that reached their notice. As [Eugene] Genovese and others have shown, slaves in the field and kitchen were shrewd observers of "old massa" and knew how to exploit his grave weaknesses, largely in answer to their grim exploitation at "ole massa's" hands. The irate owner, in helpless fury, could use the whip unmercifully—but mostly with counterproductive results. As John Blassingame has observed, under such conditions slaves became indifferent and worked less effectively than ever before, and some even risked their lives in open confrontation.
>
> On the other hand, tolerant masters watched impotently as each new privilege begged for and granted, at once became plantation tradition and precedent for further requests.

The phrase concerning the master's "helpless fury" is hardly the case—it was the slave who was helpless—but Wyatt-Brown's point is clear: the resistance of Black human beings to their slavery was constant and unrelenting, an oppositional force that white slave owners had to contend with. Yet at the same time, this counterforce was a phenomenon that the master had to deny, since slavery was supposedly part of the "natural" order of things. As they struggled with the contradictions between their supposed position as absolute master and the realities of their actual dealings with Black human beings, slave owners devised elaborate philosophic, pseudoscientific, and religious theories to rationalize and support the system of slavery. This mental production did not occur by chance, but by the conscious and constant creation, elaboration, and distribution of ideas. When the theories and rationale met the practice and suppression of the rights and humanity of actual human beings, the conflicts, contradictions, and breakdowns fueled both further mental production as well as the devising of new and greater methods of violence and terror.

In theory, the master and slave were distinctly separate entities—ontologically, epistemologically, legally, politically, biologically, theologically, psychologically, and culturally. But each day the practice of slavery indicated otherwise. The willed blindness of whites to this contradiction is part of slavery's legacy, and its influences still shape our society today. White identity is still formulated on the exclusion of or segregation by whites from the experiences, consciousness, and stories of Black Americans. Even in the present, the unwillingness of Whiteness and white people to know, much less entertain, the validity of Black knowledge is both encouraged and enforced, and yet paradoxically that willed ignorance remains unconsciously central to white identity. Whites know that they do not want to know Black reality—and yet they do not know all the ways they do not want to know or why they do not want to know.

———

In any discussion of race in twenty-first-century America, the end of slavery and the passing of civil rights laws in the 1950s and '60s are constantly cited as proof that either racism is almost entirely a phenomenon of the past or is far less prevalent in contemporary America than those making racial critiques acknowledge. Such an argument rests on defining racism as primarily a legal issue. The abandonment of legal and governmental policies of outright discrimination was supposedly the major hurdle to racial equality in this country.

But what about the thinking, the conceptual frameworks, the psychological identifications and predispositions that created all those legal and governmental racist policies of the past or the private societal and cultural rules that supported racial oppression and segregation? Did all that simply vanish once the Emancipation Proclamation was signed or civil rights laws were passed? Did the ways people think and feel about race, and more specifically, did the ways white people think about Blacks and other people of color drastically change overnight with the passing of the Fourteenth Amendment or the Voting Rights Act of 1965? Did the belief of individual whites—both conscious and unconscious—in the inferiority and lesser status of Black Americans end with any legal measure? Of course not.

Given the continued persistence of racial inequities in all areas of society, we must therefore ask, how has the thinking and psychology of whites on race in slavery's past shaped the thinking and psychology of whites on race in the present? And how does such thinking and psychology continue to distort, derail, and deny any true equality in the relationship between present-day whites and Blacks? In what ways does the gulf between a white-defined reality and a Black-defined reality—and thus, two very different epistemologies or ways of knowing the world—create a distance that still has not been breached?

Racial Epistemologies

Feminist epistemologists have argued that gender shapes and influences our conceptions of knowledge and the practices through which we attribute, acquire, and justify what is proper knowledge. This invariably involves questions of how we acquire knowledge and how we think about what we know and do not know. How does gender affect what and how someone knows? What part of gender is biological and what part performative and cultural? That is, is gender located in our DNA or in a set of social practices and beliefs? Is gender an objective set of criteria or is it subjective—that is, is it determined by history, culture, and shifting definitions of what is objective knowledge? How do a gendered male knowledge and identity claim a universality denied to female knowledge? As feminist philosopher Lorraine Code posits, "Objectivity requires taking subjectivity into account."

Similar issues arise when it comes to the epistemology of race: it shapes what we regard as valid and invalid knowledge; it shapes how we come to know and think about the world; it shapes how and whom we designate as possessing the truth of the world, both of the past and the present. Certainly, race affects our attitude toward various types of knowledge and how they are evaluated and acquired—personal knowledge; the knowledge of a group; the criteria of what is objective, true, historic, legal, scientific, of aesthetic value, etc. Or as Robin DiAngelo, author of *White Fragility,* puts it, paraphrasing Code, "From whose subjectivity does the ideal of objectivity come?"

People of color understand that a basis of white identity is always this: nothing people of color say about whites or Whiteness can be the truth (valid knowledge) unless whites and Whiteness decree it. Ultimately, whites believe it is their right to decide not just the nature of their reality, but that of Blacks and other people of color, too. It is their white epistemology, their way of knowing the world, that must remain supreme.

One purpose of this book is to examine the epistemological sources and practices of white supremacy—the questions of who gets to determine what is true knowledge, objective knowledge, official knowledge, legal knowledge, historical knowledge, and so forth—and the questions of how such knowledge is acquired and validated. To dig out the deepest roots of white supremacy, we must dismantle a racist epistemology where white Americans are the sole arbitrators of objective truth and the legitimate judges of the knowledge and the stories of Native Americans, African Americans, and other people of color. For it is a fundamental rule of white epistemology that the knowledge and stories of white America can never be legitimately challenged by Americans who are not white.

At a deep level, what both white conservatives and liberals share is a common psychology of denial and shame concerning race, a deep desire not to confront the racial realities that shape their lives and the lives of people of color. As a result, most whites don't understand, and they don't want to understand, the Whiteness of their epistemologies and ontologies—how they have come to think about their own thinking on race; how the lenses and terms through which they view their own racial identity and those of people of color have been constructed; how that construction is rooted deep in our history.

In all this, Whiteness is not just a political issue but a problem of psychological identity and denial, both individually and as a nation. This makes Whiteness a problem that can't simply or solely be addressed through legislation or policies. If passing a law to reform police practices and rules of engagement is already extremely difficult, transforming the racial consciousness of police officers is even more difficult—indeed, at least for now, nearly impossible.

The vast and far-reaching racial inequities in our society have not appeared overnight, have not been created by chance. *These inequities exist because white people have wanted them to exist and because they have acted in accordance with this desire.* In other words, these inequities do not continue to exist simply by accident or mere oversight or because of a few well-meaning mistakes or "a few bad apples."[1]

Even a cursory, honest examination reveals that present-day white identity in America is deeply rooted in our history. If there is a central theme to this book, it is that whites have been taught a false version of how race shaped not just past events or conditions but the very ways whites continue to think of themselves. In order to exert power in their interactions with people of color, whites have actively invoked and reinforced myths about themselves and the past; at the same time they have actively tried not to remember disturbing historical truths about what whites actually did to and thought about people of color in the past.

A cruel irony of this white epistemology is that Black America has always seen and understood the workings of American racism more clearly than whites. Over and over in our history, Black America has always been more morally prescient on race than white America. And yet white America has never turned finally to Black America and said, "We've gotten it wrong so many times before. You, not us, were on the right side of history. So we're just going to listen to you, really listen; we're going to recognize that you possess a knowledge that is not only vital to understanding who you are but who we are as well. And because of all this, we're going to follow your lead now."

But to acknowledge all this would be to acknowledge that in many ways the moral center of America on race has never been white America; it has always been Black and Indigenous America, the America of color. These are the portions of America who have seen and admitted the true and full extent of America's racist past and present, who truly know white Americans for who they are, for how they have acted toward their racial others; Americans of color know that white Americans are not who whites think, wish, or proclaim themselves to be. And this

---

1. Indeed, when applied to the police, the "few bad apples" phrase demonstrates how little America actually cares about Black lives. As Chris Rock has pointed out, no one would want to be operated on by a surgery department or to fly on an airline that had "a few bad apples."

America of color has always believed in America's promise far more than white American has, for they have continued to believe that that promise *could* be fulfilled, whereas white America never truly wanted to fulfill that promise. That is why it has always declared the goal of equality achieved when it clearly was not.

There's an old Black saying, "I don't believe what you say because I see what you do." But this adage also works in reverse: "You whites believe what you say because you don't see what you do."

Racial Ontologies

Ontology is the philosophical study of being or existence and the categories of being and their relations. This involves the questions of what entities can be said to exist and how those entities can be grouped and related in a hierarchy and categorized through similarities and differences.

Most people in America—but clearly not all—now accept that the categories of race are not based on essential and significant biological differences. Instead, these categories are established through superficial, if often ambiguous, differences in appearance. This leads people to argue that the categories of race are not "real," that they posit a difference that does not exist. Some people, mainly whites, further argue that because the categories of race are not real, they should not be used in current discourse. Thus racism can no longer exist since the categories of race supposedly do not exist.

At the very start of any discussion on race, there is generally a debate on what is meant by "real," that is, what is the nature of our reality. The definition of racial categories as "unreal" relies solely on whether or not there is an essential biological basis for racial categories. But such a position completely ignores the fact that America and Americans still evaluate and treat each other differently based on the categories of race. And just as important, these categories have deeply shaped America's history, its politics and institutions, its legal system and societal arrangements, its cultural practices and beliefs, how white and Black people have thought about themselves. Wishing away race and its categories does not make it so.

Richard Wright once remarked that Black America and white America are engaged in a struggle over the description of reality. Even if whites believe that their description of reality is the correct one, it is clear that this struggle still exists. And it exists on the level of how we categorize that reality, the terms we use to do so, and the meaning we assign to those terms.

––––––––

In American society, race constitutes a fundamental term through which people think they know the world and form their knowledge of themselves. However, the categories of race and their meaning can both seem obvious to all and yet be invisible in their workings, in the ways they shape our thinking, our identities, and our actions. Indeed, in this context the meaning and power of racism are often working more so at an unconscious rather than a conscious level. In part, this is what allows so many whites to deny how deeply the categories of race are embedded in our psyches.

The recent studies, for instance, of implicit or unconscious racial bias, especially in policing, represent but one example of this. Yes, there are explicitly racist police, who privately avow racial hostility and white supremacy. But there are also police who consciously avow racial equality and yet still act unconsciously in ways that enact and enforce racial bias. (Similar studies have shown unconscious or implicit bias in health care providers, teachers, and other members of society.)

But there are also less obvious and deeper unconscious racial structurings. For example, most white contemporary literary authors see themselves as progressives and opposed to political conservatives, especially on race. And yet starting with their practice of not racially identifying their characters and how they circumscribe their fictional worlds to a whites-only America, the ways these white writers practice their craft and the portraits they create are much more in keeping with the traditional rules of Whiteness, rules that have historically undergirded and supported racial inequities. Moreover, all this is accomplished in ways these white authors themselves are generally not aware of. Thus, we need to understand how Whiteness structures the aesthetic and narrative premises employed by these white authors in telling their stories. At the same time, we need to see how the stories these authors tell, as well as the stories they don't, help create white identity in both conscious and unconscious ways. In this closed loop, the fictional worlds and stories Whiteness creates help create Whiteness. White people believe in these stories and see them as reflections of and representations of themselves and of the society we live in.

But people of color understand that these white worlds and stories are incomplete at best, that at some fundamental level these white stories are based on lies, evasions, and distortions, on a blindness to both our history and our present. People of color understand that the versions of the world that white people tell themselves depend in part on the absence or denial of the consciousness of people of color, of our history and our lives. People of color question those white worlds and stories because we do not see ourselves in them—nor do we find certain truths we witness every day in our encounters with Whiteness and white people. People of color understand that nonwhite narrators have their own truths and stories to tell.

———

In the past few decades, the academic school of Afropessimism has posited that the ontology of slavery continues into the present and still structures our thinking and our perceptions of the differences between Whiteness and Blackness. The language of this theory is often dense and foreboding; aside from questions of academic jargon, this difficulty is meant in part to prevent the type of simplifying or translating I will attempt to do here. Yet the ideas underlying this theory are both useful and resonant and can aid us in understanding how deeply our racist past is embedded in the present. Indeed, when Afropessimist scholar Frank B. Wilderson III spoke to a community group in Oakland, an older black woman came up to him and said something like, "I didn't graduate from college and I'm not a scholar like you, but when you talk about how slavery is still with us, I know you're right. That's exactly the way I feel. Like a slave."

In his book *Red, White & Black: Cinema and the Structure of U.S. Antagonisms*, Wilderson argues that the structures of modernity, our post-Enlightenment concepts of what is human and what it means to be free and what it means to be a citizen or part of civil society, are all predicated on the ontological opposition of White and Black—or more pointedly, the relegation of Blackness to a realm of social death, outside the human and outside the definitions and relations of civil society. In other words, the meaning and category of Whiteness cannot be regarded as separate from the meaning and category of Blackness; the former is ontologically dependent on the existence of the latter:

> *African,* more precisely Blackness, refers to an individual who is by definition always already void of relationality. Thus modernity marks the emergence of a new ontology because it is an era in which an entire race appears, people who, a priori, that is prior to the contingency of a "transgressive act" (such as losing a war or being convicted of a crime), stand as socially dead in relation to the rest of the world. This, I will argue, is as true for those who were herded into the slave ships as it is for those who had no knowledge whatsoever of the coffles. In this period, chattel slavery, as a condition of ontology and not just as an event of experience, stuck to the African like Velcro. To the extent that we can think the essence of Whiteness and the essence of Blackness, we must think their essences through the structure of the Master/Slave relation, but I am also drawing a distinction between the experience of slavery (which anyone can be subjected to) and the ontology of slavery, which in modernity (the years 1300 to the present) becomes the singular purview of the Black. In this period, slavery is *cathedralized.* It "advances" from a word which describes a condition that anyone can be subjected to, to a word which reconfigures the African body into Black flesh. Far from being merely the experience of the African, slavery is now the African's access to (or more correctly, banishment from) ontology.

Wilderson cites how the work of scholar David Eltis asserts that it would have been cheaper to institute chattel slavery among white Europeans than enslave Africans; thus the choice not to make slaves of serfs or prisoners or those in poorhouses was a "bad business" decision. This less profitable decision was made on the surface for political reasons, but it entailed a deeper and more complex ontological rationale: "what Whites would have gained in economic value, they would have lost in symbolic value, and it is the latter which structures the libidinal economy of civil society." Making whites chattel slaves would have stripped them from the social contract, and this stripping would have problematized and infected the relationships between whites in ways that Europeans ultimately could not contemplate and act on. It would have destroyed or severely diminished Whiteness as a force of social cohesion and group identity, and thus the ability of whites to oppress and Other those of different races.

But with the expulsion of Blacks from civil society, Whiteness and civil relationships between whites were unified rather than reified. A white person was human, part of civil society, and therefore designated a citizen or potential citizen. Violence against Whiteness or whites could not be arbitrarily enacted but required justification; it needed to be legitimized as an act of war or as caused by legal transgression. Thus, whites, argues Wilderson, "are not 'generally dishonoured,' meaning they are not stigmatized in their being prior to any transgressive act or behavior. . . . they are not 'natally alienated,' meaning their claims to ascending and descending generations are not denied them; and they have some choice in their relation, meaning they are not the objects of 'naked violence.'"

In contrast, Blackness or Blacks are not human and therefore can never become citizens or act with the rights of citizens. Blackness is marked as being beyond civil society in a wholly separate and opposing category—that of the slave who is a priori dishonored and banished. Violence against the Black body needs no justification, requires no prior act of transgression, no act of war, no breaking of the law, for the Black does not own their body and because that body is not human; in that way, it is "dead" to society.[2]

At the same time, the Black body is fungible—that is, it can be owned and thus bought and sold; it belongs to its owner, whether that owner is

---

2. In a *New York Times* op-ed piece about the young black man, Ahmaud Arbery, who was killed while jogging by three armed white vigilantes in Glynn County, Georgia, on February 23, 2020, black philosopher George Yancy writes: "Historically, white people have always had this sort of power over black life, functioning as judge, jury, and executioner. To understand Arbery's death as anything other than predictable is to miss the persistent history of white supremacy in Georgia and throughout the United States. . . .

What if I told you that as a black man living in white America I feel as if I am already dead? I imagine that your first response would be disbelief. . . . But what is perhaps even stranger is that as a marked black man, I mourn my death in advance. . . .

To be black in America is to spend a lot of time talking about how to avoid death."

a person or the state. Therefore, while the parents of a white child constitute a sacrosanct relationship between progenitor and progeny, the offspring of the Black parent is the property of Whiteness and the white owner, or the white state; there is nothing sacrosanct or inviolable in the relationship between the Black parent and child, who are forever "natally alienated"—that is, ontologically (and therefore legally) separated and severed at birth.

When that working-class older Black woman addressed Wilderson after his talk on Afropessimism, she intuitively understood and felt the connections among this difficult theory, the history it represents, and the conditions of her life and of those in her neighborhood. She understood that the state and the police regard Whiteness and whites as part of civil society, that White-on-White or state-on-White violence is checked and requires justification. In contrast, White-on-Black or state-on-Black violence does not require such justification and is, in both conscious and unconscious ways, not regarded as a crime in the justice system. She understood that the Black body is always suspect because the Black body is not a priori part of the body politic, that Blackness is the category of the noncitizen, the outsider, the stranger, the threatening body. She intuitively understood the connection between this ontology and the acts of the police and justice system and the racial disparities within the legal system and disproportionate and overwhelming numbers of Blacks in the prison population. She understood why there is a disproportionate number of Black children whose parents are missing or in prison. She understood why someone named Donald J. Trump could question whether someone named Barack Hussein Obama could be a citizen, much less the legitimate President of the United States. This old black woman wasn't a scholar, but she was an experienced witness to what it means to be Black in American society, and that witnessing made her feel as if slavery was still a structuring presence in her life. She knew who created the categories of Whiteness and Blackness, and she knew that while those white-created categories may determine the conditions of her life and, indeed, whether she lives or dies, she also knew that those categories do not describe who she is and who her fellow community members are. She knew that Blacks define the categories of Whiteness and Blackness in very different ways from whites, and that a different set of definitions lies at the heart of Black culture and the stories Blacks tell themselves.

Every encroachment or potential encroachment of Blackness and the Black into civil society is a threat not just to the rights and privileges of whites, but to the very definition and ontology through which Whiteness is established. As created and promulgated by whites, including the Founding Fathers, the category of Whiteness does not make sense without the category of Blackness, and so far no amount of proclaimed good will or intention has made that distinction disappear.

To understand how this ontology was conceived and promulgated, we need to go back to the beginnings of America and how the creation of our democracy was intricately yoked to the racist ideology of slavery.

Jefferson, the Enlightenment, and the Purposes of History

FROM THE START OF SLAVERY TO THE PRESENT, THE STARK ONTOLOGI-
cal division between Whiteness and Blackness became deeply etched in the ways white Americans think of themselves. This division established a set of relations defining what is human, what it means to be a citizen, what it means to possess civil rights such as freedom of movement or freedom of assembly or the right to vote, or who had the right to enact violence upon another, what it means to own property, and what it means to be property. With the latter it is not just that whites could own Blacks and enslave them; it meant that Whiteness (with all the rights and privileges that entailed) became an ontological entity, and this entity was also the sole property of white people.

In the 1993 *Harvard Law Review* article "Whiteness as Property," legal scholar Cheryl Harris details how a white racial identity—and Whiteness itself—established not just a social or political value but also an economic value: "Because whites could not be enslaved or held as slaves, the racial line between white and black was extremely critical; it became a line of protection and demarcation from the potential threat of commodification, and it determined the allocation of the benefits and burdens of this form of property. White identity and whiteness were sources of privilege and protection; their absence meant being an object of property."

Clearly, such a social, political, and economic demarcation between Whiteness and Blackness was fundamental to the institution of slavery. It reflected the self-interest of the slave owner, a class that included many of America's Founding Fathers. It derived too from the fear of Blackness, of what the slave might do in retaliation for their bondage. "We have the wolf by the ear, and we can neither hold him nor safely let him go," wrote

Thomas Jefferson in an 1820 letter to Maine politician John Holmes, in contemplating the Missouri Crisis and the question of whether slavery should be extended to Missouri. But it also required that Blackness and Black people be regarded as inherently inferior, as biologically suited and destined for slavery. "This unfortunate difference of color, and perhaps of faculty, is a powerful obstacle to the emancipation of these people," wrote Jefferson in his 1785 book *Notes on the State of Virginia*.

In *Stamped from the Beginning: The Definitive History of Racist Ideas in America*, Ibram X. Kendi argues that in considering the history of race, many people believe that "ignorance/hate" led to "racist ideas" led to "discrimination." In contrast to this common belief, Kendi contends that racial discrimination caused the development of racist ideas, which then led to ignorance and hate, and that discriminatory policies were motivated by economic, political, cultural—and therefore psychological—self-interest:

> Politicians seeking higher office have primarily created and defended discriminatory policies out of political self-interest—not racist ideas. Capitalists seeking to increase profit margins have primarily created and defended discriminatory policies out of economic self-interest—not racist ideas. Cultural professionals, including theologians, artists, scholars, and journalists, were seeking to advance their careers or cultures and have primarily created and defended discriminatory policies out of professional self-interest—not racist ideas. . . .

While Kendi may contest certain Afropessimists as to what came first—discriminatory practices or racist ideas—obviously the two elements have been intricately intertwined throughout our history. Clearly, Kendi is not saying that racist ideas weren't a crucial factor in the history of American racism or that once those ideas were created they did not influence thinking, behavior, policy, and practices:

> When we look back on our history, we often wonder why so many Americans did not resist slave trading, enslaving, segregating, or now, mass incarcerating. The reason is, again, racist ideas. The

principle function of racist ideas in American history has been the suppression of resistance to racial discrimination and its resulting racial disparities. The beneficiaries of slavery, segregation, and mass incarceration have produced racist ideas of Black people being best suited for or deserving the confines of slavery, segregation, or the jail cell. Consumers of these racist ideas have been led to believe there is something wrong with Black people, and not the policies that have enslaved, oppressed, and confined so many Black people.

Just as important, racist ideas and racist thinking did not just occur spontaneously: just as whites had to devise the practice of slavery and discrimination, whites had to create racist ideas to justify those practices. In his book, Kendi examines the creation and etiology of these ideas that were initiated in the past, yes, but many of these ideas have lingered long after some of the practices that spawned them have been declared illegal and/or transformed into later, less harsh, but legally justified discrimination.

———

In the eighteenth century, both philosophers and scientists assured whites that they were proven superior to Blacks, and this superiority ran the gamut of human traits—intelligence, character, the ability to create civilization and act in a civilized manner, the reception of God's word and Christianity, physical beauty. Figures like Voltaire in philosophy and Linnaeus in biology voiced such views supporting a racial hierarchy with whites at the pinnacle and Blacks at the bottom.

Still, neither Linnaeus nor Voltaire had extensive contact with Black Africans. The case was quite different for a slave owner like Thomas Jefferson, who owned more than six hundred slaves during his lifetime and who had several children with his slave Sally Hemings. For Jefferson, the Blacks he kept prisoner and enslaved were not simply abstract scientific or philosophic concepts of racial inferiority. No, he encountered them daily at his famed Monticello, ruled over them and supervised them, and with at least one slave fell in love or lust or both with her. (Whatever his views on whether whites and Blacks were separate species, his progeny demonstrated that "mulattoes" were not the product of two separate species.)

Much has been made of Jefferson's supposed loathing of or misgivings about slavery, and various statements by him give evidence of this. But nothing Jefferson wrote indicates that he believed whites and Blacks were equals and equally human; whatever ambiguous thoughts and feelings he had about slavery did not sway his belief that Blacks were inferior and thus did not merit the same political rights as whites. Nor did his misgivings cause him to free his slaves with the exception of two during his lifetime. In this, Jefferson was, as they say, a product of his times. And yet so often, when people say this they are using both Jefferson's mixed feelings about slavery and the concept of historical relativism to distance or obscure his clearly racist beliefs and thinking.

Such distancing certainly mitigates the mental gymnastics and sleights of hand Jefferson required to pen "All men are created equal" while enslaving fellow human beings or promulgating his belief in Black inferiority: "The blacks, whether originally a distinct race, or made distinct by time and circumstances, are inferior to whites in the endowments both of body and mind," wrote Jefferson. In his 1785 book *Notes on the State of Virginia,* he asserted that whites were more beautiful and this was demonstrated by Blacks' "preference of them." (Jefferson's assertion would be echoed a few years later by Samuel Stanhope Smith in his 1787 lecture "An Essay on the Causes of the Variety of Complexion and Figure in the Human Species," where he asserted the hot climate of Africa had bred "physical disorders—like kinky hair, which was 'the farthest removed from the ordinary laws of nature.'") And yet, a few years later Jefferson would be engaged in sexual relations with a Black woman that produced not one but at least five children. Clearly, he had some sexual preference for the Black Sally Hemings.

Jefferson claimed he could "never . . . find that a black had uttered a thought above the level of plain narration; ever saw an elementary trait of painting or sculpture." He was aware of Phillis Wheatley but stated, "Religion indeed has produced a Phillis Wheatley, but it could not produce a poet." In this he did not go the route citing the racial exception, the one Black who proves by her intelligence or learning or deportment that she can mirror the "civilized" behavior of whites, an exception that is then used to prove the inferiority of the majority of Blacks (a tack used by many white intellectuals who encountered Wheatley and her poetry).

Instead, Jefferson went the route of the literary critic who judges the production of a Black artist as imitating but not achieving what white artists achieve.[1]

Kendi asserts that for the next fifty years Jefferson served as the leading American voice on "Black intellectual inferiority." And yet this contradiction remained:

> Jefferson did not mention the innumerable enslaved Africans who learned to be highly intelligent blacksmiths, shoemakers, bricklayers, coopers, carpenters, engineers, manufacturers, artisans, musicians, farmers, midwives, physicians, overseers, house managers, cooks, and bi- and trilingual translators—the workers who made his Virginia plantation and many others almost entirely self-sufficient. Jefferson had to ignore his own advertisements for skilled runaways and the many advertisements from other planters calling for the return of their valuable skilled captives, who were "remarkably smart and sensible," and "very ingenious at any work." One wonders whether Jefferson really believed his own words. Did Jefferson really believe Black people were smart in slavery and stupid in freedom?

In the last sentence Kendi is referring to Jefferson's assertion that not only were Blacks inferior in reason, but that if eventually they were ever emancipated—which in some instances he purported to envision—they should be sent back to Africa: Blacks could never be incorporated into

---

1. A contemporary corollary was the late Harold Bloom, who railed against "the school of resentment, the feminists, Afrocentrists, Marxists, Foucault-inspired New Historicists, or Deconstructors" and claimed that they weren't interested in literature but instead desired to "advance their programs for social change." If you think Bloom was a dinosaur from a previous time, you can still hear white writers muttering in private the same thoughts: the Black writers currently winning literary prizes and recognition aren't being judged on their merits but are representatives of a literary affirmative action. When Toni Morrison won the Nobel Prize, some critics attributed her award more to her race than to her literary achievement. While we might hope that such views may be regarded as in the minority in contemporary America, the persistence of the trope that what Black writers produce isn't literature or up to the standards of white writers and the traditional canon attests to a racist literary heritage that dates back centuries. Yet contemporary white critics who make negative critical assessments of Black literature believe that they themselves cannot possibly be extensions of this history—even if they do not adequately know or understand it.

America as citizens, since "the real distinctions which nature has made" rendered such incorporation impossible.

Whatever Jefferson's mixed views on slavery, he did not see fit to free the vast majority of his slaves. Moreover, it is important for us to see the inherent contradictions not just in Jefferson's political, scientific, and cultural thoughts on race; we must also acknowledge the ways he could only retain his racist views by contradicting or denying what he saw before him each day on his plantation and what he experienced in bed with an actual Black human being. He both saw and did not see the Black people who were intimately connected with the workings of his plantation and his life. He had to make himself engage in a vast and deep psychological denial; he had to willfully and consciously blind himself to their humanity, to their qualities, to their souls. He could not view accurately and truly their consciousness, their thoughts and feelings, and acknowledge their complex humanity; instead, though clearly one of those most brilliant minds of his day, he had to make himself stupid and blind, unable to see what was before his eyes.

One aspect of Jefferson's moral depravity—which was a constant for other slave owners—was that he kept his own progeny as slaves. Rarely does contemporary white America think about the moral vacuum and twisted psychology that allowed Jefferson and other slave owners not just to disavow their sons or daughters but to keep them in bondage. Sally Hemings was a quarter-Black and the half-sister of Jefferson's wife, Martha. Hemings and Jefferson's children were one-eighth Black. People remarked on their resemblance to Jefferson. The ethical obfuscations and depths of psychological repression to maintain such a system should astound us if we think about this system in terms of day-to-day human relations—which is why most white Americans do not want to think about it.

———

It's not difficult to see that Jefferson and his eighteenth-century Enlightenment views on race continue into the present in a variety of forms. Take Jefferson's appraisal of the physical appearance of Blacks: his views show up in present-day evaluations of Black appearance and controversies and acts of employment discrimination over Black hair; they show up in the ranking of African American women as the group least chosen on OkCupid; they show up in those places in the media where Black faces and bodies are not given equal representation.[2]

As for the mentality of Blacks, consider Jefferson's views that Blacks were more "adventuresome" than whites and less likely to give thought to "danger till it be present" and that they felt less physical pain than whites; he stated that they were inclined "to sleep when abstracted from their diversions, and unemployed in labor" and yet, in seeming contradiction, they "will be induced by the slightest amusements to sit up till midnight." He criminalized Blacks in the Declaration of Independence, since any attempt by Blacks to win their freedom was actually stealing their master's property; he believed their incorporation into the body politic would result in violence and most likely end "in the extermination of the one or the other race." Such views show up today in common explanations of Black poverty: "they are lazy and lack industry"; "they're more interested in their drugs and gangster rap and partying"; "if only they'd work hard like we whites." Similar views also show up around Black incarceration ("they are violent and dangerous"; "they're more likely to be thieves or criminals") and Black engagements with police (Rodney King was believed to not even feel the pain of police batons on his body). Through both conscious/explicit bias and unconscious/implicit bias, similar views also show up systemically in health care, with longer ER waiting periods and reduced pain medication for Blacks compared with those for whites with similar conditions.

Of course, President Barack Obama, who held the same office as Jefferson, was and is subjected to the same sorts of racist discourse: he isn't actually a citizen, which is why he hasn't shown his birth certificate; he should be sent back to Africa; he is the Black exception that proves and highlights how ill qualified, unexceptional, and uneducated the majority of Blacks are and so his achievements ought to be doubted; he didn't get the grades to get into Harvard Law School and he didn't get the grades to be head of the law review, which is why he hasn't shown his transcripts; he should be depicted on posters as an ape or associated with apes; his

---

2. Similarly, the outing of staunch segregationist Senator Strom Thurmond and the daughter he fathered with his family's Black maid cannot help but echo Jefferson and Sally Hemings.

election represented the attempts of Blacks and those of color to take over the country and remove whites from power and thus signals the potential extermination of the white race.[3]

From the beginning, the whole concept of the United States and the man who framed many of the ideas and words and the Constitution that initiated this country's beginnings were steeped in racism, entailing logical contradictions, psychological denial, and a conscious and willed blindness to the humanity of African Americans. If we have built this country on Jefferson's words of freedom, equality, and democracy, we must also address and confront his words on race and his racist ideas. These too are our legacy, our history, and they continue to speak to us and shape the present, whether we recognize it or not.

———

The current debates about history, such as the sudden made-up fears concerning Critical Race Theory in education, are as much a debate about the present as about the past. One of five historians who objected to the *New York Times*'s "1619 Project: A New Origin Story" is Gordon Wood. In a generally positive review of Alan Taylor's 2016 book *American Revolutions: A Continental History, 1750–1804*, Wood plaintively asks, "Can a revolution conceived mainly as sordid, racist and divisive be the inspiration for a nation?" But the implications of this question are more manifold than Wood perceives, for such a question actually involves or implies several unasked questions. What is the purpose of history? Is it truth or the creation of a myth? And just as important, whose history are we telling? For when Wood doubts that a more truthful, more complex

---

3. In 2011, approximately half of Republican voters believed Obama was not born in the United States. As Adam Serwer writes in *The Atlantic*: "Trump's dalliance with birtherism did not harm his presidential prospects when the 2016 primary came around, because, unlike most conspiracy theories, birtherism was never meant to answer a factual query. . . . Birtherism was a statement of values, a way to express allegiance to a particular notion of American identity, one that became the central theme of the Trump campaign itself: To Make America Great Again, to turn back the clock to an era where white political and cultural hegemony was unthreatened by black people, by immigrants, by people of a different faith. By people like Barack Obama. The calls to disavow birtherism missed the point: Trump's entire campaign was birtherism. Trump won the Republican primary, and united the party, in part because his run was focused on the psychic wound of the first black presidency. He had, after all, humiliated and humbled Obama. None of the other Republican candidates could make such a claim. None could say, as Trump could, that they had put the first black president in his place."

and contradictory history will be inspiring, who are the people he thinks will have trouble being inspired by such a history? Whom is he interested in inspiring? Does he wonder if an African American might have problems with viewing Thomas Jefferson or George Washington as spotless heroes and an unequivocable inspiration when these two men participated in a system that enslaved their ancestors? Or is the inspiring of African Americans not part of Wood's definition of the American project?

Obviously, I believe that we can, and indeed must, be able to hold two seemingly conflicting ideas in our heads at the same time. The Founding Fathers were brilliant thinkers, courageous and heroic in their fight against British tyranny, and they advanced the concepts of equality, freedom, and democracy in ways we all benefit from today. And at the same time, a good portion of the Founding Fathers were not only involved in the monstrously evil institution of chattel slavery, but some, like Jefferson, were instrumental in creating a defense of that institution and all of the others assented to the continued existence of that institution even if they didn't own slaves. Certainly, none of them seriously considered making Black people citizens. Similarly, the creation and spread of the United States depended on the denial of the rights of Indigenous Americas and on their slaughter and the enacting of genocide against them.

This much should be obvious: history should be a search for the truth and not for idealized heroes. It should not be the creation of a myth, though it has often served that purpose, as in the false history of the Lost Cause. The creation of myth is a project of nationalism, and as far as I know, no university has a Nationalism Department, though some may wish so.

But just as important, what is clear about Wood, and certainly a more strident critic of the 1619 Project like Senator Tom Cotton, is that they still conceive of the story of America as a white story—as a story of Whiteness. To various extents, they cannot view history with an integrated lens where the lives and sufferings of Black and Indigenous Americas are also part of our history, and they surely don't identify themselves with the people who are not white but also part of American history. The resilience and resistance, the courage and intelligence, the strength and spiritual force that Black people have displayed to survive slavery and American racism represent something truly heroic; so did the efforts of

Indigenous Americans to maintain their freedom and land. Indeed, Black Americans have always been fiercely fighting for equality, freedom, and democracy, though we still do little to honor the slave rebellions in our history—just as Indigenous Americans fought bravely for their independence and freedom. But the rules of Whiteness say we cannot view those American populations as central to or even a part of American history, and the implication is they are *not* us, not part of the body politic; they are extraneous characters or even enemies, what we needed to defend against. We cannot identify with them; we cannot admire them as our heroes—at which point, a Black, Indigenous, or person of color might ask, "Who is this we?" "Who gets to define what *we* includes?" There is a white answer to those ontological and epistemological questions and a BIPOC answer to them.

In a *New York Times* magazine article defending the the 1619 Project against critics like Wood, Jake Silverstein cites Harvard historian Nathan Irvin Huggins, who called "for new myths"—yes, I find problems with that phrase—"and a revised master narrative that better inspire and reflect upon our true condition":

> Such a new narrative would find inspiration in an oppressed people who defied social death as slaves and freedmen, insisting on their humanity and creating a culture despite a social consensus that they were "a brutish sort of people." Such a new narrative would bring slavery and the persistent oppression of race from the margins to the center, to define the limits and boundaries of the American Dream. Such a new narrative would oblige us to face the deforming mirror of truth.

As an African American, Huggins does not have great difficulty in identifying with Black slaves and finding inspiration in their struggle, nor does he have great difficulty seeing their masters as perpetrators of an inherently evil system, whether the master ran a small farm with a half-dozen slaves or the master was Founding Father Thomas Jefferson, who ruled over hundreds of slaves. And such an assertion does not alienate Huggins from American history or make him feel more ashamed of or less inspired by the ideal of America as an attempt to establish equality, freedom, and democracy. He has always known that ideal has not been achieved and he has always known that white supremacy has prevented that ideal from being achieved.

No, it is whites like Wood or Cotton who want their white heroes unblemished and who cannot identify with the struggle of Black or Indigenous Americans or see that struggle as heroic and inspiring. The limits of Whiteness dictate that such identification cannot take place, cannot be part of the definition of what America is and what it means to be an American. For such white people, history has always been, and must continue to be, psychically and narratively segregated.

Black History

The Master/Slave Dialectic and the Signifying Monkey

I HAVE POINTED TO JEFFERSON'S PSYCHOLOGICAL BLINDNESS OR DE-
nial of the complexity of the human beings whom he held in bondage. We
can better understand this blindness through the philosophical and psychological differences and contradictions embedded in the relationship
between the Master and the Slave. These differences and contradictions
continue to shape the relationships between whites and Blacks into the
present and still shape the ways they create and constitute their psychological identities and perceptions of each other. This in turn helps us
explain differences in the linguistic structures of Standard White American English and African American English, and the cultures founded on
them—even as those cultures have mixed and intertwined throughout
American history.

Let me start with a version of the Master/Slave dialectic first posited
by Hegel. This dialectic exposes how ontology (the terms through which
we define the things of our world and how they relate to each other)
creates epistemology, the methods and means through which we come to
know the world and define our knowledge of it, how we determine what
is a true belief and what is opinion.

For the Master, only one set of definitions delineates the relationship
of the Master and Slave. The Master is the one who rules and orders the
Slave to do the Master's bidding. The Slave is the one who obeys the
Master. The Master is a free human being. The Slave is neither free nor
completely human. (See the Founding Fathers' agreement that a slave
could be counted as three-fifths of a person.)

For the Slave, the Master's definitions of Master and Slave are a reality and a truth that the Slave must acknowledge in order to remain alive. The definition of the Slave as a slave is the Master's definition.

The Slave also has another set of definitions. The Master is the oppressor. The Slave is the oppressed. The Slave is not a slave but a free human being who has been imprisoned by the Master. The Slave's freedom lies in his or her ability *not* to see themselves as a slave. The Slave's freedom lies in his or her ability to disobey the master. The Slave's freedom lies in creating definitions of both the Master and the Slave different from the definitions the Master uses.

There is therefore a difference between the consciousness of the Master and that of the Slave. The Master must believe that the only valid set of definitions of Master and Slave are the ones the Master devises and assigns. The Master cannot admit that the Slave can create and possess an alternative set of definitions concerning the terms of their relationship. Therefore, the Master can only admit the existence of his own consciousness as a full consciousness. The Slave's consciousness can only exist as far as the Master defines it. The Master cannot see or imagine the Slave to possess the same ability to be as conscious as the Master. For the Master there exists only one way of viewing the world—that of the Master. The view of the Slave, the view of the Other, does not exist; indeed, it cannot exist if the Master is truly the Master and the Slave truly the Slave.

In contrast, the Slave is aware that their relationship consists of two separate but human consciousnesses. The Slave is aware that the Master looks at their relationship differently from the way the Slave looks at their relationship. Moreover, in order to claim any freedom—that is, the ability to disobey the Master—the Slave must be aware of the limits of the Master's consciousness. It is within those limits that the Slave can find any freedom of action and any alternative consciousness to the Master. The Slave therefore exists in a world of a dual consciousness—that of his or her self and that of the Other, the Master.[1]

For my purposes here, I want to point out that how the Master approaches language is fundamentally different from the Slave's approach.

---

1. This relates to the statement concerning the double consciousness of the Negro in W. E. B. Du Bois's classic essay "Strivings of the Negro People."

For the Master, each word has only one meaning—the meaning decreed by the Master. For the Slave, each word can possess a dual or even plural meaning—that assigned by the Master and those created by the Slave.

———

Within the constant threat of violence and death and various means of enforcement used by their white masters, Black slaves were not only forced to work long arduous hours, at times to the point of death; they were also constantly on "display" for the master: their actions, deportment, and language had to conform to the master's requirements and confirm the master's position and mastery over the slave. Since the Black slave was constituted as existing outside the body politic or any notion of citizenry and was instead relegated to the status of nonhuman, the Black slave confirmed and defined the rights of whites as humans and citizens and their place as masters over the Black body and mind. Thus, even when the Black slave was not working, they had to constantly reflect and affirm the will and power of the master; any untoward sign that might challenge this relationship had to be obliterated through discipline and punishment—or death.

In *Scenes of Subjection: Terror, Slavery, and Self-Making in Nineteenth-Century America*, Saidiya V. Hartman argues that a white-defined Blackness was anchored in and given flesh through the performances of the Black body. These performances involved not just direct plantation labor but every aspect of the Black slave's life, even in moments outside direct labor, such as in Sunday or nighttime activities. In other words, the Black slave was always reciting and acting for the master; there was no free or down time. Outward and recognizable resistance, such as escape attempts or slave rebellions, or even oppositional speech or manners, ensured physical punishment or death. Conversely, the space for inward and camouflaged resistance was severely limited and required both conscious and unconscious strategy on the part of the slave:

> These performances of blackness are in no way the "possession" of the enslaved; they are enactments of social struggle and contending articulations of racial meaning. . . . The emphasis on the joining of race, subjection, and spectacle is intended to denaturalize race

and underline its givenness—that is, the strategies through which it is made to appear as if it has always existed, thereby denying the coerced and cultivated production of race. . . . If, as I have argued, the dominant performances of blackness are about the spectacle of mastery and the enactment of a willed subjection, then can the instance in which the dominant is used, manipulated, and challenged be read as disruptive or refigured articulations of blackness?

When the Black slave was on display before the master, either in plantation labor or in slave activities outside the fields such as religious ceremonies, what the white master saw had to affirm his mastery in the master's consciousness. There could be no "performance" before the master—whether when directly at work or off—when the slave could indicate any knowledge of a past existence or a conception of a past existence where the slave was once free or could be free. In contrast, slaves knew a world where they were once free—either from direct experience in Africa or stories about Africa—and could envision an existence where they were free from the master's yoke. But whatever resistance the slave was thinking, feeling, or conveying to their fellow slaves had to be communicated in ways the master could not detect.

As an example of such communication, Hartman analyzes how the Juba work song, with its seeming nonsense syllables and repetition, was "a coded text of protest." This is reflected in Frederick Douglass's famed observation that in the South where whites heard Black songs of joy as joyful and Black songs of sadness as sad, Black slaves heard these songs as conveying the opposite of their ostensible emotion and how whites interpreted them; the songs held for the Black slave an ironic and resistant intertwining of emotions, both revealing and concealing.

———

In his groundbreaking work *The Signifying Monkey,* Henry Louis Gates Jr. explores how African American literature and culture in general are informed by a view of language where meaning and interpretation are plural and unstable rather than singular and stable. In linguistic interchanges with their master, African American slaves were aware of and created two sets of meaning and interpretation. What they said meant one thing to the master and seemingly expressed their obedience to the master and an acceptance of his definition of their relationship. But what slaves said meant another thing to their fellow slaves and signified various ways in which they were challenging the master's rule and his definition of their relationship. Moreover, the enslaved African Americans camouflaged or "masked" this second set of meaning and interpretation from the master. They used language as a code whose hidden meanings and interpretation they could decipher and the master could not.

Gates argues that in this duality, this masking, African Americans were continuing a set of African cultural and linguistic practices embodied in and employed by the trickster figures in traditional African mythology. But these practices were employed by free Africans for a different purpose from that of African Americans who were enslaved by whites and used these practices to "trick" and defy their white masters.

Gates focuses on the figure of the Monkey in African American mythology and literature; over and over, the Monkey employs "signifying," the use of language trickery and indirection, of dual meanings, to gain the upper hand on the Lion. For instance, in one oral poem the Monkey tells the Lion about how the Elephant has insulted the Lion and the Lion goes off in anger to fight the Elephant and gets beaten, "more dead than alive." In this way, the Monkey has succeeded in getting the Lion to do what the Monkey wants (for the Lion to be beaten by the Elephant), all the while seeming to be speaking for the Lion's interests.

Gates characterizes signifying in the following ways:

1. Signifyin(g) "can mean any number of things."
2. It is a black term and a black rhetorical device.
3. It can mean the "ability to talk with great innuendo."
4. It can mean "to carp, cajole, needle, and lie."
5. It can mean "the propensity to talk around a subject, never quite coming to the point."
6. It can mean "making fun of a person or situation."
7. It can "also denote speaking with the hands and eyes."
8. It is "the language of trickery, that set of words achieving Hamlet's 'direction through indirection.'"

9. The Monkey "is a 'signifier,' and the Lion, therefore, is the signified."

The final quality refers to the ways in which the linguist Ferdinand de Saussure broke down the way language works. For our purposes, it is enough to know that the Lion's mistake is that he interprets language as having only one meaning. Thus, the Lion believes what the Monkey says about what the Elephant said about the Lion. But for the Monkey, what he is saying is meant to be interpreted by the Lion in one way, while the Monkey interprets it in another. The Lion thinks the Monkey is speaking to achieve the Monkey's avowed purpose—to inform the Lion—while the Monkey is speaking for another purpose—to trick the Lion.

To state the obvious: the Monkey here is a representative of the African American or Slave while the Lion represents the white Master.

———

These signifying practices, Gates argues, have informed the culture of African Americans through slavery, after emancipation, and have continued to the present. They are a result of African Americans, both in slavery and after, developing a language and a linguistic practice to counter, disarm, and disempower the master and the whites who held power over them after slavery:

Black adults teach their children this exceptionally complex system of rhetoric, almost exactly like Richard A. Lanham describes a generic portrait of the teaching of the rhetorical *paideia* to Western schoolchildren. The mastery of Signifyin(g) creates *homo rhetoricus Africanus,* allowing—through the manipulation of these classic black figures of Signification—the black person to move freely between two discursive universes. This is an excellent example of what I call linguistic masking, the verbal sign of the mask of blackness that demarcates the boundary between the white linguistic realm and the black, two domains that exist side by side in a homonymic relation signified by the very concept of Signification. To learn to manipulate language in such a way as to facilitate the smooth navigation between these two realms has been the challenge of black parenthood, and remains so even today. Teaching one's children the fine art of Signifyin(g) is to teach them about this mode of linguistic circumnavigation, to teach them a second language that they can share with other black people.

African American linguistic practices are rooted in African culture and the history of slavery as well as the history of segregation and oppression. These practices start with a recognition that there is the language of the master, the language of whites, and there is the language as it is employed, refashioned, and created by African Americans throughout their history. The two different languages represent two different practices, two different consciousnesses, two different epistemologies. This is true even when the words used by African Americans and whites are the same—that is, when they share the same linguistic signifier.

———

One final point here needs to be emphasized concerning how the cultural linguistic practices of African Americans trace certain roots back to slavery, and the relationship between the Master and Slave: the Slave could never tell the Master directly and undisguised how the Slave regarded bondage, how the Slave regarded him or herself, and how the Slave regarded the Master. In other words, the Slave could never tell the master the Slave's truth as the Slave saw it.

To this day, in almost any situation African Americans know they can never tell the whole truth to whites concerning their lives and their experiences or how they regard whites or race relations in this country. Every Black person stopped by the police understands that their ability to signify may not only determine what will happen to them legally but whether they will live or die. In a more general sense, silence or linguistic genuflection or linguistic indirection, camouflage, and secrecy still function as tools of survival for African Americans—and not just with the police. Barack Hussein Obama knows this: he could never talk directly about race without losing political capital, without being branded as a radical with a racist agenda. But almost any Black employee in any institution or business knows they cannot be completely honest about how they regard the racial issues of that institution or business; certainly that

Black employee can rarely give free vent to the emotions they feel about the existence of those issues and the racial inequities they see.

This holding back of the truth as Black Americans see it also extends to friendships between Blacks and whites; there is almost always a zone of rawness and silence, a space of problematic negative emotions, a place of contention with a deep-seated awareness of the prevalence of racial inequities in our society that Blacks rarely express to white friends unless they are willing to risk the end of that friendship. This is why whites who may feel they are friends with Blacks often think that the state of race relations are better than Blacks actually think they are. In communications between Blacks and whites, signifying continues into the present.

That whites do not hear what Blacks are saying beneath the ostensible meaning of their words; that they do not recognize that signifying and fooling the Lion are still a basis of communication between whites and Blacks; that they take the surface of the interracial conversation as all there is to it—all this indicates that there is always a power imbalance in contemporary exchanges between whites and Blacks. This imbalance of power extends back to slavery as do the linguistic practices of African Americans developed in the face of white power. What this state of affairs gives evidence to is multifaceted: on one level, whites don't hear the undertones or what is camouflaged in interracial exchanges in part because they don't want to hear them; they don't want to know how Blacks actually feel about them and the state of race relations in contemporary America. At the same time, whites are incapable of hearing this because they aren't familiar with these linguistic practices. But more important, whites have rendered themselves incapable of hearing and seeing the realities of Black life because to do so would force whites to reassess who they themselves as whites might be and how they have benefited from our society's treatment of Blacks. Moreover, in order to gain any hint of how signifying works or whether it is present, whites would have to be intimate—that is, involved in an open and honest discussion—with Black consciousness, and this would require both an effort toward and an establishment of relationships with Black Americans that most white Americans do not desire and/or do not know how to accomplish.

As a result of this situation, which is in part a profound difference in linguistic practices and epistemology, whites do not see or understand the complex reactions of Black people to the conditions they live under and the ways they must negotiate around and through the power white people and Whiteness hold over their lives. Whites still make the Master's mistake of underestimating the complexities of Black consciousness and Black people themselves. Power is certainly a worldly tool, but it can often make one blind and deaf.

The ontological categories of Whiteness and Blackness that justified and organized the establishment of slavery; the history of our country's racist ideas stemming from and embedded in the mind of the slave owner who wrote the Declaration of Independence; the dialectic between the consciousness of the Master and the Slave; the differences between Standard White American English and African American English: all of these continue to shape the present-day consciousness of both white Americans and Black Americans.

Whiteness in Storytelling

Amistad, the Film and the Novel

What makes power hold good, what makes it accepted, is simply the fact that it doesn't only weigh on us as a force that says no, but that it reverses and produces things, it induces pleasure, forms knowledge, produces discourse. It needs to be considered as a productive network which runs through the whole social body, much more than as a negative instance whose function is repression.

—Michel Foucault, "Truth and Power"

HOW DOES WHITENESS TELL STORIES OF ITSELF? HOW DOES BLACKNESS?

In our history, it has been whites who determined the rules and power relations between whites and Blacks and thus whites who defined what Whiteness meant and what Blackness meant. In the times when American society was more openly racist, the use of these terms and their assigned meaning was neither questioned nor hidden. They were publicly employed to enforce racial inequities and disparities, to maintain white power.

Around the time of the civil rights movement, the openly racist definitions of White and Black began to be questioned; using openly racist language was deemed in some parts of society to be unacceptable. Eventually, the use of openly racist language in public to support racist laws or racist policies or racist practices became mostly taboo.

But what conservatives, and indeed many liberals, discovered was that the existence of racial inequities or segregation could be hidden or ameliorated if any talk about racial categories was deemed to be in and of itself inherently racist. If it was no longer permitted to talk about differences between Blacks and whites, pointing to any differences between Blacks and whites was supposedly racist. This would then make it more difficult or even impossible to point to the continued existence of racial inequities or how those inequities were enforced.

Of course, the terms *blackness* and *whiteness* do have meanings, and these meanings affect the ways each of us thinks and acts. For Blacks these terms have a certain meaning; for whites they often have another. The differing definitions of these terms is not simply some abstract academic debate. The definitions—and our disagreement about these definitions—affect the beliefs, practices, and policies of our society. They create differing interpretations not just of our present reality but of the ways we frame and construct stories about America's racial past.

To illustrate how this difference manifests itself, I want to start with a classic work of American liberalism, Steven Spielberg's film *Amistad*. A white Jewish American parent who has adopted two black children, Spielberg has shown an intense interest in African American culture and history; he has also directed the movie adaption of Alice Walker's classic novel *The Color Purple* (though it was panned by a number of Black critics).

When Spielberg's production studio DreamWorks began working on *Amistad*, it commissioned my friend the African American novelist Alexs Pate to write the novelization of the film, basing it on the film's script. Though Pate included almost all the elements of the script, the novel he wrote differs from the script in significant ways and starts from an entirely different premise regarding the ontological meanings of Black and white.

———

Spielberg's film *Amistad* starts in the hold of a slave ship during a storm at sea. The Black men are in chains and to most Americans are speaking an unknown language; there are no subtitles—we, the American audience, do not understand what they are saying. The camera focuses on one of the Black men who seems to be a leader. Some of the men manage to escape from their chains, and they grab weapons and attack the white sailors. This scene is violent and bloody, and the first act of violence is not the violence that enchained these men but the violence they take upon the Spanish sailors. But since we are not shown the violence that inaugurated and instituted their bondage, the unconscious or unspoken message is that the Blacks have initiated the violence since theirs is the first violence we see.

Most audience members, particularly those who were white, did not think of the implications of this opening, the ways it shut out the audience from the language of the Black men in chains or the ways it depicted the violence of the Blacks. But Alexs Pate found all this troubling, and he chose not to begin his novelization of the film script with this opening scene. From its very beginning, Pate's novel challenges unspoken assumptions concerning race embedded in the film's script.

Pate's consciously Black novel starts not on a slave ship but in Africa. More important, it begins from the point of view of Sengbe Pieh, a free African who wakes up at night in his village:

> The darkened sky spoke sweetly as they slept. The stars, like cinders, glowed. But something caused Sengbe Pieh (who would come to be called Cinque) to wake up abruptly. Perhaps it was the powerful stillness that had settled around them. He could hear no sound outside his cone-shaped, thatched-roof house. This was quite unusual because he lived on the edge of his village, so close to the swampy forests and jungle which began just beyond. The predawn morning was usually alive with the sounds of foraging animals on the hunt, the ever-present chatter of the monkeys and the call of various birds.
>
> Sengbe, a tall, twenty-four-year-old, muscular man who could hide among ebony and not be detected, pulled himself from his bed. He didn't even take the time to put on his protective charms, but moved gently so as not to disturb his wife and sleeping children. When he reached the threshold he could feel his thumping heart. He stepped out into the clearing. He felt a presence. There was something or someone nearby. And then Sengbe saw it. A lion . . . .

Sengbe kills the lion and saves his village. Pate has stated that in his novelization he tried as much as possible to present events through Sengbe's point of view. In doing so, despite the obvious counterdirection and focus of the script, he constructed the novel as Sengbe's struggle to free himself and return home. That is the goal of Pate's protagonist and the story Pate is trying to tell—often against the goals and story of the script formulated by its white screenwriters.

In the film *Amistad,* after the first scene of the slave rebellion and a couple of scenes of the slaves sailing their ship to America, the point of view is generally that of Roger Sherman Baldwin, played by Matthew McConaughey, the young white lawyer who takes up the case of Cinque (Djimon Hounsou) and the African slaves. It is Baldwin's goal—to free the Africans—that structures and centers the story of the film. Eventually, Baldwin enlists the help of ex-President John Quincy Adams (Anthony Hopkins) to present the case. Most of the screen time is shared by either Roger Baldwin or John Quincy Adams. Cinque is the third most prominent character, but the focus of the film is on the white lawyers attempting to obtain the release of the African slaves. Even one of Spielberg's partner at DreamWorks, David Geffen, has commented that the film is less about slavery than about "white people saving black people."

The same historical events, the same script—but two different tales.

In Pate's novelization, the protagonist—the hero—is Sengbe, and the events of the novel are presented as much as possible through his viewpoint. His goal is to free himself and return to his home. In the Spielberg film, the protagonists are first Roger Baldwin and then John Quincy Adams, and the point of view is mainly that of the young white lawyer. Baldwin's and Adams's goal is to win their law case with the argument that Sengbe and his fellow Africans are not slaves.

Wrestling with a script written by two white men that established the two white characters as protagonists, Pate tried in his novelization to create an African American novel and not the white film script he was handed. As Pate has observed to me, if a film had been made from his novelization, it would have been a Black film. Of course, such a film would have been much harder, if not impossible, to be produced. Many if not most whites would simply not go see a Black film.

What makes one work Black and the other white?

From a storyteller's viewpoint, the answer is, on the surface, simple: a different protagonist and a different point of view, and with two different protagonists, there are of course two different goals for each protagonist. All this leads to two different tales, one white, one Black.

————

But a question then arises: why couldn't Spielberg and the two white screenwriters have created a story with Sengbe as the protagonist and told this story from his point of view? Is the only reason Spielberg did not create a film with the same premise as Pate's novel simply that white audiences would not go see such a film? Or is it that Spielberg and his screenwriters could not conceive of the story in the ways Pate did—as a tale of a free African trying to return home?

The boundary between Spielberg's film and Pate's novel marks *the boundary between the white imagination and the Black imagination,* between the white version of history and the Black version of history. For the white creator, the white imagination, the white version of history is the dominant, if not the only, possibility. A Black creator, like Pate, is well aware of the white imagination and its limits, well aware of the white version of history.

But Pate imagined a very different version of the story from the one Spielberg and his team created. At the same time, Pate's worldview includes both the white imagination and the white version of history and the Black imagination and the Black version of history. He consciously understands that duality. After all, the white imagination wrote and shaped the script he was working from.

What is the cause of this difference between the imagination of Spielberg's team and Pate's? Obviously it must stem from their different life experiences, particularly in the area of race. What is less obvious is that Spielberg and his screenwriters start from a very different set of assumptions and categorizations regarding race. The difference in the stories they tell stems from an *ontological* disagreement.

————

Why does Pate start the novel in Africa? The opening scene of his novel is nowhere in the script. Pate does this because he sees Sengbe Pieh first and foremost as a free African man with a family and a village and a culture to which he belongs (he has a first name and a family name). He is a man of courage and strength who helps save his village. He is a hero.

What's important to note here in terms of ontology is this: in this setting, Sengbe's Blackness *has no meaning.* It is not a question or an issue; it is not part of his identity; it is not, to use W. E. B. Du Bois's famous phrase, a problem. Sengbe exists outside any white conception of who he might be and any definition of Blackness as signifying inferiority or identity as a slave.

When Pate comes to the scene with Sengbe in the slave ship, he presents it through Sengbe's point of view. The qualities of Sengbe introduced in the African opening scene of Pate's novel remain present; there is no mystery about who Sengbe is, no question that he does not see himself as a free man. And he sees his fellow prisoners as individual free men. Most significant, he possesses a fully realized consciousness and—unlike in the movie where the audience doesn't understand his language and thus cannot enter any of Sengbe's thoughts, even when he speaks—this consciousness is presented to the reader in Pate's novel:

> His entire reality had been replaced by chains and the stifling air of slave ships. He'd been plucked from his life in Mani by kidnappers who'd sold him into slavery. He was aboard the *Amistad,* the second slave ship in a journey of wretchedness and pain. He was packed in a hold with fifty-three other Africans, many of them from his Mende tribe, but from other tribes as well. The crying and moaning came in Temne, Sherbo, Kissi, Fula, Lokko, Ibo, Mandinka. It was June 29, 1839, and the *Amistad* was being thrown about in the turbulent waters off the coast of Cuba. They had been only three days out of port, but the storm that raged around them pushed the ship, its crew, and cargo farther and farther off course.
>
> Since his abduction, Cinque had been engaged in an ongoing fight to keep from drowning in the vile effort to turn him into a piece of property. He was chained and tightly packed into a small two-masted schooner outfitted for carrying slaves from Havana to various locales. The *Amistad* was headed for Puerto Principe down the coast of Cuba. He would probably be sold as a fieldworker in

the sugarcane fields there. He was bound to live the rest of his life that way, in service to his white master. But he was fighting it with everything he had. And it *was* like drowning. A descent into an abyss of misery. Of having so many unknown and unanticipated things happen to you at one time that it was hard to remember who you had been. He held on to his wife's image in his head. He remembered the sound of his children as they played in the yard. He would not forget. He would do what he had to do to try to get them back.

Again, contrast the above with the opening of the film. There the images are stark, disorienting, and without context. A Black man is presented in chains. He speaks a language the audience does not understand; he is indecipherable. He and the other Black men attack and kill the white men on the ship in a scene of bloody carnage. The audience's introduction to the Black men yokes them to violence, and violence enacted upon whites (again as opposed to the violence that brought the Black men to the slave ship, the violence of the Black slave traders and the Spanish slave traders). In the film, the Black man is first seen as a slave or prisoner and a figure of violence. He has no name, no family, no village. He has no culture. His language is unknown. He kills and imprisons white men. This is what the film starts with as the meaning of his Blackness: as a slave, a prisoner. Beyond civilization. Unintelligible. Dangerous. Violent.[1]

There are questions here that may or may not come up in a viewer's mind. Is this violence justifiable? If the audience knows what the film is about, the audience will assume the Black man is a slave, but he could also very well be a prisoner and have committed some crime. Moreover, in the film's racial ontology, only the white American courts can decide if this violence is justifiable. Similarly, only the white American courts can decide whether these Blacks are slaves or free men. The Black man is not seen as free until the white man decides. The Black man does not have *a prior existence to his entrance into the white world*. He does not have a full name, a family, a village, a culture. He is not the hero. We cannot see the world through his eyes. He is mysterious, dangerous. The tale is

---

1. Question: Does such a meaning of Blackness have anything to do with the behavior of police toward Black men? My response: How can it not?

not about him. Again, all this is tied up in the way the film presents and employs the meaning of Blackness.

———

Two different racial ontologies and epistemologies, two different tales.

Yes, this film is about a historical event, and some readers may argue that I'm doing what people of color frequently do—bringing up the past. "All that is over," they will say. But the film *Amistad* was created *in the present.* It is the white present's viewpoint of the past. Moreover, it is based on a racial ontology that is still working in our society. And it's not just racist whites who subscribe to and employ this ontology. It's also the demonstrated ontology of a liberal Jewish filmmaker with two adopted Black children.[2]

All this can be reduced to a simple statement: only by identifying and then changing the basic racial ontology of this society can we create and thus *live* a different tale concerning race. Otherwise, we will tell the same racially biased tales of our history and our present. We will continue to see the white characters as free humans and Black characters as beings whose humanity is in doubt and can only be certified by the white characters. We will continue to see whites and Whiteness as the ultimate and final arbitrators of our racial reality and social relations. This change in racial ontology and epistemology will only come about through a shift in power in the other areas of our society: political, economic, social, and cultural changes will force us to change the ways we define and use racial categories.

Or not.

Certainly the intractability of this ontology and its resultant epistemology, their persistence beyond the time of slavery into the present, tells us how deeply they are woven into the ways we think and speak about race. Just as important, this racial ontology and epistemology are not simply part of our vocabulary. They are the basis on which we build

---

2. When Pate presented his novelization to DreamWorks, they approved it but he could tell they also felt somehow uneasy about it in a way they could not articulate. The novel Pate created was another form of what Henry Louis Gates Jr. calls "signifying"—seeming to say one thing to the white world while actually saying something else to the Black world (and, in disguise, to the white world).

our stories about race. And stories are far more effective in creating our identities—our view of ourselves and the world and the way the world works—than statistics. To repeat: *this racial ontology and epistemology inform and shape the stories we tell; they permit certain stories to be told and prevent others from being imagined or countenanced by white people.*

In the film version of *Amistad,* created by a white director and two white screenwriters, a Black man is seen initially as an indecipherable instrument of violence and as a slave; he cannot be declared a free human being unless the white man declares him to be, unless he is judged by the superior white epistemology. In the novelization of the same script, written by an African American fiction writer, the African man is first and foremost a free human being—with a family, a wife, and a child; he exists and lives within the context of his home village and culture. He does not possess a race because no conception of race exists in his society—he is outside the ontology of race. Within his village, his knowledge, his sense of his world is shared and valid and is not subject to the judgments of white epistemology. This difference in viewpoints, originated in slavery, still embodies and creates the divide between the ways whites and Blacks process and understand race in America.

Portraits of Slavery

Faulkner and Morrison

IN 2009, MORE THAN A HUNDRED WRITERS AND CRITICS CITED WILLIAM Faulkner's *Absalom, Absalom!* as "the greatest Southern novel ever written," and in 2012, in the *New York Times* magazine, John Jeremiah Sullivan opined that the novel "has been well described as the most serious attempt by any white writer to confront the problem of race in America." Yet the novel was published in 1936, more than seventy-five years before Sullivan's declaration.

In contemporary American literature, white writers have generally avoided dealing directly with the issues of race. Indeed, in most novels by white authors, they avoid the presence of characters of color, and if such characters do appear, they do so as backdrop or social "color." But while contemporary American writers can often avoid the issues of race and the presence of African Americans in portraying their white version of contemporary America, it is more difficult to do so when directly confronting the particulars of our mutual racial history, especially with slavery. Perhaps this is one crucial reason why few contemporary white American authors or artists have engaged this subject—in contrast to the many African American authors and artists who have done so.

Indeed, perhaps the last major instance where a white author tried to depict slavery, William Styron's *The Confessions of Nat Turner*, has come to serve as a cautionary tale for contemporary white writers. As the white novelist Jess Row writes of his own literary training in his book *White Flights: Race, Fiction, and the American Imagination*:

One of the stories I was told in my first fiction workshop—I was seventeen, at Yale Summer School in 1991—detailed "what happened to" William Styron after the publication of *The Confessions of Nat Turner* in 1967. . . . I don't remember exactly how [my teacher Lee K. Abbott] framed it . . . but the conclusion was unambiguous: white writers, meaning all the writers in the classroom, had no business writing about race, because Styron had tried to do it, in good faith, and had been publicly attacked and scorned, and his career had never recovered. I remember the phrase "kiss of death." That was twenty-five years ago, and the same fatalism, the same fear of the impolitic, still circulates in American creative writing.

Row's account here is one of those instances where Whiteness is instituted and enforced and yet is presented in a way that disguises or camouflages the import and ramifications of such enforcement. As a beginning fiction writer, the young white Row was instructed not to address race, and yet he was instructed in such a way that such avoidance would place him as one of the racially enlightened. He would not make the mistake Styron did; he would remain "innocent."

Before Styron, the last book by a white author on slavery that etched itself into the American literary imagination was probably William Faulkner's *Absalom, Absalom!* created nearly a century ago. The Mississippi-born-and-raised Faulkner both lived in and benefited from the segregation instituted in the South. Faulkner grew up in a time and place where an accusation of his being racist did not threaten his vulnerability or position as a white man (as it would a writer of Row's generation). Faulkner could admit what white contemporary authors have such a hard time admitting: that neither he nor the South were innocent. Indeed, it is the curse and damnation of being Southern that shape the central vision of his work. (Think of Faulkner's fictional character Quentin Compson, who as a student at Harvard in the early twentieth century tells tales of the South to his roommate and insists, "I don't hate the South, I don't hate the South.")[1]

---

1. In this way, despite the racial distortions that were an integral part of his vision of race, and in part because of these views, Faulkner could confront the institution of slavery with a sense of necessity that his contemporary white forebears still largely cannot. A contemporary white

I believe *Absalom, Absalom!* to be one of the great American novels. But both the novel and its creator were certainly flawed in their racism. (A casual example of Faulkner's racism: when J. Robert Oppenheimer met Faulkner in 1958 and asked the writer what he thought of television, Faulkner replied, "Television is for niggers.") I can certainly understand a critique, similar to Chinua Achebe's critique of Joseph Conrad's *Heart of Darkness,* which argues that the racism of *Absalom, Absalom!* prevents it from being considered a great novel. But I would argue that Faulkner, like Conrad, enters territories, both literal and figurative, where many of their white contemporaries were unwilling to go or simply ignored; their work investigates key elements of history where race and commerce and violence intertwined in ways many white writers still feel are too untoward or too unsettling to confront.[2] Because Faulkner grew up in an era where the racism of the South was not questioned or forbidden, he was able to at least acknowledge the enormous fact of slavery in ways contemporary white authors are far more reluctant to do. But that does not mean he was able to depict the true nature of slavery and the relationships between white and Black Southerners; the racism of his time that had formed his identity forbade this.

Faulkner's treatment of the Southern past and the legacy of slavery is certainly worthy of analysis and critique. But it is useful to examine Faulkner's *Absalom, Absalom!* in contrast to Toni Morrison's novel on slavery *Beloved,* to illustrate significant differences in the way the white imagination has dealt with the institution of slavery in contrast to the imaginative re-creations by Black American novelists.

---

writer would not be as certain as Faulkner of his racial views or inherent position of power and does not write in an America where their white views on race would never be significantly challenged. Hence, as Row found in his writing workshop, contemporary white fiction writers believe that slavery and, more generally, race are subjects they should best avoid.

2. In *Playing in the Dark,* Toni Morrison writes: "For the horror that the 'one-drop' rule excites, there is no better guide than William Faulkner. What else haunts *The Sound and the Fury* or *Absalom, Absalom!*? Between the marital outrages of incest and miscegenation, the latter (an old but useful term for 'the mixing of races') is obviously the more abhorrent. In much American literature, when plot requires a family crisis, nothing is more disgusting than mutual sexual congress between the races. It is the mutual aspect of these encounters that is rendered shocking, illegal, and repulsive."

Faulkner's *Absalom, Absalom!*

My first encounter with a portrait of a white slave owner was not Faulkner's *Absalom, Absalom!* but the movie *Gone with the Wind,* based on Margaret Mitchell's novel, which in many ways epitomizes the myth of the Lost Cause. In both the film and the novel, slavery plays a secondary and minor role to Scarlett's romantic intrigues, the joys and pleasures of antebellum plantation life and its society, the supposedly unjust destruction of that way of life by the Civil War and the North, and the attempts by Scarlett and her brethren to retrieve and reestablish the glories of their antebellum existence after the war. The slaves were either comical figures, stereotyped buffoons, or docile figures who readily accepted their masters' status and their enslavement and who even felt great affection for and loved their masters. That the film was a totally ahistorical whitewashed version of slavery and the antebellum South did not quite penetrate my consciousness at the age of twelve, nor did I understand that these very qualities were part of what ensured the enormous success of both the film and the novel. That both were extremely popular all across the country, in the North and the South, indicates how pervasive and ensconced the myth of the Lost Cause had become in the American psyche, well into the second half of the twentieth century.

Then in high school, I was assigned Faulkner's *Absalom, Absalom!* and its portrait of the slave owner Thomas Sutpen. Born of the rural Virginia poor, as a young man, Sutpen travels to Haiti and through marriage establishes himself as a plantation owner—only to discover to his horror that his seemingly white bride possesses Black blood. And so he abandons her and his son, Charles Bon, and eventually ends up in Jefferson, Mississippi, where he again tries to establish himself as a plantation owner and brings with him a French architect and Haitian slaves to build his mansion.

As a high school student, I was confounded by Faulkner's use of multiple narrators and multiple retellings of what seemed to me the same story. But *Absalom, Absalom!* stuck with me, and I've reread it several times since. What I first remember from the novel was the way Faulkner describes the Haitian slaves, who are distinguished from the Mississippi slaves by the Haitians' mysterious origin and language. When one of Jefferson's townsmen looks underneath the wagon hood transporting the slaves he finds "a black tunnel filled with still eyeballs and smelling like a wolfden," and this animal imagery is carried on in further descriptions:

> So the legend of the wild men came gradually back to town, brought by the men who would ride out to watch what was going on, who began to tell how Sutpen would take stand beside a game trail with the pistols and send the negroes in to drive the swamp like a pack of hounds; it was they who told how during the first summer and fall the negroes did not even have (or did not use) blankets to sleep in, even before the coon-hunter Akers claimed to have walked one of them out of the absolute mud like a sleeping alligator and screamed just in time. The negroes could speak no English yet and doubtless there were more than Akers who did not know that the language in which they and Sutpen communicated was a sort of French and not some dark and fatal tongue of their own. . . . General Compson told his son, Quentin's father, while the negroes were working Sutpen never raised his voice at them, that instead he led them, caught them at the psychological instant by example, by some ascendancy of forbearance rather than by brute fear. . . . Without dismounting (usually Sutpen did not even greet them with as much as a nod, apparently as unaware of their presence as if they had been idle shades) they would sit in a curious quiet clump as though for mutual protection and watch his mansion rise, carried plank by plank and brick by brick out of the swamp where the clay and timber waited—the bearded white man and the twenty black ones and all stark naked beneath the encroaching and pervading mud.

The town and county look at Sutpen with disapprobation for many reasons: because he is not from the town; because his funds are not accounted for and stem from a mysterious source; because he uses a French architect and speaks a form of French; because he shows no direct or sufficient deference to the ruling elites of the area; because he asks no permission for what he is doing, such as his purchasing land from a Chickasaw Indian agent and building a mansion on "a hundred square miles of some of the best virgin bottom land in the country."

But it is Sutpen's behavior with and attitudes toward his slaves that primarily outrage the citizens of Jefferson and the county. Supten clearly doesn't observe certain distinctions of attitude and deportment that the other white slave owners observe when dealing with their slaves. In the eyes of the county, Sutpen's seemingly less directly brutal method of controlling his slaves results from an unholy and blasphemous closeness to them, which goes far beyond his working naked with them in their nakedness (a fact someone later surmises is because he doesn't own a trove of clothes). This unholy connection is evidenced by his seeming understanding of their psychology, their mysterious language (a French Creole), and his blithe readiness to work and consort with them. (Later, one of the scandals that surround him is that he not only pits his slaves in fights against each other—something the other slave owners might do—but that he actually fights against them himself.) One of the effects of Sutpen's characterization and these West Indian slaves, whether consciously intended by Faulkner or not, is to "normalize" the other Mississippi slave owners and their version of slavery; it is Sutpen and his slaves who are aberrant and deviant, not the system of slavery.

For, of course, in none of this does Faulkner indicate that Sutpen or his fellow disapproving slave masters even contemplate that the "negroes" in their bondage possess any sort of complex consciousness that might approach, much less equal, their white masters. There is no evidence in the Black characters of any concentrated and camouflaged revulsion and rebellion against their own condition. Though Faulkner writes many decades after slavery's abolition, almost nothing in his work even approaches a vision where whites and Blacks are considered equals and the power of whites over Blacks is not simply an inherited and long-established dispensation, a biblical and societal enforcement and acknowledgment of Black inferiority.

Movements for racial equality did take place in Faulkner's lifetime, but in his famous essay defending the modern South, he argued for a policy of patience, to go "slow" on any push for racial equality. And little in his work demonstrates that he had any deep understanding of the racial others around him, any sense that they might look at him and his fellow Southern whites with anything approaching a clear-eyed understanding of what these Southern whites had done to their forebears and were now doing to them in the present. (Even a cursory reading of, say,

James Baldwin's essays on the South and the civil rights movement re-veals Faulkner's blindness to the psychology and character of Southern Blacks and the ways they viewed white people.) Faulkner sometimes acknowledged in Southern Blacks a spiritual fortitude, as in his one sentence about the Compson family's Black servant Dilsey in *The Sound and the Fury*. "They endured" is all he has to say about her consciousness and biography. Faulkner was not interested in the complexities of their tale, for in his mind those complexities did not exist.

———

The plot of *Absalom, Absalom!* revolves around Thomas Sutpen's biracial Haitian-born son, Charles Bon. When Henry, Sutpen's son with Jefferson resident Ellen Coldfield, goes off to college at the University of Mississippi, he returns with his good friend and fellow student, Charles Bon. During his stay, Bon eventually charms Sutpen's daughter, Judith (Henry's sister). It turns out that Bon is seeking his father's recognition or acknowledgment, and Bon states to Sutpen that he will renounce his engagement to Judith if this happens. Sutpen cannot and will not publicly acknowledge his mixed-race son, and he tells his white son, Henry, that Bon must not marry Judith because he is her half-brother. During the Civil War, in the fighting far from Mississippi, Henry reaches a point where he thinks that he can accept this incestual relationship because of his love for Bon. But when Sutpen informs Henry that Bon is part-Black, that he fathered a Black son through an octoroon wife, Henry knows he must prevent their union. Eventually, after fighting together in the Civil War, Henry kills Bon before he can enter the gates of the Sutpen mansion.

In this killing, the novel's moral framework posits that miscegenation entails a far worse blasphemy and revolt against the natural order than incest (and of course than slavery). The taint of Black blood is insurmountable, forever sullying those who possess that blood. In this, Henry is upholding the Southern code of honor. In *Honor and Violence in the Old South*, Bertram Wyatt-Brown writes:

> In slaveholding cultures, the contrast between the free and unfree—the autonomy of one, the abjectness of the other—prompts an awareness of moral, as well as political and social stratification. . . .

The very debasement of the slave added much to the master's honor, since the latter's claim to self-sufficiency rested upon the prestige, power, and wealth that accrued from the benefits of controlling others. . . . The most psychologically powerful expression of Southern honor was the sexual dread of black blood in a white womb. In the patriarchal imagination, no humiliation was greater.

In the culture of the South, "the political and social stratification" of slavery also required a moral stratification. Whites were morally superior to Blacks, and the code of honor was a crucial linchpin in this superiority, a code that rested on various factors: the power of the slave owner; the slave owner's inherent biological and moral superiority; the belief that Africans were heathens with the taint of the biblical curse upon the children of Ham and thus a fate ordained by God. But the fact of miscegenation—which was evident throughout the system of Southern slavery, as Thomas Jefferson's example attests—challenged the assertion of white moral and biological superiority and difference.

Moral purity and honor required a projected public sexual segregation, and so the private fact of sexual unions between whites and Blacks had to be kept hidden and unmentioned. Sutpen has fathered a child, Clytemnestra (Clytie), with one of his slaves, but the people of the county focus their disapprobation not on this but on Sutpen's bare-chested fights with his slaves.[3]

In certain ways, one can view *Absalom, Absalom!* as an example of gothic Southern slave potboilers or bodice rippers but written with the skills, language, and imagination of a major American novelist. But despite

---

3. In *Honor and Violence in the Old South,* Wyatt-Brown observes that honor was regarded as stemming from social judgment, by public approval rather than private behavior or one's internal moral compass. This notion of white moral superiority as well as the ethos of honor continue to shape the political psychology and rhetoric of present-day Southern politics, just as do the theories of nullification (states may opt out of "unjust" federal laws and regulations), states' rights, and the tyranny of the majority—concepts created by defenders of slavery like South Carolina's John C. Calhoun. Even the language carried a conservative racist bent. As Wyatt-Brown writes: "The language of politics was less devoted to rational explanation than to rituals reaffirming shared values; the style of oratory for which the South was famous served to remind listeners of common principles rather than to challenge existing beliefs. Both deeds and words of this character helped to create structure, hierarchy, race control, and social discourse."

Faulkner's genius, the immorality and insanity of racism and slavery are never directly challenged in his novel but are instead constituted as the "tragic flaw" of the novel's characters, along with their excessive pride. Faulkner vividly and brilliantly *depicts* the ways his white characters and their community view both themselves and Blacks, both in the antebellum South and after slavery, but he does not and cannot *challenge* their white worldview. He cannot in the end depict the true reality of the slavery and racism that formed that worldview. For in order to do this, he would have had to enter or at least acknowledge the consciousness of the Blacks who were victimized and oppressed by these white Southerners.

He cannot do this because deep down he does not view their consciousness as equally complex and three-dimensional as that of his white characters. But he also cannot do this because if he had fully been able to enter and re-create the consciousness of Southern Blacks, either in slavery or after, the gap between the white conceptions of reality and the Black conceptions would reveal how the flaws of his white Southern characters are not just "tragic" but stem from a participation in and an acceptance of a monstrous evil. The whole system of slavery was based on the premise that Blacks were less human than whites, less intelligent, less moral, less complex, less feeling, less evolved; so how could Faulkner depict his Black characters as three-dimensional? If he had actually done that, his whole view of the South as noble and tragic, as honorable and flawed, would have collapsed, and he would have entered a political and psychological territory almost no Southern white of his time—and few even in the present—could enter. He would have been depicting not just the fall of the antebellum South and its myths but the entire collapse of white identity and the premises on which it is based and rooted. Faulkner was too much a white Southerner and a white American to enter such territory, even if throughout his works his unconscious and buried edges of his fictional world sometimes hint at its existence.

If Margaret Mitchell created romance out of slavery, Faulkner created faux gothic tragedy; but neither author examined slavery and its legacy for its intrinsic horror and evil, for its vast and systematic establishment of white supremacy and power that created the society in which both authors lived and wrote. Faulkner may have viewed slavery as a "curse" on the South, but in doing this he implicitly absolved white

Southerners: a curse is something delivered on someone—that is, by another entity—and thus the curse is not something one creates, perpetuates, and justifies as the natural order of things. Indeed, in Faulkner, the curse of slavery ennobled the slave owners and the South, even as it damned them and bestowed on them the role of tragic heroes.

On some levels, Faulkner understood that this curse was brought on the South by Southerners. But by failing to focus on the true horrors of slavery and by primarily focusing on the stories of white Southerners, Faulkner never truly confronted the exact nature and cause of this curse. Indeed, he could not because such a confrontation would run contrary to the myths of the South and the Lost Cause—stories of gentility and honor, of civility and freedom—which bolster and uphold the Southern amnesia concerning slavery, and thus the nation's amnesia. This mythology cannot entertain or admit what slavery actually entailed, and the violence and justification for such violence that enabled it to exist.

———

Just as Thomas Jefferson's racial ideology is essential to understanding our history, so too is Faulkner's. If Faulkner's willed blindness to the complexity of his Black characters and the Blacks he encountered in Mississippi didn't encompass an acceptance of slavery as Jefferson did, Faulkner's blindness was of the same source and lineage and only slightly less deluded in its vehemence and contradictions.

At the same time, guarded in part by the obscurity of his writing style, Faulkner's novels reveal, as Jefferson never did except in his bedroom, that slavery involved not just forced labor but sex trafficking, rape, sadism, and interracial desire. As Thomas Powers writes in a review of a biography of Faulkner in the *New York Review of Books*: "What Faulkner contributes to this knotted history [of the South's racial divide] is the understanding that slavery's grip on white masters was sexual, and that the coping mechanism of the white South was denial." Powers quotes the diary of Mary Chestnut, both the daughter of a slave owner and wife of another slave owner: "Like the patriarchs of old our men live all in one house with their wives and their concubines, and the mulattoes one sees in every family exactly resemble the white children—and every lady tells you who is the father of all the mulatto children in everybody's household, but those in her own she seems to think they drop from the clouds." The white master's sexual license was a source of his power and slavery's allure and thus a secret and seemingly forbidden taboo—which in turn was normalized in everyday practice.

White rape was integral to the practice and sustainability of slavery. But the violence inherent in this rape points to another sexual aspect of Southern slavery: the abhorrent sadism in the discipline and punishment of slaves formed an intrinsic bond with a pleasure that rooted itself deep in the slave owner's psyche, his sexuality, and sense of masculinity. In *Scenes of Subjection: Terror, Slavery, and Self-Making in Nineteenth-Century America*, Saidiya V. Hartman quotes this observation by an ex-slave: "Whipping darkies was the joy of the white man in those days." In other words, the psychological embrace and thrill of sadism was deeply intertwined with Southern conceptions of masculinity and sexuality.[4]

Great powers of white denial on the part of both sexes were required to maintain such a system. In Thomas Jefferson's case, others remarked on the uncanny resemblance between his son by Sally Hemings and Jefferson himself, and this resemblance was only exacerbated by the fact that Hemings was a quadroon and their offspring octoroon—nearly white in appearance. And we're not even touching on the enormous psychological twistings required to keep one's own offspring as a slave. Until very recently, when most whites thought of Jefferson, they didn't automatically see a man who kept human beings as slaves. But even now, most white Americans do not think of Jefferson as a rapist (what choice did Sally Hemings have to refuse his advances?) and a man who enslaved his own son, daughter, and grandchildren.

This denial carries on into the present. As the poet Caroline Randall Williams writes in her brilliant 2020 *New York Times* opinion piece "You Want a Confederate Monument? My Body Is a Confederate Monument": "I have rape-colored skin. My light-brown-blackness is a living testament

---

4. The contemporary equivalent is found in stories of police who take pride and revel in their freedom to inflict pain on Black bodies. As former African American police officer Cheryl Dorsey stated in a 2020 ABC interview: "We had a term in the LAPD called stick time, and I know I have heard officers talk about it, wanting to get in some stick time. In other words, this is an opportunity for me to hit you with my baton. I don't have to worry about completing a use of force report [when confronting protesters] because everybody is going to be hitting folks, so there are officers who look forward to getting in some stick time."

to the rules, the practices, the causes of the Old South." Williams is the great-great-granddaughter of the infamous Edmund Pettus, who was a Confederate general, slave owner, and the grand dragon of the Ku Klux Klan, the man whose name is famous for Selma, Alabama's Bloody Sunday and the bridge that bears his name. So much for the harmless nonracist nostalgia of Southern heritage and the noble myth of the Lost Cause.

Turning back to Faulkner, it's clear that he wrote about the system of chattel slavery and its sexual taboos with a focus and skill unrivaled by other white authors of his generation. And yet the question remains as to whether he adequately engaged with the suffering caused by the system of slavery, its violence, desecration, and the ways it sullied both the masters and their victims. Our country's history of white terrorism is still far removed not just from the world of Faulkner's fiction but from most mainstream accounts of our past; certainly such a past is not viewed as an essential element in the ways most white Americans conceive of their racial identities.[5] Nor has slavery become an essential and central focus of white fictional portrayals of our past, as it has for Black American authors, including recent works by Colson Whitehead, Octavia E. Butler, Edward P. Jones, Yaa Gyasi, David Anthony Durham, Charles R. Johnson, and many others. The stories Whiteness tells itself seemingly cannot accommodate such a reckoning with our racial past.

Morrison's *Beloved*

In Toni Morrison's *Beloved,* set mainly in 1873, the traumas of slavery still haunt the novel's Black characters. Morrison's inspiration for the novel

---

5. The violence of slavery on African Americans occurs in tandem with the violence toward Native Americans, which is also occluded from white history and myths about our country's past. Reviewing Claudio Saunt's *Unworthy Republic: The Dispossession of Native Americans and the Road to Indian Terrory,* a study of the treatment of Native Americans during the 1830s, Caitlin Fitz writes in *The Atlantic* of how Andrew Jackson's policies toward Native Americans, which included the Trail of Tears, was echoed by government acts and the private actions of white citizens: "Jackson's deportation act didn't operate alone. It worked in tandem with calls for outright and sometimes even 'exterminatory' warfare, including the U.S.–Sauk War (fought in the Midwest in 1832 and the Second U.S.–Seminole War waged in Florida from 1835 to 1842). It also worked alongside state laws in Georgia, Alabama, and Mississippi that asserted sovereignty over Indigenous nations in the late 1820s and the 1830s, subjecting them to the South's racial hierarchy and denying them legal protection. The states' goal: to terrorize Native people until they fled."

came from the story of Margaret Garner, who escaped slavery in Kentucky in 1856 by crossing the Ohio River to the free state of Ohio; when Garner was captured, she killed her child to prevent the child from being taken back into slavery. In *Beloved*, during slavery and before the present of the novel, the main character Sethe escaped from her master's plantation, Sweet Home, to try to join her children at her mother-in-law's home. But when Sethe was about to be recaptured, she tried to kill her children and succeeded in killing her youngest at the time, a two-year-old. As Sethe explains to Paul D., a former slave at Sweet Home who becomes her lover, she was "trying to put my babies where they would be safe."

Later, in the present time of the novel, a young woman shows up, Beloved, who may or may not be a ghost or spirit. Sethe comes to believe that Beloved is the daughter she killed: at one point Sethe says to herself, "I won't never let her go. I'll explain to her, even though I don't have to. Why I did it. How if I hadn't killed her she would have died and that is something I could not bear to happen to her." For Sethe, slavery rendered her and her children into a state of nonexistence worse than actual death, and it severed the natural bond between parent and child— literally, figuratively, and ontologically (that is, natally alienated).

When Paul D. questions Sethe's decision, another former slave Stamp Paid tries to explain Sethe's reasoning and state of mind. Stamp tells of how he thought of killing his wife who had been repeatedly raped by their owner (whether he actually has done so is left uncertain): "I looked at the back of her neck. She had a real small neck. I decided to break it. You know, like a twig—just snap it. I been low but that was as low as I ever got." As a slave, Stamp is unable to stop the repeated violence and sexual crimes wreaked upon his wife or take vengeance against his masters. For him, the stain of the master's actions reaches beyond the actual physical violence: "That anybody white could take your whole self for anything that came to mind. Not just work, kill, or maim you, but dirty you. Dirty you so bad you couldn't like yourself anymore." There is shame in Stamp Paid's words, a shame that stems both from his own humanity and his sense of himself as a man, but it is also a shame shared by other slaves. Similarly, Sethe is unable to protect her children from being sullied by slavery, and she believes that her child is better off dead than taken back into bondage.

Morrison's novel focuses on the lives and consciousness of her African

American characters. What is left relatively unexamined is the shame of the white men and women who enslaved these African Americans and who "dirtied" themselves in their ownership, cruelty, and desire not just to discipline and sexually violate the slaves but to rob them of their humanity, their families, and the bonds between them. But then Morrison is not particularly interested in writing stories of Southern whites, partly because Southern whites like Faulkner have done so, but even more because those writers never did justice to the Blacks in their midst.

For example, Faulkner could only contemplate the effects of the rape of slaves and sexual miscegenation through the offspring of such liaisons, such as Charles Bon in *Absalom, Absalom!* or Joe Christmas in *Light in August*—not the effects on slaves or Black women who gave birth to these offspring. Perhaps Faulkner's deepest yet most murky treatment of rape and miscegenation occurs in *Go Down, Moses,* particularly the novella *The Bear.* After a vivid and fairly clear account of the hunting of a mythically destructive and enormous bear, the novella's fourth section is a dense and highly rhetorical dialogue between twenty-one-year-old Isaac McCaslin and his cousin McCaslin Edmonds. Their talk centers on Isaac's decision to reject his inheritance of the family plantation.

Embedded in this dialogue are entries from a ledger kept by his Uncles Buck and Buddy noting the purchases of their slaves and some events in their lives. Given the obscurity of this section—in certain ways a purposeful obfuscation on Faulkner's part—it was only recently that I came to understand the significance of a brief fragment noting that Eunice, one of the brothers' slaves, committed suicide by drowning herself. Isaac's grandfather, Carothers McCaslin, has impregnated Eunice's and Carothers's daughter, Tomey, and Eunice kills herself just before the birth of Tomey's daughter, Turl.[6] Thus Isaac's inheritance involves not just miscegenation but incest and rape, and it highlights a gaping blasphemy in the Southern code of separation between the races.

Not unexpectedly, Isaac remains a bachelor his entire life and rejects not just the idea of property but sexuality as well. His identity as a Southern white male contains contradictions and contortions of the psyche

---

6. Commenting on Faulkner's famed obscurity, Thomas Powers points out that the denseness of Faulkner's prose kept most of his Southern neighbors from understanding some of the ways he was investigating the racism and sexual underbelly of Southern history.

that he cannot untie and would rather avoid. At the same time, in Isaac's tale Eunice and Tomey are mere footnotes, one-sentence entries in an account ledger, and the rape and incest they have suffered and the pain in their psyches are never examined or depicted. Faulkner can barely allude to the rape and incest committed by Carothers; he cannot contemplate it in any detail, and he cannot even begin to enter the experience of Eunice or Tomey or, in particular, the horrifying despair that leads Eunice to drown herself, existing in a society where she is regarded as inhuman and natally alienated from her child. To do all this, as Morrison has done, would completely destroy any pretense in the Southern code of honor that Faulkner's fictional vision upholds and celebrates even while lamenting its demise. It would shatter not only his attachment to the myths of the South and the Lost Cause but also tear apart his very identity as a Southerner and the legacy of that history. His Whiteness would no longer mean to him what he believes and wishes it to be. And it is here that the ideology of Whiteness defeats the imagination of one of America's greatest authors.

––––––

In a preface to a later edition of *Beloved,* Morrison writes:

> In trying to make the slave experience intimate, I hoped the sense of things being both under control and out of control would be persuasive throughout . . . that the order and quietude of everyday life would be violently disrupted by the chaos of the needy dead; that the herculean effort to forget would be threatened by memory desperate to stay alive. To render enslavement as a personal experience, language must first get out of the way.

Like Faulkner in *Absalom, Absalom!* but for different reasons, Morrison chooses to approach slavery not through a direct present. Instead slavery appears through memory, through the presence of the past within the present of the novel and through the psychic and physical scars the formerly enslaved African Americans continue to carry and give witness to in their so-called emancipation. Faulkner generally eschews depictions of the violence used to enforce slavery, because to do so would stain and muddy the concept of honor on which Southern identity and racist nostalgia rely. In contrast, a central and problematic issue for Morrison is the aesthetic and moral question of how to approach the violence inherent in slavery. She does not want to shy away from the violence, but she also does not want to present it in a way that exploits her characters or diminishes their humanity.

To understand the parameters of this issue, it's instructive to look at the ways recent studies on African American history have approached it. In *Scenes of Subjection,* Saidiya V. Hartman complicates our contemporary reaction to direct accounts of the brutality of slavery. She cites the "terrible spectacle" that Frederick Douglass presents in his account of the beating of his Aunt Hester. Hartman then questions "the routine display of the slave's ravaged body" and asks: "Are we witnesses who confirm the truth of what happened in the face of the world-destroying capacities of pain, the distortions of torture, the sheer unrepresentability of terror, and the repression of dominant accounts? Or are we voyeurs fascinated with and repelled by exhibitions of terror and sufferance?" In other words, do these accounts of violence restore the humanity of the slave or do they keep that humanity at a remove, still trapped within the system and violence that was intent on obliterating that humanity?

It is in light of such questions that we should regard various aesthetic choices Morrison makes in her novel, in terms of its language, temporal perspective, and movement beyond the strict boundaries of social realism. *Beloved* is written in a poetic language that tries to render not so much the everyday realities of slavery but the deep inner trauma that slavery savaged upon African Americans. *Beloved* and its characters are haunted both by the memories of slavery and by actual spirits, and in the narrative the two are intimately and inextricably connected.

———

At the opening of the novel, the presence of the ghost of Sethe's child is believed to inhabit Sethe's house: "124 was spiteful. Full of a baby's venom. The women in the house knew it and so did the children. For years each put up with the spite in his own way." The novel's given reality is one in which the spirit haunting 124 is a real and palpable presence, which both Paul D. and Sethe acknowledge and which Paul D. eventually seems to exorcise. Where Paul D. and Sethe part is on the question of whether Beloved is the spirit of the daughter Sethe killed resurrected in the flesh. It is here that the different registers or realms of existence and the narrative each of these characters constructs of their lives and history both intertwine and diverge. This multilayering of realities, which is much more complicated than the literary term *magic realism* suggests, allows Morrison to individuate her characters and their stories; in this she moves far beyond the mode of social realism to convey the lives of these two former slaves.

While a more prosaic and reductive reading of Morrison's text is to decide which character's interpretation of reality is true, in contrast a complete reading must acknowledge that for both Sethe and Paul D. their own reading is the literal truth—and that both interpretations constitute the whole truth the reader must take in. In Faulkner, the prolix contortions of his language, especially when it comes to the actualities of slavery and his Black characters, often seem intent on mystifying and obscuring; certainly he intends to mythologize if not glorify that past. In contrast, Morrison's aim is to move language "out of the way" through the metaphoric qualities of her language and her mélange of literary techniques; these qualities help her draw her African American characters with greater precision and depth. Her purpose is not to obscure or reduce slavery or the slave but to reveal them.

That she does all this through a literary technique that goes beyond the boundaries of social realism, that her Black characters acknowledge and live within a "paranormal" reality that the whites around them do not see or acknowledge is a conscious and in many ways a necessary aesthetic choice.[7] The reality of Black life in America has always been very apparent to Blacks and has been shaped in fundamental ways by the powers of whites and white supremacy—but the white ability to see that reality has always been consciously and unconsciously repressed. What is "paranormal" for whites, what is fictional or nonexistent, what is "ghostly" are the truths Black people know about their lives—and the truths Black people know about white people. What Black people see are

---

7. Morrison's literary technique is not unrelated to the practices of signifying and linguistic assumptions as outlined by Henry Louis Gates Jr. in *The Signifying Monkey*.

the ghosts and hauntings of the past; to whites, these ghosts do not exist; there is nothing to be haunted about.

Later in the narrative, Sethe shows Paul D. the scars of whippings, which she refers to as a chokeberry tree and tells him, "I got a tree on my back and a haint in my house." In this scene there is no question of Paul D.'s viewing Sethe's scars through the lens of voyeurism or a gaze that casts the slave as the other; indeed, it is the absence of the white presence or gaze that allows the scene to exist beyond that presence and gaze and that creates an alternate existence and intimacy. Sethe is not telling her story to a white audience but to Paul D., a fellow former slave who has witnessed and suffered similar violence. Paul D. hopes through his love to free or ease Sethe from the isolation, scars, and alienation slavery has wrought within her. That he is not able to accomplish this is understandable, tragic, and to some extent expected. In this, Morrison's novel does justice to Paul D.'s and Sethe's humanity and their individualized responses to the pain and memories they both carry from their enslavement and their continued attempt to escape the realms of the dead—the literal, the figurative (spirits), and the ontological. Recall Sethe's "If I didn't kill her she would have died": Sethe refuses to enter the natal alienation and death of her baby's humanity that are a key component of the ontology of the slave.

Morrison dedicates her novel to those who lived in slavery: "Sixty Million and more." By thrusting her novel firmly within the American canon through the brilliance of her writing, she has opened a door into our past and the lives lost, violated, and traumatized by slavery and the ghosts of those who represent an essential constituency of our mutual past—a counterpart to the white slave owners and their supporters. Just so, the beliefs of those white slave owners and their thinking on race that was part of the establishment and defense of slavery continue to haunt us, to infect and influence our present—our politics, our institutions and systems, our language and culture. We still have not come to terms with that legacy or fully recognized how its ghosts continue to live among us. In a certain sense, the spectral and spiritual world of Sethe and her fellow slaves remains part of the paranormal, the other world or existence that white America cannot yet fully acknowledge or see, even if Morrison has enacted that reality there on the page.

Lincoln Was a Great American, Lincoln Was a Racist

Reality, however one interprets it, lies beyond a screen of clichés. Every culture produces such a screen, partly to facilitate its own practices (to establish habits) and partly to consolidate its own power. Reality is inimical to those with power.

—John Berger, *And Our Faces, My Heart, Brief as Photos*

WHEN I WAS SEVEN, MY FATHER, A RESOLUTELY PATRIOTIC SECOND-generation Japanese American and a tiger dad, assigned me the Gettysburg Address to memorize. Or, rather, he offered me fifty cents, but only if I memorized the whole speech, which I never quite did. Still to this day, I recall the first line, "Four score and seven years ago our fathers brought forth, upon this continent, a new nation, conceived in Liberty, and dedicated to the proposition that all men are created equal." That line and bits of the speech are intertwined in my memory with the image I learned in school of Lincoln as the Great Emancipator, the President who freed the slaves. And those images in turn were added to by the noble portraits of Lincoln in films like *Abraham Lincoln, Young Mr. Lincoln*, and *Abe Lincoln in Illinois*.

Indeed, it was only recently, setting out to write this essay, that I looked up statements of Lincoln that fundamentally alter any reading of the phrase "all men are created equal." In actuality, Lincoln's own words contain a truth that in many ways America still has not quite accepted: Abraham Lincoln was a racist.

Such an assertion leads us to several unsettling questions. What does the fact that Lincoln's racist views are not part of his popular image say about our present moment? Why is it so hard, even for contemporaries, to say, "Lincoln freed the slaves and was a great president. And Lincoln was a racist."?

―――――――

When I was growing up, my image of the Lincoln–Douglass debates was formed by their portrayal in *Abe Lincoln in Illinois,* where Raymond Massey as Lincoln gives a rousing speech with the phrase "a house divided against itself cannot survive." What the film leaves out are the more ambiguous and problematic views Lincoln expressed during the time of those debates:

> I will say then that I am not, nor ever have been in favor of bringing about in any way the social and political equality of the white and black races.

> I have never had the least apprehension that I or my friends would marry negroes if there was no law to keep them from it, but as Judge [Stephen] Douglas and his friends seem to be in great apprehension that they might, if there were no law to keep them from it, I give him the most solemn pledge that I will to the very last stand by the law of this State, which forbids the marrying of white people with negroes.

> Our republican system was meant for a homogeneous people. As long as blacks continue to live with the whites they constitute a threat to the national life. Family life may also collapse and the increase of mixed breed bastards may some day challenge the supremacy of the white man.

> There is a physical difference between the white and black races which I believe will forever forbid the two races living together on terms of social and political equality.

In 1862, a group of five freed Black ministers visited the White House, the first time ever that Blacks were admitted there in a role other than as servants; their aim was to discuss public policy with Lincoln. But instead, Lincoln did not so much talk with them as lecture them:

> You and we are different races. We have between us a broader difference than exists between almost any other two races. Whether it is right or wrong I need not discuss, but this physical difference is a great disadvantage to us both, as I think your race suffers very greatly, many of them, by living among us, while ours suffers from your presence. In a word, we suffer on each side. If this is admitted, it affords a reason at least why we should be separated. . . .
>
> Even when you cease to be slaves, you are yet far removed from being placed on an equality with the white race. . . . The aspiration of men is to enjoy equality with the best when free, but on this broad continent, not a single man of your race is made the equal of a single man of ours. Go where you are treated the best, and the ban is still upon you. . . .
>
> It is better for us both, therefore, to be separated.

Given his belief that Blacks could not be incorporated in the American body politic, Lincoln at various times entertained the notion that Blacks should either be sent back to Africa, to a colony in Panama, or elsewhere in the Americas.

When remarks like these by Lincoln are brought up today, a common response is that it is unfair to impose the standards of the present on this noble figure and great president, a man who more than anyone else was responsible for freeing the slaves. Obviously, Lincoln lived more than a century and a half ago, and in so many ways he rose above his times. But he was also of his times. In a *New York Times* review of George M. Fredrickson's *Big Enough to Be Inconsistent: Abraham Lincoln Confronts Slavery and Race,* Barry Gewen writes:

> [Lincoln] would stand on principle in opposing the extension of slavery into the territories. . . . But he would do nothing to undermine the Peculiar Institution where it was already legal, hoping instead that it would die a natural death some time in the future. This is a stand that will not sit well with those modern readers who

prefer luxuriating in the purity of their ideals (especially if those ideals don't cost them anything) rather than trying to understand the difficult compromises a pragmatic politician is forced to make. But in Lincoln's day a refusal to compromise led to the terrorism of John Brown—just as in our own time it leads to other kinds of fanaticism.

More problematic were Lincoln's views on race. . . . "Whether Lincoln ever went beyond being an anti-slavery white supremacist," Fredrickson writes, "is a question that is difficult to resolve."

So should we tear down his memorial on the National Mall? Only if we are ready to impose a present-day absolutism on a realistic and deeply empathetic politician who took matters one careful step at a time to try to keep them moving in the right direction. Fredrickson closes his book by quoting from [Frederick] Douglass's 1876 address, and here Douglass got it exactly right: "Viewed from genuine abolition ground, Mr. Lincoln seemed tardy, cold, dull and indifferent; but measuring him by the sentiment of his country, a sentiment he was bound as a statesman to consult, he was swift, zealous, radical, and determined."

Gewen skips over the dual-sided nature of Douglass's words, which both critique and praise Lincoln; instead, Gewen rails against "modern readers who prefer luxuriating in the purity of their ideals (especially if those ideals don't cost them anything)"—implying that such readers are unrealistic and unaware of the political exigencies Lincoln faced.[1] Nowhere does Gewen call Lincoln a racist.[2]

---

1. As for figures like General Robert E. Lee, Douglass objected to the reconciliation with former Confederates who failed to truly renounce secession and slavery, and he bristled at the "bombastic laudation" of Lee after his death in 1870: "We are sometimes asked in the name of patriotism to forget the merits of [the Civil War], and to remember with equal admiration those who struck at the nation's life, and those who struck to save it—those who fought for slavery and those who fought for liberty. . . . May my tongue cleave to the roof of my mouth if I forget the differences between the parties to that . . . bloody conflict" (Declaration Day ceremony speech, Arlington National Cemetery, May 30, 1871). Douglass was Lee's contemporary: no historical relativism here.

2. Gewen here is also making an argument about the present in his reference to "the terrorism of John Brown." In our contemporary America, *terrorism* is a loaded word, and one could defend Lincoln without calling John Brown a terrorist, as Gewen does. Gewen sets up a

Here I want to ask Gewen a question: why must a belief in the equality of the races be "a present-day absolutism"? Gewen and others like him would argue that Lincoln's views were far more progressive than whatever was typical of his historical moment. We should view Lincoln against the moral and political standards of his times.

But what are we to make of the fact that there were whites of Lincoln's time who also believed the races were equal? Such a view was not impossible for a white man of Lincoln's time, as John Brown and other less violent abolitionists attest. And there were those in Europe who thought slavery a sin; there is the obvious fact that Britain had abolished the practice before Lincoln did. In Charles Dickens's *American Notes*, published in 1842, Dickens concocts a snarling takedown of slavery and the hypocrisies involved in defending that institution. He lists notice after notice of runaway slaves, notices that belie the absurd contention that slaves are happy in their lot, and he ends with a list of physical abuses associated with slavery:

> I may observe that a distinguished abolitionist in New York once received a negro's ear, which had been cut off close to the head, in a general post letter. It was forwarded by the free and independent gentleman who had caused it to be amputated, with a police request that he would place the specimen in his "collection." I would enlarge this catalogue with broken arms, and broken legs, and gashed flesh, and missing teeth, and lacerated backs, and bites of dogs, and brands of red-hot irons innumerable. . . .

After one trip to America, Dickens could make a condemnation of slavery that so many other white Americans, including Lincoln, could not bring themselves to make, and Dickens made it nearly twenty years before Lincoln became president.

Beyond this, when those in the present invoke historical relativism, they are implicitly only thinking about *white* people. There's a way Gewen

---

telling opposition: belief in equality leads to terrorism; belief in inequality—pragmatic and of its times—is the quality of a statesman and an empathetic politician. It's hard not to get the impression that Gewen seems more worried about the "terrorism" of John Brown than that of the Southern slave owners.

can imagine himself in Lincoln's place, but he can't imagine himself as one of the Black ministers listening to Lincoln lecture them on race. Gewen can bring empathy and historical relativism to Lincoln. But what of the Black minister who left that meeting with Lincoln feeling demeaned, humiliated, and ostracized? Or the Black minister who hoped to have a dialogue with the President only to be told that he would never be part of America, and that he may or may not be equal to the white man—but that really wasn't the question that needed to be considered—and yes, if truth be told, there is not a Black man equal to even the worst white man? Why wouldn't those Black ministers' judgment of Lincoln be relevant? After all, that judgment would be coming not from a twenty-first-century sideline idealist with no stake in the matter but a contemporary of Lincoln with a very large and recognizable stake in the matter.

One could argue that Frederick Douglass, Harriet Tubman, Sojourner Truth, and other Blacks of Lincoln's time saw the equality of races in a way that neither Lincoln nor perhaps any white man of the time could, and yet Douglass, Tubman and Truth were their contemporaries. In other words, why would it be unreasonable to say that the Blacks of Lincoln's time saw the racial question far more clearly than Lincoln and were not hampered by so-called historical limits? Moreover, if the Blacks of Lincoln's time understood the equality of the races in ways whites did not, why isn't their view more prominent in our conception of the times, and why are we so loathe to admit that they were more morally prescient than Lincoln?

And what does that say then about our elevation of Lincoln as the moral ideal? Doesn't that simply replicate a false racist hierarchy, where the less morally clear white man is raised above more morally clear Blacks? Isn't that the essence of racism, using unequal standards to raise up one race and then neglect, devalue, or denigrate another? In the same way Major League Baseball was once a place where Blacks and their abilities were outlawed, Gewen seems to want a moral realm where Blacks will not be considered and by implication where Blacks are not part of the moral conscience of our nation—thus, unconsciously perhaps, Gewen excises Blacks from being fully part of America.[3]

---

3. Again, this can be seen as duplicating the ontology of slavery: Blacks cannot be citizens or full citizens; only whites can.

Yet it's hard to see any time in American history where Blacks weren't far more prescient and morally correct about the racist practices of whites than the majority of whites were. In racial issues of the past, it wasn't the majority of whites who had the correct moral position: it was a majority of Blacks.

———

In many ways, we still possess two versions of our history—the white version and the Black version. To imagine the Black version of history, though, one must step out of a number of assumptions that for most whites remain unconscious.

Such a Black-balanced history involves the creation of a narrative that is certainly not part of the mainstream view of history that exists in our present culture and social discourse, and waits to be created (though scholars and artists, especially Black scholars and artists, are doing just that). This psychological block certainly involves the white inability or refusal to imagine the Black past. But ultimately this block has as much or even more to do with the white inability to reimagine the white past.

What do I mean by this? *In so many ways, whites of today can't imagine or accommodate white evil in the past, only white good. In contrast, Blacks of today have no trouble imagining and acknowledging historical white evil.* This is in part because Blacks in the present identify with Blacks in the past who were victims of white evil. At the same time, most Blacks have experienced racism in the present in ways most whites have not; Blacks understand that racists are far more prevalent in the present than most whites are willing to admit (thus the white liberal surprise at Trump's election and his resounding encouragement of racism and white supremacy).

But there is a difference in how Lincoln configures in white identity as opposed to Black identity. Lincoln's racism does not threaten a Black person's self-image or identity. In contrast, the average white person is perfectly willing to see him- or herself as an heir to Lincoln the emancipator, to see themselves reflected in that image (which is why present-day Republicans remind others of their shared party). But Lincoln the racist? Why would a white person want to see that as part of their heritage, much less their identity as a white person? *That* Lincoln must be kept far away from the average white person's conception of themselves. The best way of doing that is to either deny that Lincoln was actually a racist or minimize as much as possible Lincoln the racist from their conception of the man.

The bracketing of Lincoln the racist as outside the bounds of proper historical discourse is integral to the contemporary white conception of their own white identity. But that is not true of the way most African Americans view our history. Black people today obviously celebrate Lincoln and his signing of the Emancipation Proclamation—what is Juneteenth all about but that? And at the same time, most Blacks have little trouble seeing Lincoln the racist or seeing whites of today as heirs of his racism and the racism of the past.

But what does it mean to be an heir?

Black people today have little trouble seeing whites as benefiting from the racism of the past, whether the racism of slave owners like Jefferson or the great emancipator Lincoln or later generations of whites, just as Blacks have little trouble citing white wealth and Black poverty as part of the legacy of slavery. In contrast, whites today object to such a viewpoint; they argue that they enjoy little or no benefits from racism of the past, that racism is not part of their inheritance. And in order for them to maintain such a belief, whites today have to believe that they are only connected to Lincoln the emancipator, not Lincoln the racist— much less to those who owned slaves or condoned slavery.

In other words, if whites of today were truly convinced that they enjoy little or no benefits from the racism of the past, they would have little trouble acknowledging Lincoln was a racist. That acknowledgment would not be the threat it obviously is to their self-identity as whites. Instead, their idealized portrait of Lincoln would seem to be essential to their idealized portrait of themselves.

————

If you can't openly admit the racism of the past, how can you see clearly the racism of the present?

The answer is you can't. That is why the truth of our racist history is important. That is why admonitions that all that was long ago ("Why can't you just let the past go?") are actually essential aspects of Whiteness. White moral relativism defends racism in the past *and* the present.

It lies about how our racist past created and thus fuels and supports the racism and racial inequities of the present.

Whether President Lincoln was morally wrong or at least obtuse is a debatable point for liberal whites; whether General Robert E. Lee was a treasonous or honorable man is a debatable point for conservative whites. Though debates about these figures concern our past, these debates take place *in the present.* Moreover, they shape who speaks for America, who determines not just what America has been but what it is now. Such debates determine even who can properly be considered an American or a true American, since according to some a true American would not harshly judge Lincoln if you're liberal or Lee if you're conservative. And so Blacks and others who critique both Lincoln and Lee do not represent the true spirit of America and therefore cannot be trusted in any critiques they might make of contemporary America.

In this way, the distorted moral relativism by which we view the past infects our present and shapes and enforces rules about what is moral and rational racial discourse in the present. You lower the moral bar in judging the past, you can lower it accordingly in the present. The result is moral blindness. In other words, when evaluating Lincoln or Lee, moral relativism protects the power of Whiteness as it exists in the present. Similarly, if you mitigate or deny the severity and pervasiveness of the racism at any point in America's past, it makes it easier to argue or pretend that past racism has no influence on the present. Why defend the racism and racists of the past if your views of the present have no connection to that past?

Again, what white liberals or conservatives will rarely focus on is this: the Blacks of Lincoln's and Lee's time were far more prescient, far more truthful, and far more morally accurate about the conditions under which Blacks lived and had a truer understanding of why the whites of their time were morally wrong and racist.[4] But if you deny the existence

---

4. If Lincoln was not a racist or cannot be considered a racist, then it makes sense that the slave-owning, slave-beating, and slave-killing Robert E. Lee can be considered an honorable man, that Lee is worthy of memorial statues and a place in the heart of President Trump and his chief of staff, former Lieutenant General John F. Kelly. If the racism of slave owners in the past or white supremacists or neo-Nazis in the present is, at the very least, a debatable question, then there can be no question that the rest of the white population must almost always be innocent of the charge of racism or moral condemnation since they do not own slaves.

of Black moral prescience in the past, it makes it easier to deny the possibility of Black prescience in the present.

In the debate about Lincoln's or Lee's moral failings, almost all whites, no matter their stance on these issues, tacitly agree: these issues can never be ultimately settled by Blacks, either in the past or the present. In other words, Whiteness always sets the terms of the argument so that no matter what is decided Whiteness always wins. Whiteness always defines what America is, and thus by implication Blacks are ancillary, bit players and can never be said to constitute or be part of the essential America. History is supposedly made and judged by white people. That is America's true moral relativism.

Honoring racists of the past and protecting or diminishing the racism of the past provide protection and camouflage for racists and racism in the present. On another note, when a nation has many public monuments to leaders who were slave holders and few for slaves or leaders of slave rebellions, that should tell us something about the way that nation narrates its past and whom it sees as legitimate members of its society or not.

Racial Regression

Trump, Obama, and the Legacy of Reconstruction

In the Trump administration, white men will be in charge (virtually his entire transition team, and practically every name offered for a potential cabinet post, is a white man). You could say that's nothing new, that white men have been in charge forever. This is true, but now with a gigantic difference. This time the white men in charge will not simply happen to be white; they will be governing as white, as taking America back, back to before multiculturalism.

—Nell Irvin Painter, "What Whiteness Means in the Trump Era"

Between me and the other world there is ever an unasked question: unasked by some through feelings of delicacy; by others through the difficulty of rightly framing it. All, nevertheless, flutter round it. . . . To the real question, How does it feel to be a problem? I answer seldom a word.

—W. E. B. Du Bois, *The Souls of Black Folk*

If you can convince the lowest white man he's better than the best colored man, he won't notice you're picking his pocket. Hell, give him somebody to look down on, and he'll empty his pockets for you.

—Lyndon Johnson to Bill Moyers

I

One definition of the Trump era: Whiteness is now a problem.

Thus, in a reversal of Du Bois's question, we may now ask whites: how does it feel to be a problem?

Power is strongest when it does not have to declare itself to maintain itself. However, today America's future demographics and the loss of white majority status predicted after 2040 loom over our political landscape. Because of this growing awareness of a steady diminishment of white demographic power, Whiteness has had to come out of hiding. It has had to declare itself. A significant number of whites have decided that this is the only way they're going to maintain their white power and status, the only way they're going to ensure the continuation of white supremacy.[1] The prominence of racial coding as well as the unvarnished racism in Trump's rhetoric is in a way an admission: in order to maintain their Whiteness and the privileges and supremacy that go with it, whites will have to self-identify in ways they have not been forced to since the civil rights era.

It's as if there's always been this little glass box affixed to the offices of white America: UNABASHED WHITE SUPREMACY—BREAK OUT IN TIMES OF EMERGENCY. Today, with 2040 looming, many white people feel a certain unease or even panic about their coming minority status. Indeed, a distinct portion of whites and a significant white portion of the Republican Party are terrified of this prospect. (In various studies, when whites are told of these demographic changes, they respond more conservatively not just on questions concerning race but on nonracial issues like climate change.) These white people wish to return to a previous phase in American history where their power as a majority was secure and there

---

1. An update since I first began this essay: in "Many GOP Voters Value America's Whiteness More Than Its Democracy," *New York* magazine's Eric Levitz writes: "Trump's refusal to keep his assaults on democracy constrained within limits . . . has scandalized a significant minority of Republican elites. But his high crimes and misdemeanors have made little impression on the party faithful . . . a new paper from Vanderbilt University political scientist Larry Bartels suggests. . . . Many Republican voters value 'keeping America great' more than they value democracy—and, by 'keeping America great,' such voters typically mean 'keeping America's power structure white' . . . . he found that ethnic antagonism is a better predictor of a Republican's indifference to democratic niceties than anything else." Put another way: for a significant portion of white America, white supremacy is more of a core value than democracy.

were fewer people of color. But this return in time and its mythological pull—"Make America Great Again"—require a portrait of our past where our true history of race is either occluded or transmitted in a palatable and, yes, white-washed version, a history where the past racist actions and tools are either glorified, muted, or diminished. Whether it's Trump's love for the decidedly racist Andrew Jackson and Jackson's genocidal actions against Native Americans, or Trump's support for Confederate statues, or the general white amnesia about slavery and Jim Crow, a majority of white Americans continue to believe in a past where the experiences of people of color do not exist or exist only as a distant and muted minor background.

———

In analyzing this renewed resurgence of white supremacy, many have observed the election of Donald J. Trump to the presidency was spurred in part by a white racial backlash against the presidency of Barack Hussein Obama. In a very pointed and obvious way, Obama's election highlighted for many whites our changing demographics and its threat to white dominance and white supremacy. Tellingly, in an article in the *New Republic*, "Breaking the Grip of White Grievance," John A. Farrell writes that this backlash took place even among whites who voted for Obama:

> In 2008, with the nation suffering its greatest bout of economic turmoil since the Great Depression, John McCain lost among all male voters by 1 point. Four years later, Mitt Romney won their nod by 7 points. But Trump carried men by 11 points and beat Clinton among white men by 31 points. It was the worst performance among white men by any Democrat since the Reagan era.
>
> The election of a black president, it turns out, was more divisive than it looked when the Obamas took the stage before 240,000 people at Grant Park in Chicago on election night 2008. Whites soon commenced to drift, in significant numbers, from the Democratic Party. According to the surveys of the Pew Research Center, the identification of white voters as Democrats or Republicans was evenly split when Obama took office. By 2010, whites were 12 points more likely to be Republican. And the most prominent members of

the caravan of political refugees trudging rightward were white voters with no college education. They began the Obama years evenly split, but were 24 points more likely to declare for the GOP as the 2016 election began.

Yes, the election of Obama did mark a significant progress toward racial equality in America. Yet it also prompted a resurgence of white grievance and a series of actions and policies—from anti-immigration measures to laws limiting voting rights to election challenges to the privatization of public education—designed to thwart the growing demographic power of people of color and to more firmly establish a threatened white dominance by whatever means could be devised.

Like so much in our history, the reaction to Obama was conditioned by the two irreconcilable goals of the America story—to establish freedom, equality, and democracy; and to establish white supremacy. The opposing responses to Obama embody this: Obama as promise versus Obama as threat. Obama as hope versus Obama as fear. Obama as the American dream versus Obama as the American nightmare.

Racial regression is a two-step dance in American history that reflects these divided contradictory goals: a movement forward in racial progress is always accompanied and followed by a movement backward. In many ways, it seems almost inevitable that after America elected its first Black President, he would be followed by a white President proclaiming, "Make America Great Again." Trump based his campaign on a return to a time when the power of the white majority was not threatened by a shift in demographics and a movement toward racial progress.

But in order to properly contextualize and understand this present moment, we need to see clearly its historical roots: Whiteness in American has confronted similar crises before. Recall that whites in the South after the Civil War understood they were a potential voting minority. And the result was a thorough and widespread repudiation and nullification of the racial progress instituted in the Emancipation Proclamation and the Thirteenth, Fourteenth, and Fifteenth Amendments. Yet in our history books and cultural representations of this past, it is the Emancipation that is celebrated and the backlash that is occluded or glossed over.

Thus, whatever their political persuasion, almost all whites have a far easier time accepting and viewing our history as one of racial progress. What they have a far more difficult time acknowledging and accepting is our history of racial backlash. That portion of our history remains a repressed central element in the story we tell ourselves of America. The history of racial backlash says as much about who we actually are as a country as our movements forward in racial progress.

II

The history of race from the Civil War and Reconstruction to the formal establishment of Jim Crow and segregation through *Plessy v. Ferguson* in 1898 is not simple. In certain ways this makes it much easier for most Americans to avoid confronting what happened to race relations in America during this time period. But the complexity of this history is telling. The reestablishment of white supremacy after the Emancipation Proclamation was not an easy task. It required decades of concentrated effort not just in the legal and political realms but in all arenas of society. It required strategy and thinking, new laws and legal arguments; it required a great deal of violence and organization to enforce white will through violence; it required the creation of a new myth of the South and a way of telling its history—that is, a new overarching narrative to bind the South together and, indeed, to bind the South to the North in ways we still don't quite realize; it required a reconfiguration of what the terms *white* and *black* meant—that is, a new statement of ontology. In sum, it required a new formulation of what white supremacy constituted and the form it would take in a society where chattel slavery now appeared to be banned.[2] White Southerners sat at desks or around tables or in gatherings and plotted and planned this new dispensation; it did not occur by accident or unconsciously; it was not created simply by those who might fit some stereotypical image of racist Southerners as uneducated or a mob of roughnecks. The whole of Southern society participated in

---

2. When white South Africans in the twentieth century chose to model apartheid after the example of the Jim Crow South, white South Africans were in part acknowledging the work white Southerners had done in support of white supremacy, using it to organize and govern their society. White South Africans didn't have to invent apartheid; white Southerners had already accomplished that.

this endeavor; indeed, it was the educated elites who contributed most to the forming of a new postslavery version of the South. If Jefferson and other Founding Fathers helped install the ideology of white supremacy through their arguments for slavery, the South of the Reconstruction period formulated white supremacy 2.0 and Jim Crow.

In order to understand this period, we must view it in part from the perspective of those in the South who went to war over slavery and who after defeat continued to believe that slavery was a just and natural order, who felt great terror and animus toward the prospect of any Black progress—politically, legally, socially, economically. After the abolition of slavery by Lincoln's Emancipation Proclamation and the passage of the Thirteenth and Fourteenth Amendments, the response of racist whites to these steps toward racial equity may be phrased this way: how can we return, as closely as possible, to the prior state—to the time before these laws or court decisions were made? More bluntly, how can we reinstitute the conditions of Black chattel slavery?

Thus began the recurring American phenomenon of racial regression or backlash. Indeed, in subsequent periods after Reconstruction, the terms and details of this problem have shifted, but the basic goals and strategies have remained the same. How do we turn back the racial clock? How do we chip away at or dismantle this apparent or incipient racial progress so that it has as little effect as possible on the system of racism we have had in place, even though recent legal measures may have declared parts of this racist system illegal?

A key factor in this effort relied on the power structures and struggle within the legal system. In this realm, regressive whites had to battle seemingly progressive whites, but much more often than not, regressive whites carried the day and progressive whites wearied of the struggle or even ended up agreeing with or at least placating regressive whites.[3] Moreover, to both groups it was assumed that Blacks would never have equal access to the workings of the legal system, much less to the power to overturn decisions by whites.

---

3. Surveys indicate that a telling portion of whites who voted for Obama soon began to sour on him and turned back from the Democratic Party to the Republicans. As in Reconstruction, our history of backlash has always involved a portion of progressive-seeming whites stepping back and rejoining those whites who want to reestablish the prior state of white supremacy.

Given the racial imbalance of power, the basic strategy for racially regressive whites has always involved subverting and overturning the legal system to the disadvantage of Blacks: use whatever resources possible to ensure that the declared legal progress for racial equity in any time period is weakened or made nearly null and void. In other words, so-called progress should be more in name than in deed. To accomplish this, whites had to devise legislative and legal measures designed to limit the enactment of such efforts to advance racial equity. The varieties of maneuvers to achieve this have obviously included direct challenges in the courts or in legislatures; such challenges involved making exceptions to the legal or legislative measures toward racial progress and creating other measures limiting the scope of such progressive measures.

To achieve these aims during Reconstruction and afterward, regressive whites came to employ a cunning legal strategy: limit the powers of the federal government where the control of regressive whites was diluted and expand the powers of state and local government where regressive whites had nearly total control. Similarly, regressive whites worked the legal system to limit the public realm where new racial laws could be enforced; at the same time, they moved to expand the private realm, where new laws would be rendered moot and without legal force. Thus, redefinitions of what is public and what is private have also served as tools against legal measures for racial progress.

Finally, at various points in American history, in order to make backlash efforts to impede racial progress successful, whites have had to alter the vocabulary and language in which they argued for and enacted such efforts. They did this for legal, political, and social reasons: they had to make such measures acceptable not only to those who wanted to impede racial progress but also to those who might want to support such progress. Often, among those who shared their political sentiments, the proponents of racial backlash could openly use prior terminology and reasoning. The new terminology and reasoning were intended more for those who might not share such sentiments.

———

In the period after the Civil War, the Southerners who wanted to return as closely as possible to the conditions and terms of slavery faced an obvious problem: they could not say directly in their legislative, political, and social appeals, "We will reinstitute slavery!" However, they could establish arrangements that duplicated many of the terms of slavery by calling such arrangements by another name. Moreover, the use of these new terms allowed them avenues to new, seemingly more racially neutral arguments that served to justify the retraction or restriction of Black rights. In other words, a certain camouflaging and linguistic trickery was needed—not to fool themselves but to fool and flummox those who might oppose their racist goals, or to placate racial progressives, many of whom did not have the courage of their convictions or the will to persevere toward actual racial equality for Blacks.

One measure that Southerners took immediately after the Civil War was to declare that Black workers were now apprentices. Once they entered these apprenticeships, they owed their labor to those to whom they were apprenticed. The terms of that apprenticeship could restrict Black movement and any attempt to exercise any rights the whites who owned their apprenticeship deemed harmful or unnecessary. The Freedmen's Bureau, whose mandate was supposedly to protect Blacks in the South, still wanted to maintain Blacks as laborers and allow the South to resume work on the plantations in order to recover economically from the war; thus it supported the efforts of owners to continue to control their former slaves through apprenticeships.[4]

Besides apprenticeships, the practice of indentured servitude also kept Blacks working on plantations without pay, eclipsed their right to own land, and severely limited freedom of movement. Because Blacks in the South after the war did not own land, most could not farm their own land. Once Blacks began to work on property owned by whites, landowners could manipulate the terms of that arrangement so that the Blacks inevitably owed money to the white landowner. Of course, this was supplemented by the practice of not allowing Blacks to purchase supplies or other goods from anyone other than the landowner. In this system, Blacks were in perpetual debt to the white landowner, and that debt enabled white landowners to take away or lower any payment Blacks

---

4. Such use of apprenticeship is illustrated in the recent movie *The Free State of Jones,* in which a freed Black man finds that his son has been taken by his former owner; because of the son's apprenticeship, he cannot leave the plantation and be returned to his father.

were supposed to receive; any opposition to such arrangements was punished—either within the legal system by arrest and imprisonment, or outside the legal system by white violence and terrorism. This arrangement was not exactly slavery, but it was close enough to serve the purposes of white Southern landowners. Certainly, none of this honored the spirit of the Thirteenth and Fourteenth Amendments.

Working in conjunction with apprenticeships and indentured servitude were the Black Codes, a set of laws that threatened Blacks with imprisonment at almost any time and under any circumstance, no matter their behavior. All through the South vagrancy laws allowed local authorities to arrest freed Blacks on charges of not working or other minor infractions. In practice these laws meant that if Blacks were not actively engaged in working for whites, they could be arrested on the whim of law enforcement officers (such practices continue to this day in the form of stop-and-frisk and routine traffic stops). Moreover, in many cases any white person could make such an arrest—and thus any white person could threaten a Black person with exercising this power.[5] To be Black in the post–Civil War South did not mean you were officially a slave, but in the eyes of the law you were always inherently guilty of criminal activity simply because of your Blackness. Support for such laws, both in theory and in practice, also came from pseudoscientific studies that purported to prove the inherent and genetic criminality of Blacks.[6]

Once freed slaves were arrested, they were now prisoners of the state and could no longer be said to retain the rights of citizenship. Just as important, they could then be forced into involuntary labor without pay. All over the South a convict lease system was set up, which essentially worked very similarly to slavery, including the use of corporal punishment and torture.

This is what Douglas A. Blackmon argues in his 2008 book *Slavery by Another Name: The Re-Enslavement of Black Americans from the Civil War to World War II*. Blackmon writes of how the incipient prison-industrial

---

5. Think here of all the contemporary Karens calling the police on Black people for barbecuing, entering an Airbnb they have rented, drawing a Black Lives Matter sign on their own sidewalk, and so on. Think of Amy Cooper calling the police on the Black birdwatcher Christian Cooper (no relation) in Central Park.

6. See Khalil Gibran Muhammad, *The Condemnation of Blackness*.

complex in the post–Civil War South served to imprison—and basically enslave—a huge portion of the Black population. This system provided much-needed cheap labor to restart the Southern economy; certainly it exploited Blacks economically. But at the same time, it also disrupted attempts at upward mobility and political power on the part of African Americans:

> The total number of workers caught in this net had to have totaled more than a hundred thousand and perhaps more than twice that figure. Instead of evidence showing black crime waves, the original records of county jails indicated thousands of arrests for inconsequential charges or for violations of laws specifically written to intimidate blacks—changing employers without permission, vagrancy, riding freight cars without a ticket, engaging in sexual activity—or loud talk—with white women. Repeatedly, the time and scale of surges in arrests appeared more attuned to rises and dips in the need for cheap labor than any demonstrable acts of crime. Hundreds of forced labor camps came to exist, scattered throughout the South— operated by state and country governments, larger corporations, small-time entrepreneurs, and provincial farms. These bulging slave centers became a primary weapon of suppression of black aspirations. Where mob violence or the Ku Klux Klan terrorized black citizens periodically, the return of forced labor as a fixture in black life ground pervasively into the daily lives of far more African Americans.

The racial animus that informed the pursuit of runaway slaves similarly informed the arrests and imprisonment of supposedly freed African Americans in the South. The result was a new form of white terrorism, this time enacted by law enforcement and the legal system, a repression that was not needed in the same way during slavery.

The post–Civil War era illustrates a guiding principle of American racism: *once legal measures have been enacted to supposedly outlaw certain racist practices, any backlash attempt to thwart or retract those measures toward racial equality cannot use the same prior terms or vocabulary.* Apprenticeship, debtor or indentured-servant status, vagrancy laws, prison labor—these were the terms through which many aspects of slavery were reinstituted in the South. The goal was to reinstitute slavery, but the goal could not be named as such.

III

As can be seen in such practices as indentured servitude or the Black Codes, the process of hiding racist intentions and maintaining a pro-slavery mindset after the Civil War is quite intricate: it is even more clearly so when we examine that era in further depth. To start with, after the war the question remained as to what the rights of former slaves entailed other than ending the formal legalized arrangements of slavery. As Saidiya V. Hartman points out in *Scenes of Subjection: Terror, Slavery, and Self-Making in Nineteenth-Century America,* the abolishment of slavery opened up more questions than it answered:

> After the amendment's passage, the status and condition of the freed slave remained in question. For example, were equality and suffrage ensuant upon the abolition of slavery? Were blacks citizens? Did the abolition of slavery annul all distinctions of race? Did the abolition of slavery entail more than nominal freedom, the freedom from constraint and the right to own one's person, or did it secure to the oppressed slave his natural and God-given rights and annul invidious distinctions of color? Was slavery merely a status, condition, or private situation in which one man belonged to another and was subject to his absolute control, and thus could be abolished without conferring on former slaves the civil or political rights that whites enjoyed? Did the abolition of slavery entail an equality of rights and privileges? Were those formerly enslaved free if they did not possess an equality of civil rights and immunities?

After emancipation, the status of Blackness was no longer formally and legally aligned with slavery; thus it had to be reconsidered and reformulated. Further ontological work was needed; whites had to determine what Whiteness and Blackness meant in categorizing human beings on a political, social, legal, philosophical, and biological level. If whites could no longer be deemed the masters and Black persons the slaves—with all the implications of those designations—how should the terms *white* and *black* be regarded? The Black slave was not a citizen, but did the abolishment of formal chattel slavery mean that Blacks were truly citizens and equal to whites? Under slavery, white rule over Blacks was absolute; how much power did whites possess over Blacks in this new dispensation? Could whites discriminate against Blacks and limit Black rights? Were whites as free to do violence and terrorize Blacks as they were during slavery? Should Blacks have equal rights as whites to participate in government?

By their actions and creation of the vast machinery of Jim Crow, the answer that Southern whites (and to a lesser extent Northern whites) came up with was essentially this: Blacks may no longer be slaves on a formal and legal level, but that is the only thing that should be changed in the ways the categories of whiteness and blackness should be regarded. As Hartman points out, earlier drafts of the Civil Rights bill of 1866 and the Fourteenth Amendment "contained explicit nondiscrimination provisions," but only when this language was excluded did the amendment and bill pass. As a result, nothing in either the 1866 bill or the Fourteenth Amendment prevented racial discrimination or various methods of assigning Blacks to a status lacking many of the rights that whites enjoyed. Hartman states, "If the Reconstruction Amendments delivered the slave to the 'plane of manhood' and brought him within 'the pale of the Constitution,' they certainly did not imply that distinctions of race were annulled or that all were equal on the plane of manhood."

But in order to ensure this inequality, race as a formal and legal classification needed to be maintained and inscribed into law and public and private practices (though the last was more easily accomplished). Hartman writes:

> Now that race no longer defined status, classificatory schemes were required to maintain these lines of division. The effort to maintain the color line, or, properly speaking, black subordination involved securing the division between the races and controlling the freed population. Central to this effort was the codification of race, which focused primarily on defining and containing blackness.

In other words, after the Civil War those who wished to subjugate Blacks and take away their rights as citizens had to develop legal and extralegal measures in order to do so; they also had to create measures that enacted and encoded the semantic and ontological opposition of Whiteness and Blackness.

This is how regressive Southern whites worked to limit the public and federal sphere and expand the private, state, and local spheres hand in hand with Black Codes and the establishment of Blackness as a separate category from Whiteness. Prior to the Civil War, Blackness was seen as the mark of slavery and all the political, philosophical, and economic framework that went with slavery. After the Civil War, Blackness now became a mark of disapprobation; a site of prejudice, discrimination, and animus; a limited, provisional, and easily revocable citizenry, having no essential rights in the private sphere whatever the law said about the public sphere. There was a consistent move to restrict any measures toward racial equality by defining areas of conduct and practice beyond the reach of the law: racial animus and discrimination came to be deemed as private acts that could not be ruled or prevented by public law.

At the same time in a corollary move, matters of individual conscience needed to be defined as superseding notions of public rights. By limiting the realm of the public, proponents of racial discrimination and prejudice could continue to practice them as part of the private realm and, just as important, as a protection of the collective and individual power of whites. The distinction between whites and Blacks in the public and private realms had to be maintained as part of the legal system and laws regarding public and private life. The value of Whiteness had to be upheld, even more so with the formal end of slavery and the reign of the white master. This in turn relied on the denigration of Blackness, with that denigration inscribed into the law and the ways that laws were enforced.

Such definitions of the public and private were intrinsic to the logic of *Plessy v. Ferguson,* the 1896 Supreme Court decision that legalized segregation and established the falsely labeled "separate but equal" doctrine in the South. In formalizing and sanctifying Jim Crow laws, which began in the 1870s, *Plessy* firmly and formally established the legal precedents that drastically reduced or even effectively eliminated the rights granted by the Thirteenth, Fourteenth, and Fifteenth Amendments. *Plessy* was the culmination not just of a legal battle concerning segregation but of a decades-long effort to reestablish the racial norms of slavery—if not the exact institution of slavery—and to fortify the structures, ideologies, and narratives of white supremacy. Again, the necessity for this latter work and its significance has generally been overlooked, certainly within the popular historical imagination. For as Saidiya Hartman writes of *Plessy*, the denigration and abhorrence of Blackness institutionalized in slavery did not suddenly disappear post-Emancipation, either in terms of legal precedents or of social and cultural practice:

> If the citation of *Roberts* [*Roberts v. City of Boston*, 1849–50] and other pre–Civil War cases in the majority opinion of *Plessy v. Ferguson* attests to the longevity of antebellum attitudes towards blacks and neglects the changes instituted by emancipation, it similarly confirms the impermanence or fragility of the law as compared with the durability of sentiment and the peculiar fashion in which the law established its autonomy—that is, the authorizing and ambivalent gesture in which the law affirmed and seceded to sentiment. For *Plessy*, in acquiescing to the sway of sentiment, echoed *Roberts*: "Prejudice, if it exists, is not created by law and cannot be changed by the law." Yet if the law cannot change prejudice, is its role to affirm it? Following this logic to its end, it appeared that "simple chattelism" was only to be supplanted by legal subjections to the dominant race. For the progeny of the Civil Rights cases and *Plessy* was a dwarfed and stigmatized black citizenry. The slippery logic that spawned this defiled offspring contended that racial discrimination was not a badge of slavery; in short, the enduring condition of subjection had nothing to do with slavery. It was claimed that these racial taxonomies were neutral and noninjurious and thus they bore no relation to the degradation of slavery. The reasonableness of racial classifications reached its grotesque apogee in *Plessy v. Ferguson,* and the spatial segregation sanctioned in this case must be situated within the negrophobic obsession with health and security that infused antimiscegenation statues. Sentiment, instinct, and affinity were called upon to justify the compatibility of perfect equality and racial distinctions.

In *Plessy,* the Supreme Court ruled that racist beliefs and the practice of racial discrimination and white antipathy toward the Black race *were not intrinsic and essential elements of slavery.* They were not created by the law and therefore could not be placed under the stricture of the law. Therefore, the Thirteenth Amendment did not make them illegal.[7] Moreover, according to the dictates of *Plessy,* the health, morals, and comfort of the white population and thus of the public required the segregation of Blacks from the public domain. White supremacy, the key legacy of slavery, would continue to prevail—and that is the conclusion not just of *Plessy* but of the whole Reconstruction period.

————

The Black Codes and other statutes and court rulings like *Plessy* did not take place in a vacuum; the reinstatement of Black servitude and extraction from the body politic took place within and outside the legal system. In direct opposition to the Fifteenth Amendment, numerous measures, both legal and extralegal, were enacted to ensure that Blacks in the South could not vote: practices such as poll taxes and voting quizzes involving questions concerning the Constitution; longer residency requirements; shifting election procedures; and literacy tests.[8] Such blocks to Black voting rights were more formally instituted in the 1898 Supreme Court decision in *Williams v. Mississippi,* which ruled that efforts to disenfranchise Black voters like the poll tax or literacy tests did "not on their face discriminate between the races." In his written opinion, Justice Joseph McKenna alluded to a South Carolina supreme court decision that stated that "the Negro race had acquired or accentuated certain peculiarities of habit or temperament, and of character which clearly distinguished it as a race from the whites; a patient, docile people, but careless, landless, migratory within narrow limits, without

———

7. Part of the insane logic of *Plessy* was that Plessy himself was seven-eighths white. As Hartman explains: "Having been accused of forcing himself into the company of a 'race to which he did not belong,' despite his seven-eighths Caucasian blood, Plessy countered that he had been deprived of his property in whiteness—that is, the reputation of belonging to the white race. Thus, he contended, 'he was entitled to every right, privilege and immunity secured to citizens of the U.S. of the white race.' Ultimately, the Louisiana statue decided who was entitled to enjoy the entitlements of whiteness and, by extension, the universal rights of citizens."

8. Regarding literacy tests, recall that it was illegal to teach a slave to read.

forethought, and its criminal members given to furtive offenses, rather than the robust crimes of whites."

But the legal realm was but one arena of attack on Black rights. These legal measures were accompanied by beatings, killings, lynchings, burnings, and other forms of intimidation. These private acts of white violence instituted a form a terrorism intended to police Blacks and keep them in accordance with white laws and rules of how Blacks should behave, such as where they could live or congregate or what work they could undertake. Most important, such violence made it clear to the South's Black population: do not ask for the rights granted to you either by your supposed citizenship or the Thirteenth, Fourteenth, and Fifteenth Amendments—under the pain of death.

In the post–Civil War era, a wave of white violence erupted in the South against Blacks and continued for decades; its ripples still affect white-Black relationships and white hate crimes today. Both randomly and in concerted planned campaigns, the Ku Klux Klan and other whites beat, whipped, raped, and killed thousands of Blacks, almost always without fear of being arrested by local law enforcement. Indeed, many local law officers and legislators were themselves members of the Klan.[9] The KKK burned Black schools and churches, set out armed patrols of polling places, and killed white Republican leaders who advocated any rights for Blacks. Southern whites devised the Mississippi Plan to suppress the Black vote and wrest back control of the government from the early Black progress in Reconstruction through violence and murder and terrorist groups like the Red Shirts, as well as economic and legal pressure.

A particularly egregious example of this violence was the 1898 Wilmington Massacre, which many consider a turning point in Reconstruction. The largest city in North Carolina at the time, Wilmington had a majority

---

9. Terrorist activities in America have largely involved violence by white Americans against Black Americans. Yet the term *white terrorist* has never been used in any account of our history. Control of ontology and language is a basic tool of white supremacy. This aversion to this term continues today as a practice and is a legacy of our racist history. Similarly, a prime symbol of the KKK and white terrorism has been the Confederate flag, and the refusal to acknowledge this is present in the contemporary South and rural areas of America, while the flag's message remains clear. As the Mississippi-born poet Natasha Trethewey trenchantly observed in a 2020 *New York Times* op-ed, the ubiquity of the Confederate flag in Southern white culture said to her and other Southern Blacks, "Know your place."

Black population; Blacks were elected to local office, had achieved prominent positions in government and business, and were creating a rising middle clas. Indeed, the city can be viewed as what the Black population of the South might have achieved if not for the efforts of white supremacists and systemic racism. After a concerted campaign of white resentment, legal battles, and organizing, a mob of about two thousand white men armed with shotguns attacked and killed at least sixty Black people, burned and destroyed Black-owned buildings and businesses, banned other Blacks, and caused others to flee. The white mob, whose avowed purpose was to kill "every damn nigger in sight," then took over the city government, establishing white supremacist Alfred Waddell as mayor. Waddell proclaimed that the U.S. Constitution "did not anticipate the enfranchisement of an ignorant population of African origin" and that "never again will white men of New Hanover County permit Black political participation." As might be expected, the massacre was blamed on a rumor that Black people had fired on a group of white people, and those whites who participated in the massacre did not face legal consequences; they were in fact celebrated by their fellow white citizens and in the white press. As in so many of our white racial narratives, it was Blacks who caused the violence not whites, even though it was Blacks who suffered the violence at the hands of whites.

Throughout Reconstruction and many decades after, the legal system in the South turned a dependable blind eye toward these acts of white terror. In terms of legal logic, this blindness was reinforced by their "private" nature, therefore not being subject to public and legal scrutiny: if racial animus and discrimination were deemed primarily private matters, legal authorities had wider latitude in ignoring even the most violently racist acts. Whites had the individual right to hate Blacks, and since that wasn't in the governmental purview, how could the legal authorities determine when that hate had gone too far? As in Wilmington, any white-on-Black violence could be justified by the creation of narratives blaming Blacks for their victimization and stating that it was the Black population that started any violence. Such narratives were not challenged in virtually any way by local legal authorities.[10]

---

10. The practice of blaming the Black victim continues to this day. We see it in police reports

At the same time as white Southerners were enacting this enormous legal work and outright terrorism, they also lobbied against the progressive movement in the North that spurred the Civil War: they created a mythology that enticed the North to move toward the South in its understanding of the war and slavery. Whatever the energy of Northern whites to end slavery through measures like the Thirteenth and Fourteenth Amendments, that momentum soon fell away under pressure from the South as the war receded in time and memory. In this way, the North became complicit with the aims of the South and allowed the original spirit of the Thirteenth, Fourteenth, and Fifteenth Amendments to be drained of their power. If there were cries to punish the South and end slavery at the start of Reconstruction, eventually the federal powers and the North receded from the region and took a much more laissez-faire attitude toward Southern race relations.[11] Let the South continue to be the South in terms of race. This symbiotic racial regression again firmly established Whiteness as a form of power and proof of citizenship and Blackness as a site of disempowerment and ostracism from the body politic.

Significant to this racial mythology and narrative, the influence of the South on the retreat of Northern progressivism was spurred by the myth of the Lost Cause. This mythology was created almost immediately after the Civil War by various sources: Southern historians like Edward A. Pollard (*The Lost Cause: A New Southern History of the War of the Confederates* [1866]); political leaders like Jefferson Davis (*The Rise and Fall of the Confederate Government* [1881]); former military figures (particularly

---

defending police brutality and killings; we see it in white vigilantes like the three white men who pursued and killed Ahmaud Arbery in Georgia in 2020; we see it in conservative reporting of Black Lives Matter and protests for racial justice. Also, local authorities have often participated in such violence, further silencing any legal challenge to the narrative. A recent example: the first two white prosecutors who examined the case of Ahmaud Arbery's killing did not press charges on the three white men and readily accepted their explanation that they were in fact threatened by Arbery.

11. In *The Half Has Never Been Told: Slavery and the Making of American Capitalism,* Edward E. Baptist writes: "For a few years after 1865, many white northerners celebrated emancipation as one of their collective triumphs. Yet whites' belief in the emancipation made permanent by the Thirteenth Amendment, much less in the race-neutral citizenship that the Fourteenth and Fifteenth Amendments had written into the Constitution, was never that deep. Many northerners had only supported Benjamin Butler and Abraham Lincoln's moves against slavery because they hated the arrogance of slaveholders like Charles Mallory. And after 1876, northern allies abandoned southern black voters."

the writings of General Jubal Early); and groups like the United Confederate Veterans, the United Daughters of the Confederacy, and the Sons of Confederate Veterans. The Lost Cause deemphasized the evils of slavery, even celebrating a vision of slavery in which slaves were contented, treated well, and were part of a natural God-given order; the myth claimed the real causes of the Civil War were the issue of states' rights and Northern aggression and greed (aggression which was then extended into the Reconstruction period). The myth pictured not just Confederate soldiers but the whole Southern way of life as chivalrous and noble, heroically valiant in defeat. At its core, the Lost Cause mythology was served as a victim story for white Southerners where the horrors of slavery and the suffering of Blacks could be erased from white memory; the war became a tale in which the suffering of white Southerners obliterated Black pain and any sense of the injustice of slavery. This sense of shared victimhood united nineteenth-century Southern whites and continues into the present.[12]

Historian David Blight observes that the Lost Cause provided a "foundation on which Southerners built the Jim Crow system," which still influences and structures much of the politics in the contemporary South. But that influence extends beyond the South. In a *New York Times* article "The South's Fight for White Supremacy," presidential historian Jon Meacham writes that the Southern narrative of the noble lost cause eventually became shared by both Southern and Northern whites:

> As early as 1874 the historian William Wells Brown had said, "There is a feeling all over this country that the Negro has got about as much as he ought to have." Slavery and race were thus pushed to the side in favor of a more comforting story of how valiant brother had taken up arms against valiant brother.
>
> In this recasting of reality, the Civil War was a family quarrel in which both sides were doing the best they could according to their lights. Right and wrong did not enter into it. White Americans chose to celebrate one another without reference to the actual causes and implications of the war. . . . To recall that the war had been about

---

12. My baby boomer wife recalls learning of the "war of Northern aggression"—not called the Civil War—in her eighth-grade Georgia history class.

what Lincoln had called a "new birth of freedom" meant acknowledging the nation's failings on race. So white Americans decided to recall something else.

As Blight argues in *Race and Reunion: The Civil War in American Memory,* through this shared distortion of history Northern whites came to choose racial unity with Southern whites over any concerted attempt to protect the rights of Black Americans. Thus the ideology of Whiteness prevailed over the quest for racial equality. In this way, the North as much as the South was responsible for establishing white supremacy as the guiding doctrine of the country.

————

In the early twentieth century, one proof of how the Lost Cause myth had taken over the national historical imagination was the success of D. W. Griffiths' film *The Birth of a Nation.* The film starts with a Black man attempting to rape a white women who kills herself to escape him, proceeds through his lynching, and celebrates the terrorism wrought by the Ku Klux Klan. *The Birth of a Nation* became a national sensation, and as President Woodrow Wilson said of the film, "It is like writing history with lightning, and my only regret is that it is all so terribly true." A couple of decades later, tourists from all over the country would make pilgrimages to Southern plantations, regaling themselves in the noble lost world of the antebellum South, sans any evidence of the cruelty and evil at the heart of chattel slavery. (Tourist visitations to these plantations continue to this day.) In a less extreme mode than *The Birth of the Nation,* the novel and 1939 film *Gone with the Wind* popularly reenacted the myth of the Lost Cause, and the film won an Academy Award for Best Picture. The film was shown on television several decades later when I was an adolescent, thus shaping the historical imagination of a generation of baby boomers. In all of these representations, Southern whites cast themselves as victims rather than the Blacks they victimized. The psychological displacement here ought to be obvious, but abusers cannot recognize their own denial if they continue the abuse—which is what white Southerners assuredly did.

Even today, the vast intellectual, political, legal, social, and cultural machinery white Southerners employed to reestablish white supremacy after the Civil War is not part of the official history taught to most Americans; it is seldom featured in our fictional re-creations of that time. And yet, as Saidiya Hartman explains:

> The nineteenth-century social is best described as an asylum of inequality, for the practices and relations allowed to flourish in this domain were liberated from the most nominal commitment to equality. . . . Thus, the federal government sanctioned the white supremacist laws of the states by resource to the separation of powers, state sovereignty, and declared noninterference. The incapacity of federal law and the remove of the state regulated the very domain they identified as beyond their reach. . . . This disavowed regulation of the private engendered the subordination of blacks while claiming the noninvolvement of the state. . . . The innocence of the law (it did not create prejudice and thus could not change it) and the state (it merely protected the public safety, health, and morals and promoted the general prosperity) was maintained by denying the public character of racism and attributing it to individual prerogatives.

Under such conditions, it's difficult to see where Southern Blacks were ever regarded as citizens. That Black Americans were able to continue to survive and work in such conditions, that they strived as much as possible to keep their families and culture intact, that they formed churches and other institutions says far more about their character and resilience, their desire for freedom, than it does about any wishes of white Southerners or Northerners that Blacks become a legitimate part of the nation or thrive as a people. Indeed, as in Wilmington or later in the Tulsa Race Massacre of 1921, the more successful Southern Blacks became, the more surrounding whites felt threatened and suppressed any measure of Black progress. Any economic or political progress on the part of Blacks brought them further punishment.

In ways that many Americans still don't realize, Reconstruction established white supremacy as a ruling doctrine in the South and the North. One could argue that white supremacy was even more pervasive than before the Civil War. Before the war, a portion of white male and female Southerners owned slaves, though slavery structured all of South-ern society, especially economically, and how all whites thought about themselves in relationship to Blacks. Still, after the war the daily life of all white Southern men, women, and children became inextricably bound up in the formalized segregation of Jim Crow; unlike with slavery, every white person in the South had to openly and willingly participate in this white supremacist system. As the North came to share the myth of the Lost Cause and placed unity with their fellow Southern whites as the morally correct way to heal the nation, the North came to sanction the white supremacy of Jim Crow, adopting similar de facto principles of segregation—even more so when Blacks began to migrate to the North. The Emancipation Proclamation supposedly took Blacks from the state of being a slave, a noncitizen, and indeed a nonhuman—not into the ac-tual rights of a citizen or an equal human being, but simply out of the formalized trappings of slavery. The barely nascent emergence of Blacks from slavery brought forth a vicious backlash, a recoiling backwards rather than forwards.

In order to understand American history, we must understand the ways the Emancipation Proclamation and the Thirteenth, Fourteenth, and Fifteenth Amendments did not change the actual lives and conditions of Blacks in the South. Certainly, the subjugation of the Black population continued in many ways unaffected by these federal legal measures. Sim-ilarly, white hatred and the desire to repress Blacks continued in many ways unimpeded. After all, the psychology of the master and the racial mindset of Southern whites was not altered by federal legal measures designed to end slavery. Laws do not change the human heart nor do they end hatred and animus. That is something white America has never quite admitted or understood.

IV

Beyond its historical time period, what the Reconstruction and its ra-cial backlash tell us is something deeper: we should understand that the general bent of current conservative Republican views is intimately intertwined with the legal and ideological arguments supporting the practice of racism in this country. This ideology includes several related phenomena: a focus on the individual versus the group; a privileging of state and local government over the national government; a call for less governance; a call for expansion of the private realm and limitations placed on the public realm; an expanded recognition of the private rights of white people as a group within the private sphere (often under the guise of white religious groups).

There are legitimate reasons for a political philosophy based on this grouping of ideas. However, any consideration of these ideas or whatever governing philosophy is based on them should acknowledge the racist uses of such ideas from our past. Because of this, there ought to be a greater skepticism and openness to critiques of these ideas when they are invoked in support of measures dealing with race. It is nothing but a falsehood to say that such ideas have nothing to do with America's racist past.

As a legacy of apprenticeships and indentured servitude, the combined use of institutionalized Black debt and imprisonment that undergirded the South during Reconstruction has been a hallmark of American racism ever since. As current studies on Black unemployment, contemporary redlining, and racist bank practices tell us, the legacy of such measures stretches from the nineteenth century into the present. The methods may be subtler and less obvious now, but their basic character remains—to prop up white economic interests and political power and to lessen Black economic interests and political power. Similarly, the segregation of Jim Crow was not abolished by civil rights laws in private and de facto realms, and the backlash to those laws has created a South where many school systems are as segregated or almost as segregated as they were back in the 1950s.

The most prominent legacy of the racial backlash of Reconstruction can still be seen in our justice system. As Michelle Alexander's *The New Jim Crow* demonstrates:

> What has changed since the collapse of Jim Crow has less to do with the basic structure of our society than with the language we use to justify it. In the era of colorblindness, it is no longer socially permissible to use race, explicitly, as a justification for discrimination, exclusion and social contempt. So we don't. Rather than rely on race, we use our criminal justice system to label people of color

"criminals" and then engage in all the practices we supposedly left behind. Today it is perfectly legal to discriminate against criminals in nearly all the ways that it was once legal to discriminate against African Americans. Once you're labeled a felon, the old forms of discrimination—employment discrimination, housing discrimination, denial of the right to vote, denial of educational opportunity, denial of food stamps and other public benefits, and exclusion from jury service—are suddenly legal. As a criminal, you have scarcely more rights, and arguably less respect, than a black man living in Alabama at the height of Jim Crow. We have not ended racial caste in America; we have merely redesigned it.

The current prison industrial complex described and analyzed by Alexander had its origins in the Reconstruction practices Douglas Blackmon describes in *Slavery by Another Name*. Not only does our present-day justice system imprison a far more significant portion of the Black population than the white, but once Blacks have entered that system, they are stripped of many of their rights as citizens, even after they are no longer incarcerated. One in three Black men in this country can expect to enter this system, as if it were only by chance that they might escape it. Indeed, it can be argued that in our justice system Black citizenship is not a birthright but a temporary state that can be voided at any moment if you encounter the police. Certainly, the vast majority of Blacks believe that in such a system they are not innocent until proven guilty, but exactly the opposite.[13]

Every day in America, when Blacks are stopped by police for minor or

---

13. There are also the horrible conditions of the prisons and the ways in which racial bias and violence are systemic within these prisons. In the prisons, racism can be explicit and virtually unchecked, can openly avow white supremacy. In a *Salon* article on November 23, 2021, "Guards Openly Brag about Being White Supremacists in Florida Prison," Trish Rooney writes: "Officers with the Florida Department of Corrections (DOC) openly brag about being white supremacists. Three white officers recently beat, pepper sprayed, and used a stun gun on a Black inmate who was screaming that he couldn't breathe, in full view of surveillance cameras. The next day, the officers did it again. In a new report from the Associated Press, who interviewed inmates of several Florida prisons and prison guards, this problem goes deeper than a couple of bad apples in the bunch. In 2017, three DOC officers, who were members of the Ku Klux Klan, were arrested by the FBI for planning the murder of a Black former inmate. This summer, one guard allowed for a meeting of white supremacists to take place."

made-up traffic violations—driving while Black—we see a reenactment of the vagrancy laws and Black Codes, which in turn were reenactments of the pursuit of runaway slaves during slavery. These encounters with the police are the state saying to Black people: "You are not truly citizens; you are not whom we are to serve and protect; you are not to be given equal treatment; you will not be regarded the same as a middle-aged white woman or a white businessman or a suburban white teenager driving his parents' car or a white farmer in rural Georgia." When these traffic stops or random police encounters lead to the death of Black people—Sandra Bland, Philando Castile, Daunte Wright, Eric Garner, Michael Brown, Alton Sterling, George Floyd—the script for these events was written in the Reconstruction backlash of the nineteenth century, and before that in the institution of slavery as a basic premise of this country from 1619 forward.

Alexander points to the appalling racial inequities in today's justice system, starting with the disproportionate incarceration of African Americans. She demonstrates how the war on drugs declared by President Reagan—echoing the lies of President Nixon's war on drugs and its racial hatred of Blacks—contributed to this. The numbers and racial disparities she finds in the justice system are horrific, and yet like many aspects of race are not part of the way most white Americans think of their country:

> In less than thirty years, the U.S. penal population exploded from around three hundred thousand to more than two million. . . . The United States now has the highest rate of incarceration in the world. . . . The racial dimension of mass incarceration is its most striking feature. *No other country in the world imprisons so many of its racial or ethnic minorities.* The United States imprisons a larger percentage of its black population than South Africa did at the height of apartheid. [emphasis mine]

Slavery ostracized Blacks from citizenship; the Black Codes attempted to restore slavery during Reconstruction; now such exclusion is accomplished through the justice system. While Alexander named her book *The New Jim Crow*, the legacy of America's racist justice system stretches even further back to the post–Civil War period. So many of the roots of our justice system stem from postwar backlash and the attempt by racist whites to reinscribe the practice of slavery into the economics, politics, legal system, and culture of the South—and more broadly into the rest of America.

The Contemporary White Literary Imagination

The Refusal to Identify White Characters as White

In my recent book on creative writing, *A Stranger's Journey: Race, Identity, and Narrative Craft in Writing*, I examine a distinct difference between the way white fiction writers and fiction writers of color introduce their characters. In general, white fiction writers do not identify their white characters as white. If the characters are named, say, Bill and Bridget, we are to assume tacitly that those characters are white. In contrast, fiction writers of color often identify their characters by race and/or ethnicity. By implication, white fiction writers assume that Whiteness is the universal—and unremarked or undenoted—default. It is writers of color and their characters of color who are an exception to this rule and this universality. Moreover, this practice of white fiction writers also assumes that they and their white characters do not see their race as essential to their identity. Their characters being white is not a significant factor in their experience or the ways they think about themselves.

These are assumptions that few writers of color make about race and their characters—and also about white writers and their white characters. At the same time, white writers often assert that many writers of color substitute politics for art—that we write in ways that are overly concerned with politics.

But this practice of white writers—that is, their avoidance of any question of what Whiteness has meant to their characters identities and lives—is in itself a political position. It is a position much closer to a conservative take on race than a progressive position on race. Moreover, making Whiteness invisible and the universal default leads to instructive differences in the ways white authors envision their work to be evaluated and the ways that work of writers of color are evaluated.

For white writers, these implications are:

White authors start with the premise that their characters are primarily individuals and not members of a racial group. Underlying this is a belief that a character's membership in a group negates or obstructs seeing that character as an individual.

The white writer does not have to indicate openly the race of their white characters. If no other racial designation is assigned to these characters, the reader is to assume they are white.

The lack of racial designation for white characters makes certain tacit assumptions: race will generally be considered not to play an important factor in the identity of these white characters or the ways they think of themselves. Nor does their Whiteness or race play a significant factor in their experiences or the course of their lives.

For most white authors and their white characters, the questions of race and white identity can only come up when those white characters encounter characters of color. Otherwise, unlike Blackness, to reverse W. E. B. Du Bois's phrase, Whiteness is never a problem—or even a question.

The white writer is not considering how people of color might view their white characters or the fact that people of color would consider their characters to be white and that racial designation is part of the way people of color would contextualize those characters. Thus the white author makes, often unconsciously, the following assumption: the gaze and judgment of the racial other will not be present or accounted for in the text.

The literary judgment of a work by a white writer does not need to take into account the lens of race. Just as significant, what is missing from the text because the lens of race is not employed can have no effect on our literary evaluation of that text.

Correspondingly, the judgment of the reader of color is not essential to an evaluation of that text.

For writers of color, a different set of assumptions is at work:

The writer of color does not see a contradiction between viewing their characters as individuals and as members of a group.

Given the fact that Whiteness is considered the universal default, the writer of color must identify her characters in terms of ethnicity and/or race if the characters are not white.

In exploring the character's ethnicity or race, the writer of color must make a decision concerning the ways a white reader, a reader of the writer's own group, and other readers of color will interpret and evaluate the text. This is an aesthetic question that most white writers do not ask themselves.

Many characters of color possess an awareness of how whites view these characters and not just how people of the character's own race view that character: the character of color possesses an awareness of the gaze and judgment of the racial/white Other, and the racial hierarchy that benefits that racial/white Other.

For many writers of color, the lens of race is essential to understanding their characters as well as the way the writer views his characters and his society.

If a writer of color specifically employs the lens of race, that places that writer at odds with the assumptions of many white writers who believe the lens of race is inessential or unimportant.

The writer's ability to read her characters and the society through the lens of race and her ability to convey the complexities of that reading often constitute significant criteria through which readers of color evaluate writers of color.

For the white reader to make such an evaluation, the white reader must be aware of the ways people of color use the lens of race to understand themselves, their communities, and their society as well as our nation's history.

Most white readers do not possess this knowledge. It goes against the white aesthetic—and political—assumption that race is not a significant lens through which to understand characters in literature, whether they are white or people of color. Such differences occur because most white readers do not assume that race is a necessary lens to view their own lives. They do not think very often of their own racial identity (which naming white characters as white would force them to do).

To maintain this view, many white writers and readers must therefore deem the lens of race as unnecessary to an essential understanding of the society they live in. Or to its literature.

Given all these contrasting assumptions by white writers and writers of color, it is therefore impossible to argue that race is not a factor in the aesthetic judgment of works by either white writers or writers of color.

There are many further implications concerning literary practice that arise from the above premises. In the context of my arguments here, it is useful to note that one current practice of Whiteness is to erase Whiteness as a group identity or render it invisible or nonessential when Whiteness benefits from such a view. For instance, in the nineteenth century, studies of criminality viewed white criminals as individuals whose race had nothing to do with their criminality or whose criminality was caused by social conditions. In contrast, Black criminals were considered to be evidence of the criminality of the entire Black race, as biologically inherent and inherited.

In the nineteenth century whites could declare their racist practices more openly, but contemporary racism generally does not declare itself openly (or at least not until the Trump presidency). In contemporary America, whites often do not see themselves as members of a racial group and reject such identification; they even declare that to do otherwise is to engage in racism. In such a dispensation, Whiteness and white group identity either cannot be said to exist or cannot be designated as racial. By design, such a view makes identifying racial disparities and racist practices much harder—and it makes it harder for white people to admit this possibility, much less this reality. In other words, Whiteness remains invisible so its power can remain invisible, camouflaged, undetectable. At the same time, the invisibility of Whiteness allows whites to ignore what whites have done to create the racial disparities and injustices that exist in our society, just as the invisible bubble of white-defined social reality allows whites to ignore what the actual lives of Black people are like in this country.

In contrast, Blacks understand that the negative stereotypes of their race continue to shape white attitudes and behaviors toward Blacks, in many cases determining the conditions of Black life. Blacks and other people of color understand that their membership in a racial group shapes their encounters with whites. They also understand that whites' resistance to see themselves as white, as members of a racial group, is part of the way individual whites and white America deny the existence of racism, consciously and unconsciously.

The practice of white authors not identifying their characters racially is very much in keeping with the beliefs of Whiteness, in the past and present.

White Flights

In *White Flights: Race, Fiction, and the American Imagination,* the white novelist Jess Row examines how contemporary white American fiction writers have depicted white identity. According to Row, many white writers do not see themselves as specifically concerned with or engaging race; when they write about their white characters living in a mainly white or all-white environment, they are not writing about race or defining their relationship with the racial other—their racial other is not a part of their characters' lives and consciousness. But such a view only makes sense when the reading of these writers takes place in a vacuum—without any consideration of the work of writers of color and a reader of color.

Row contradicts the belief of many white fiction writers that their racial identity is not a crucial element of their identity or artistic vision:

If "white flights" in the context of this book means only one thing, it means exactly that: wishful thinking as a way of life, a way of seeing, and a way of making art. The fictions I write about here represent an era when most white writers, like white Americans in general, consciously or unconsciously retreated from the "subject" of race, while writers of color did not; the result is that it often seems like there are two American literatures: one in which race is always marked, and almost always tied to the identity of the author, and one in which race seems to play no part at all. I don't think this is actually the case: stories not only deny but undeny, tell but untell themselves.

Row links this absence of race in contemporary white fiction with the question of how we tell ourselves the story of our country and how we approach our mutual racial past. He cites the reconciliation process in South Africa after apartheid ended and how that involved all constituent elements of that society telling their stories, their version of what happened during apartheid: "This was an act of collective narration, literally: testimonies collected from all sides, including apartheid-regime torturers, Umkhonto we Sizwe terrorists, Zulu royalists, ordinary citizens, and heads of state." This testimony included "harrowing" accounts of state and private racial violence and the abuses and wastes of apartheid. But just as significant, it also established the principle that the story of South Africa could no longer be told by only one voice; no longer could only one version of that history stand for the whole or stand alone, uncontextualized by competing and contradicting narratives—no universal default.

But as Row notes, the United States has not undergone such a reconciliation or reckoning, and we continue to refuse to do so. As evidenced by recent editions of history textbooks in Texas, there is a concerted effort to erase or ameliorate the racism in our past; we are now living in a country where students in Texas will learn a completely different version of our history compared to that taught to students in California.[1] The

---

1. In the post–civil rights era the trend was toward more accurate textbooks, but this has been reversed in red-state America. While California textbooks admit that many African Americans did not have access to the suburban dream of the 1950s, current Texas books do not. Similarly, California textbooks contain information on redlining and restrictive deeds; quotations from black historical personages about the white resistance to civil rights; and assertions

effect of this whitewashing is certainly political, but it also entails a psychological component. Addressing this situation, Row writes:

> The United States has never undergone the process of *officially* collecting the truth about itself, let alone the even more difficult process of figuring out how to balance opposing truth claims within something that calls itself a single society. . . . in some pregnant sense, many self-identified Americans remain in a kind of dream state—what the scholar Lauren Berlant calls "infantile citizenship"—about their common past, always open to deliberation and more often than not vulnerable to erasure and denial.

Row here echoes James Baldwin's contention that white Americans live in a state of false innocence concerning their history and that this has crippled them both psychologically and spiritually: our country's racial past is just as violent and egregious as South Africa's—if not more so. It takes a high degree of denial not to see that viewing Blacks as violent, dangerous, and vengeful entails a vast psychological projection embedded in American history. Such a view more accurately describes the behaviors and beliefs of whites since the inception of this country.[2]

––––––

While contemporary white literary writers don't express the animus and conscious prejudices of the far right, many white writers have made the choice not to see beyond their white world and not to see the reality of Blacks and other people of color. At the same time, they also share with conservatives a blindness to how much race has shaped their own

––––––

that lynchings were meant to "discourage black political and economic power." Textbooks in Texas cover none of these issues. See https://www.nytimes.com/interactive/2020/01/12/us/texas-vs-california-history-textbooks.html.

2. One excellent exception to white literary avoidance of race is poet Patrick Phillips's memoir *Blood at the Root: A Racial Cleansing in America,* which chronicles the racial violence and expulsion of the entire Black population of Forsyth County, Georgia, which began with a lynching in 1912. The book came out of a taxi-ride conversation Phillips had with the African American poet Natasha Trethewey over their mutual Southern roots. When Phillips told her where he came from, Trethewey replied, "I know about Forsyth County. I know where you are from. Why have you been silent on this? Do you think you're not involved?"

lives and the ways they think about themselves. Like conservatives, these white liberal writers would rather live in a world where they don't have to think about Blacks and other people of color. These white writers consciously and unconsciously seem to want to live in a world where Black people do not exist, where they are severed from their own history: proof of this is the America they depict and write about where Black America does not intrude.

In contrast, even if a Black writer is writing only about the Black community or Black characters, the presence of Whiteness and white people—and how Whiteness has shaped the lives, conditions, and history of the Black community—are always a constant. Yes, Black writers and writers of color may write about moments where Whiteness is not present or occupying the main stage, but that is not the same thing as saying these writers do not take Whiteness or the reality of white people into account. They must do so in order to depict the reality of their characters in order to understand the conditions their community lives under. Black life in America makes no sense without the effect of white racism on that life. So why don't white writers do the same?

When white authors do write about Black characters, almost invariably they end up reinforcing racial stereotypes. In *Playing in the Dark: Whiteness and the Literary Imagination,* Toni Morrison demonstrates that it is the racial vision of canonical authors like Willa Cather, Mark Twain, William Faulkner, and Ernest Hemingway that keeps them from seeing their Black characters clearly—without the distorting lens of racial blindness. Thus a failure to understand and critique their own biases as whites in a society of white supremacy led these white writers to failures in craft, and these failures involved their portrayal of not only Black characters but of their white protagonists as well.

Like Baldwin, Morrison argues that the white writer's failure to critique the givens of white identity means that white writers cannot see both Blacks or whites themselves clearly. Examining the nineteenth-century American gothic romance, which was shaped by what Herman Melville described as "the power of blackness," Morrison demonstrates how African Americans and their racial identity as defined by whites provided white authors with a way of "organizing American coherence," of achieving a "new cultural hegemony." The freedom of the New World was seen in contrast to the bonds and restrictions of the Old World, but also by setting the white American in opposition to Blacks who were "not-free" and "not-me." For the white settler to claim and define their freedom, they required "the presence of the unfree within the heart of the democratic experiment—the critical absence of democracy, its echo, shadow, and silent force in the political and intellectual activity of some not-Americans." Or to put it more simply, Whiteness and white freedom were established through the establishment of Blackness and its association with the un-American and un-free, with the bondage of chattel slavery.

Morrison yokes the inaccuracies and stereotypes of white authors and their distortions of race to the question of readership:

> For reasons that should not need explanation here, until very recently, and regardless of the race of the author, the readers of virtually all of American fiction have been positioned as white. I am interested to know what that assumption has meant to the literary imagination. When does racial "unconsciousness" or awareness of race enrich interpretive language, and when does it impoverish it? What does positing one's writerly self, in the whole racialized society that is the United States, as unraced and all others as raced entail? What happens to the writerly imagination of a black author who is at some level *always* conscious of representing one's own race to, or in spite of, a race of readers that understands itself to be "universal" or race-free? In other words, how is "literary whiteness" and "literary blackness" made, and what is the consequence of that construction? . . . Living in a nation of people who *decided* that their world view would combine agendas for individual freedom and mechanisms for devastating racial oppression presents a singular landscape for a writer.

While Morrison uses the qualifying phrase "until very recently," I would maintain that most contemporary white writers still do not write imagining an explicitly Black reader and thus without any consideration of how the Black reader might interpret the text or what differences might be involved in the evaluation of the text by Black reader and white readers.

In contrast, any Black writer understands that the gatekeepers of the literary world are mainly white and white evaluation of that Black writer's work will have an effect on whether and where the work is published, and how it is received and critiqued. Moreover, the Black writer knows that the white editor or publisher will be considering in a conscious or unconscious way how the average white reader will interpret and evaluate the text. This does not mean that the Black writer must write for a white readership. Indeed, Morrison made a conscious choice not to do so; she wrote for a Black readership, thinking of how Black readers would receive her fiction. But at the same time she was also acutely aware that her work would be judged by white literary gatekeepers.

––––––––

In *Killing Rage,* in her essay "Representations of Whiteness in the Black Imagination," bell hooks describes how her white students are often surprised or even angered by that fact that Black students talk about Whiteness and white people with a critical "'ethnographic' gaze." She relates this phenomenon to the legacy of slavery:

> In white supremacist society, white people can "safely" imagine that they are invisible to black people since the power they have historically asserted, and even now collectively assert over black people, accorded them the right to control the black gaze. As fantastic as it may seem, racist white people find it easy to imagine that black people cannot see them if within their desire they do not want to be seen by the dark Other. . . . Even though legal racial apartheid no longer is a norm in the United States, the habits that uphold and maintain institutionalized white supremacy linger. Since most white people do not have to "see" black people (constantly appearing on billboards, television, movies, in magazines, etc.) and they do not need to be ever on guard nor to observe black people to be safe, they can live as though black people are invisible, and they can imagine that they too are also invisible to blacks.

In considering the literary white writer and the gaze—or reading—of the racial other, it is hard not to see the corollary here to the dynamics of the Master/Slave relationship. There was a way in which the white master did not believe the Black slave could actually see the master. Or if the master's definition of their relationship were absolutely true, then the Black slave's view of the master could not be any different from the way the master saw himself. (If it was, such a difference was unnatural and a revolt against not just the master but the word of God—and so it must be incorrect.) It's well known that the Black slave was often instructed not to look the master directly in the eye and in any way that was challenging. Thus, to the master the Black slave's critique of the master officially did not exist; the slave was less than human and the slave's consciousness was not equal to the master, so how could the slave form a viable and valid critique of the master? Indeed, at the core of this relationship was almost a trust in magic on the master's part: the slave could only see what the master wanted the slave to see; if the master did not want the slave to see him or aspects of himself, the slave did not see.

Is there not a similar sort of magical wish in the choice of white literary writers to focus solely on the white world and society or in their absenting the issues of race or a consideration of their racial others in their fictional—and real—worlds? Is there not something similar to the slave owner's assumption of a master's consciousness in the white writer's denial or erasure of the Black reader and their evaluation of the text? When the white writer seems to tacitly assume that the Black reader's judgment does not exist, and thus cannot possibly contest or even on occasion supersede the judgment of the white writer or their white readers? When the white writer consciously or unconsciously erases any thought of viewing the white text through a Black and thus a racial lens? When any use of such a racial lens is deemed in creative writing workshops to be inherently illegitimate and political rather than aesthetic? Up until recently, in most writing workshops the subject of race in literature has been frequently deemed nonliterary and political and viewed as leading to agitprop or works of less aesthetic value. And excluding race from creative writing classes has helped shape the structure and content of fiction by white writers and thus contributed to a vision and version of white identity where the problems of race are avoided and/or deemed minor to the essential story of white life in this country.

Racial Absence and Racial Presence in Jonathan Franzen and ZZ Packer

Jonathan Franzen and *Freedom*

In many ways, Jonathan Franzen has become the most representative white male novelist of his generation (especially after the suicide death of his friend David Foster Wallace). Franzen writes large ambitious best-selling novels, realistic, socially observant, generally following the interactions and fates of a family and its members; he's won a National Book Award, been a finalist for the Pulitzer Prize, gained fame—or infamy—for his skepticism toward being picked for Oprah's Book Club (which led to her disinviting him and his book), and has written significant criticism on the direction of the contemporary novel. In an essay in 1996 in *Harper's*, much discussed in the literary world, he explored how he felt overly weighted by "burden of news bringing" as the aim of a socially conscious novel; he highlighted fiction's "duty to entertain" and his wish "to write about the things closest to me, to lose myself in the characters and locals I loved."

In a *New York Times* review of Franzen's 2010 novel *Freedom*, Sam Tanenhaus praises the novel effusively and celebrates Franzen's exploration of the themes of liberty and freedom:

> Jonathan Franzen's new novel, "Freedom," like his previous one, "The Corrections," is a masterpiece of American fiction. The two books have much in common. Once again Franzen has fashioned a capacious but intricately ordered narrative that in its majestic sweep seems to gather up every fresh datum of our shared millennial life. . . .

. . . As each of us seeks to assert his "personal liberties"—a phrase Franzen uses with full command of its ideological implications—we helplessly collide with others in equal pursuit of *their* sacred freedoms, which, more often than not, seem to threaten our own. It is no surprise, then, that "the personality susceptible to the dream of limitless freedom is a personality also prone, should the dream ever sour, to misanthropy and rage," as Franzen remarks. And the dream will always sour; for it is seldom enough simply to follow one's creed; others must embrace it too. They alone can validate it.

Rather than explore Franzen's definition of *freedom* and its exclusion of matters concerning race, Tanenhaus takes Franzen's exploration of his themes at face value, as evidence of the novel's intellectual and psychological depth.

So as an example of standard white literary practice, let me use the opening of Franzen's *Freedom,* which I've chosen in part because the opening setting is the Twin Cities, where I've lived since the 1970s:

The news about Walter Berglund wasn't picked up locally—he and Patty had moved away to Washington two years earlier and meant nothing to St. Paul now—but the urban gentry of Ramsey Hill were not so loyal to their city as not to read the *New York Times.* According to a long and very unflattering story in the *Times,* Walter had made quite a mess of his professional life out there in the nation's capital. His old neighbors had some difficulty reconciling the quotes about him in the *Times* ("arrogant," "high-handed," "ethically compromised") with the generous, smiling red-faced 3M employee they remembered pedaling his commuter bicycle up Summit Avenue in February snow; it seemed strange that Walter, who was greener than Greenpeace and whose own roots were rural, should be in trouble now for conniving with the coal industry and mistreating country people. Then again, there had always been something not quite right about the Berglunds.

Walter and Patty were the young pioneers of Ramsey Hill—the first college grads to buy a house on Barrier Street since the old heart of St. Paul had fallen on hard times three decades earlier. They paid nothing for their Victorian and then killed themselves for ten years renovating it. Early on, some very determined person torched their garage and twice broke into their car before they got the garage rebuilt. Sunburned bikers descended on the vacant lot across the alley to drink Schlitz and grill knockwurst and rev engines at small hours until Patty went outside in sweatclothes and said, "Hey, you guys, you know what?" Patty frightened nobody, but she'd been a standout athlete in high school and college and possessed a jock sort of fearlessness. From her very first day in the neighborhood, she was helplessly conspicuous. Tall, ponytailed, absurdly young, pushing a smaller stroller past stripped cars and broken beer bottles and barfed-upon old snow, she might have been carrying all the hours of her day in the string bags that hung from her stroller. Behind her you could see the baby-encumbered preparations for a morning of baby-encumbered errands, ahead of her, an afternoon of public radio, the *Silver Palate Cookbook*, cloth diapers, drywall compound, and latex paint; and then *Goodnight Moon*, then zinfandel. She was already fully the thing that was just starting to happen to the rest of the street.

Walter and Patty aren't specifically designated as white but in the absence of any markers indicating otherwise, that is the reader's assumption, and Franzen knows this. (Their last name Berglund reads as European American, but I know Minnesota Korean adoptees with Germanic and Scandinavian last names, so that's not a fair assumption.)

In his social portrait of the Berglunds, Franzen's task seems to be to differentiate the Berglunds from the other presumably white people—also never racially designated—in their St. Paul neighborhood and to indicate the Berglunds' socioeconomic class. The Berglunds are not like the "urban gentry of Ramsey Hill," who read the *New York Times*, nor are they like the sunburned bikers across the alley. The Berglunds are "greener than Greenpeace," listeners of public radio, users of the *Silver Palate Cookbook*, and new yuppie parents; in terms of St. Paul's geography, they are the first college grads in the neighborhood, the first pioneers in a gentrification process. Franzen's portrait carries a good dose of social satire, which continues into the third paragraph:

In the earliest years, when you could still drive a Volvo 240 without feeling self-conscious, the collective task in Ramsey Hill was to relearn certain life skills that your own parents had fled to the suburbs specifically to unlearn, like how to interest the local cops in actually doing their job, and how to protect a bike from a highly motivated thief, and when to bother rousting a drunk from your lawn furniture, and how to encourage feral cats to shit in somebody else's children's sandbox, and how to determine whether a public school sucked too much to bother trying to fix it. There were also more contemporary questions, like, what about those cloth diapers? Worth the bother? And was it true that you could still get milk delivered in glass bottles? Were the Boy Scouts OK politically? Was bulgur really necessary? Where to recycle batteries? How to respond when a poor person of color accused you of destroying her neighborhood? Was it true that the glaze of old Fiestaware contained dangerous amounts of lead? How elaborate did a kitchen water filter actually need to be?

These questions continue for several more sentences. Part of Franzen's skill in this list is to pin down with great accuracy a specific urban social class—white yuppie gentrifiers. At the same time, his version of realism also marks a limit: race is mentioned, but only in passing and of course it is the person of color—who *must* be designated as such—who brings this intrusion. There is one question about the effect of gentrification on the Blacks who have lived previously in the neighborhood. The issues brought up in this confrontation occupy the same importance in the Berglunds' consciousness as "What about those cloth diapers?" and "Was bulgur really necessary?" This implied equivalence in part satirizes the Berglunds. But at the same time it limits how far the issues of race and Whiteness will intrude on Franzen's portrait of their world—that is, race will be absent here. The Berglunds are more concerned about other matters, and Franzen is simply reflecting their vision of the world.

If I were to say that the Berglunds and their creator share a white vision of the world, what does that mean? And what does that have to say about a set of assumptions concerning race that undergird the "realist" aesthetic of Franzen's novel? The depicted reality of the Berglunds and thus the realism of Franzen depend in part on circumscribing and silencing race in the lives of the Berglunds. Franzen is giving us his version of reality; that is his right. But that doesn't mean I as a reader must remain unconscious of what his version of reality—and thus his definition of *freedom*—leaves out. As David Palumbo-Liu has argued, the concept and practice of realism rely on both agreements and challenges and are far more open to the latter than many recognize.[1] Often, white writers—especially if they do not consider readers of color—assume that there is no disagreement about the nature of social reality. Most writers of color assume there is disagreement, and race is an essential battleground within this disagreement. Unlike Toni Morrison's traditional white author who does not envision a reader of color, writers of color are also aware that their work will be interpreted and evaluated by white readers as well as readers of color.

Like most white writers, Franzen starts from an epistemological position where his take on the world when it comes to race is unchallenged. Fiction investigates subjectivity, yes, but Franzen never questions the subjectivity of his white identity or that of his characters. A writer of color understands that they are always in a position where their knowledge is regarded as subjective and open to denial, that she or he always stands in opposition not just to white knowledge but to white knowledge as the objective standard.

The epistemological roots of America's white supremacy are embedded in these contrasting racial approaches and positions in creating fictional characters—even if the white author believes him- or herself to be free of racism. On one level, white characters are supposedly raceless—and thus universal. On another level, their Whiteness is not to be subject to interrogation or examination and requires no explanation or contextualization. The meaning of the character's Whiteness ought to be apparent to any reader, whether the reader is white or not—again it is universal. Only the character of color requires categorization, contextualization,

---

1. David Palumbo-Liu explains in *The Deliverance of Others: Reading Literature in a Global Age*: "Analysis of literary realism allows us to diagnose the reputed commonality of behavior, how different people might act in concert with others, but also, this literature, *as* literature, contains a critical, self-reflective element. If literature has been charged with delivering the lives of others to us for our enrichment and betterment, how, if at all, does this new otherness change our assumptions about what is realistic, about what is common to all human beings in their behaviors, choices, actions, judgments?"

explication, and interrogation in terms of race; only the character of color requires the author of color to assume this is necessary; only the character of color is a question or, to use W. E. B. Du Bois's term, a problem. Of course, Franzen is not alone in making these assumptions; he shares this epistemological stance with almost all white American authors who present their white characters with no racial designation.

From this opening, Franzen's *Freedom* moves on to focus on an adulterous triangle and an affair between Patty Berglund and Walter's best friend, Richard, a rock-and-roll musician. Later in the novel, Walter becomes involved in ecological issues that engender clashes with the his and Patty's son Joey. The social portrait that starts the novel and the shifting economics of the Berglunds' neighborhood are never really revisited in any detail, nor are the changing demographics of that area of the city, which has included the influx of Southeast Asian immigrants and, more recently, East African immigrants. (Since I live in the Twin Cities, I know how much willed blindness must be enacted in order to keep these racial demographics from intruding on the reality and lives of the Berglunds.)

Rather than the neighborhood, Franzen's novel is about the breakdown of one family more than anything else, and this is a perfectly fine subject for a novel. I merely want to point out that Franzen eschews the lens of race to examine the lives of the Berglunds. They're middle-class white people. Why should race matter to them at all?

————

In an interview for *Slate,* Franzen was asked, "Have you ever considered writing a book about race?" Here's Franzen's answer:

> I have thought about it, but—this is an embarrassing confession—I don't have very many black friends. I have never been in love with a black woman. I feel like if I had, I might dare. . . . Didn't marry into a black family. I write about characters, and I have to love the character to write about the character. If you have not had direct firsthand experience of loving a category of person—a person of a different race, a profoundly religious person, things that are real stark differences between people—I think it is very hard to dare, or necessarily even want, to write fully from the inside of a person.

To his credit, Franzen speaks more candidly about his lack of contact with Blacks than many white writers might. Reading Franzen's remarks, I recall an article by the poet Major Jackson several years ago in the *American Poetry Review* in which he is asked why white poets didn't write more about race. One cause Jackson listed was that most white poets don't have many or any Black friends.

Later in the interview, talking about his novel *Purity,* Franzen observes that having lived in Germany for two and a half years and knowing the literature was not enough to be able to write about German people. It was the fact that he started making German friends that established an entry: "The portal to being able to write about it was suddenly having these friends I really loved. And then I wasn't the hostile outsider; I was the loving insider."

To me, a logical question is why doesn't Franzen have Black friends? Why is it more possible for him to have several friends he loves who are German but few who are Black Americans? After all, Franzen is an American and not a German. Are the barriers of race greater for him than those of culture and nationality? Franzen doesn't ask or reveal if he has unconsciously or consciously decided not to seek out friendships with Black Americans. Nor does he wonder if his lack of friendships with Black Americans has something to do with the ways he approaches both his own identity and theirs; this would involve the question as to whether or not Black Americans who meet Franzen do or do not feel that he is a white man with whom they could have an authentic relationship, one where they as Black Americans could be themselves and trust that he accepts and values who they are. Tellingly, Franzen doesn't seem to acknowledge in the interview that he actually has written about race. In *Freedom*, Walter Berglund eventually has an interracial affair with a twenty-five-year-old Bengali Indian American, Lalitha. Does this relationship break or not break the personal rule Franzen seems to set up in the interview? I may be wrong, but I seriously doubt that he has a trove of South Asian friends. He may possibly have had a love affair with an Indian American woman, though from the evidence of this novel I doubt it.

Whatever Franzen's personal relations, his portrait of this affair between an older white male and a younger Asian American female is problematic at best and certainly bears more scrutiny than most critics have given it. Lalitha is portrayed as adoring Walter. She praises his "vision" for a problematic project that purports to be environmentally minded but is devised in partnership with a coal company; she tells Walter he's clearly superior to his college friend Richard, who has slept with Walter's wife. After an encounter with Richard, Lalitha tells Water, "All I could see when we were talking was how much he admires you."

As a reader familiar with Edward Said's *Orientalism* and other post-colonial critical works, I can't help but be troubled by the way such a relationship echoes various Orientalist tropes, tropes Franzen doesn't seem aware of. As Said has shown, the trope of the powerful, superior, and masculine West and the less powerful, inferior, feminine East was an integral ideological tool in the conquering of Brown and Black people across the globe and the establishment of colonialism. But rather than invoking this history or the skepticism it might bring up, the novelist presents Lalitha's adoration and this affair at face value, or, rather, in the way the older white male regards it.

To be fair, the novel remains outside the subjectivity of the young Indian American woman; the novel is told from the viewpoint of Walter and his family, not Lalitha's. Still, within a limited omniscient narrative, the novelist can make clear the limitations or blind spots of the protag-onist's consciousness. I cannot find any signals or hints that any racial reading or critique is at play in the novel.

It is true that Asian Americans in general, and Indian Americans in particular, are positioned racially differently from Black Americans in American society and culture. These differences are myriad and far too complex to go into in this essay. But on a larger level, I would maintain that a young Indian American who enters a relationship with an older white American male must consciously or unconsciously process their racial differences in experience and identity; these differences are at play whether or not she is aware of how those differences have shaped her sexual desires. This would seem especially true given that Lalitha gets involved with Walter right after ending her relationship with Jairam, an Indian American who, according to Walter, "was thick-bodied and some-what ugly but arrogant and driven, a heart surgeon in training." Note that "ugly" here is Walter's assessment, and yet the question of racialized standards of appearance never arises in the text.

In her idolization of Walter, Lalitha sees a figure of power, and this power cannot be separated from his position as a white male or in how she views both Indian American men and other men of color. One would reasonably suspect that this affair may stem in part from her relationship with her family, but there's no investigation of this in the novel (how her family views Jairam or Walter isn't explored). As I've said, nothing in this novel critiques the relationship and its absence of racial investigation; there's no one else in Walter's world who might bring an alternate racial reading to this relationship, much less anyone who would question the colonial tropes of Orientalism.

But even beyond the problematic relationship, Franzen's portrait of Lalitha lacks a specificity that can only be derived from a lens that takes into account ethnicity and race. For instance, Lalitha apparently speaks with a "lilt" of an accent, but we are never told at exactly what age she came to America. That detail would indicate something of how she might process her identity and would affect her relationship to American society and culture. To arrive as an immigrant at seven or twelve or sixteen are entirely different experiences, but my suspicion is Franzen hasn't considered such differences.

———

Shortly after Walter throws his wife, Patty, out of the house, Walter and Lalitha make love for the first time. The description does nothing to dispel suspicions that the Orientalism here is not only Walter's but also the author's:

> He needed the quick fix simply in order to keep functioning—to not get leveled by hatred and self-pity—and, in one way, the fix was very sweet indeed, because Lalitha really was crazy for him, almost literally dripping with desire, certainly strongly seeping with it. She stared into his eyes with love and joy, she pronounced beautiful and perfect and wonderful the manhood that Patty in her document had libeled and spat upon. What wasn't to like? He was a man in his prime, she was adorable, and young and insatiable; and this, in fact, was what wasn't to like.

Note here how in Walter's mind the differences between him and Lalitha are their positions in power—she is his assistant—and age. Race is not worth remarking on. But then this follows:

> His emotions couldn't keep up with the vigor and urgency of their animal attraction, the interminability of their coupling. She needed to ride him, she needed to be crushed underneath him, she needed to have her legs on his shoulders, she needed to do the Downward Dog and be whammed from behind, she needed bending over the bed, she needed her face pressed against the wall, she needed her legs wrapped around him and her head thrown back and her very round breasts flying every which way. It all seemed intensely meaningful to her, she was a bottomless well of anguished noise, and he was up for all of it. In good cardiovascular shape, thrilled by her extravagance, attuned to her wishes, and extremely fond of her. And yet it wasn't quite personal, and he couldn't find his way to orgasm. And this was very odd, an entirely new and unanticipated problem, due in part, perhaps, to his unfamiliarity with condoms, and to how unbelievably wet she was.

As Toni Morrison demonstrates in *Playing in the Dark: Whiteness and the Literary Imagination,* the unconscious racial assumptions of white authors can reveal themselves in myriad ways. One is terrible prose. The prose is so bad here—"almost literally dripping with desire," "bottomless well of anguished noise," "in good cardiovascular shape." I at first wondered if the passage were simply satirizing Walter, but Franzen's brand of satire is not Tom Wolfe's. Beyond the poor prose, there's an undergirding to this passage that's clearly racialized. If this were writing from a student of mine, and not one of the most celebrated novelists of his generation, I can't imagine not flagging this passage (though I can imagine that in certain white instructors' workshops, a student of color commenting on this passage would be called out for "political correctness").

In Walter's mind, Lalitha "needed to be crushed underneath him." Now this might be contextualized simply as a patriarchal attitude, but then what does one do with the awful Downward Dog reference? On one level, Walter is aware that Lalitha is of a different race and culture; indeed, a drunk white man in a restaurant has previously made crude racist remarks about the pair, using the N-word. But any deep contemplation of race never really enters Walter's consciousness. And yet what would the reader think if Lalitha were Black and Walter believed she "needed to be crushed underneath him"? Racial alarm bells would go off everywhere. One surmises that Franzen hasn't imagined an Asian American reader or even simply a reader of postcolonial studies for whom the interracial relationship would set off similar alarms.

Perhaps it's in part because Lalitha is an Indian American that Franzen can enter this territory without getting flagged—for his lack of knowledge of the psychology, culture, and history of Indian Americans; for his one-dimensional characterization of Lalitha and her desires; for never questioning the racist assumptions that underlie the Orientalism here and in the whole relationship; and for Walter's own perceptions of Lalitha.[2] In *Playing in the Dark,* Morrison faults Willa Cather for absenting race in *Sapphira and the Slave Girl* and not examining the white female protagonist's struggle with power and sexuality. Similarly, the unexplored aspect of Walter's identity involves not only his class and age but his Whiteness.

———

In *White Flights: Race, Fiction, and the American Imagination,* Jess Row connects white agency and privilege with the deracination of history and the present; this connection extends to a deracination of space, which he contends is integral to white conceptions of imaginative freedom. In the work of various white novelists such as Marilynne Robinson and Don DeLillo, and the work of a memoirist like Annie Dillard, Row marks those plot points and instances where white characters and writers and their narrations move away from elements of history involving race and ethnicity and retreat to spaces where they are free from such considerations. In investigating these movements, Row yokes these fictional and nonfictional moves with the spatial demographics of the post–civil rights

---

2. Tanenhaus's review of *Freedom* on the front page of the *New York Times Book Review* mentions "an adoring and nubile Bengali-American" only once in passing and never names her.

era—to the phenomena of white flight and the maintenance and even increase of racial segregation in America.

Racially, the Whiteness of white literary imagination is obviously linked to this segregation: people of different races in this country often do not go to school together; they do not often worship together; they do not often socialize with each other. Beyond this, the very conception of imaginative freedom for many of these white authors and their characters seems to necessitate a certain social or imaginative retreat, but also a retreat from any confrontation or interaction with a racial other. Row writes:

> In a country that today is about as far from homogenous as it is possible to be, it's fascinating and deeply telling that the impossible desire for deracination still has such a deep hold on the white American psyche. . . .
>
> All my life, it seems sometimes, I've been absorbing one story after another—from *My Side of the Mountain* to *Huck Finn* to *Lord Jim* to *The Snow Leopard* to *Housekeeping*—in which a person who looks like me defines him- or herself against a rocky crag, a pathless desert, a glacier, a remote Montana Valley. It feels unquestionably like the necessary and natural scale of my own experience, against which my life should be measured. . . .
>
> What does it mean to call white flight—the white flight of the mind—an "aestheticization of social reality?" To begin with, it's a posture of avoidance or evasion: the desire not to have one's visual field constantly invaded by inconveniently different faces— relationships that are fraught, unfixed, capable of producing equal measures of helplessness and guilt. Via the fantasy of deracination, however, that avoidance turns into a desirable thing, a psychic good: because white people feel, so often, that in order to think and feel good, in order to be their "true selves," they have to find themselves in a landscape that silhouettes them, that flatters their individuality by allowing them to mediate freely. In this sense the most troubling part of deracination as an imaginative practice is not even that it draws writers toward all-white environments but that it can happen, as it does in [Robinson's novel] *Home,* even when the troubling face

of a person of color is present. Guilt, helplessness, the longing for redemption, the presumption of racial benevolence marked as, or indistinguishable from, innocence—those things linger around the white subject like trace elements in the air, like our own private Idahos, and turn longings for justice and reconciliation into something foreshortened and already foreclosed. . . .

When you refuse to allow for the presence of others, you lose the ability to be seen by them. At that point, a social bond, a human bond, is severed. This is a form of imaginative violence Americans practice so routinely that it has become, in the biopolitical sense, second nature, or just nature.

Franzen's *Freedom* starts not with white flight but a similar phenomenon: gentrification, the imposing or colonizing of a space previously occupied by people of color and/or people of lower income so that those inhabitants are removed or forced to move from that space by various means. But under his white aesthetics and the rubric of the white imagination, Franzen does not use his novel to investigate the lives of or tensions with those the Berglund family has uprooted or dispossessed: there is only the single mention of the "poor person of color" who might still live on the outskirts of their neighborhood.

On a related plane, the novelist occupies a similar imaginative space in his own personal life. Franzen can come to love and write about Germans but not Black Americans because white Germans do not presumably intrude on or limit his white space; they do not fuck with his imaginative vision and freedom in the ways American people of color would. Beyond that, in order to protect the white space of his white characters, when a South Asian Indian American enters the social realm of the Berglunds, she must be deracinated and de-ethnicized. Such a move retains the white space of the novel; it presents the racial other without actually integrating that character into the imaginative or politicized vision of the novel—rather than exploring the racial implications of such an integration, Franzen ignores or evades those racial implications.

I'm focusing on Franzen's weaknesses here not because they are particularly or exceptionally egregious, but because they are representative and common; far more egregious examples show up in writing workshops where writers of color must make the decision of whether to point out racial stereotypes and distortions in their fellow white writers and risk being branded as troublemakers, censors, and proponents of the politically correct. The Whiteness of fiction produced by white American novelists is just a small portion of our society and culture, but it is still an essential portion through which the basic rules of white identity in our society are created and maintained—and thus the white supremacy that identity undergirds.

In the world of fiction created by Franzen and other white American writers, Michael Brown and Ferguson, Missouri, or Freddie Gray and Baltimore, or the poor person of color who accuses the Berglunds of destroying her neighborhood are distant figures, inhabiting a backdrop that rarely intrudes on the private lives of these white characters—thus defining and confining the public space of the book solely within white consciousness. This is not a move that can be readily shared by authors of color and their fictional characters and worlds, even when the novelist's world is centered on characters of color. White writers can and do consciously or unconsciously blind themselves to the presence of the racial in the worlds they create, and this reflects their power to enforce white norms of thinking about race. In contrast, in order to survive and succeed at any level of society, writers of color and their characters must always be aware of white people, their presence and power, however much these people of color might wish otherwise.

ZZ Packer and Black Existential Danger

As an example of the differences between Franzen's white literary imagination and that of a Black writer, let me present the opening of "Drinking Coffee Elsewhere," the title short story of ZZ Packer's collection of short stories:

> Orientation games began the day I arrived at Yale from Baltimore. In my group we played heady, frustrating games for smart people. One game appeared to be charades reinterpreted by existentialists; another involved listening to rocks. Then a freshman counselor made everyone play Trust. The idea was that if you had the faith to

fall backward and wait for four scrawny former high school geniuses to catch you, just before your head cracked on the slate sidewalk, then you might learn to trust your fellow students. Russian roulette sounded like a better way to go.

"No way," I said. The white boys were waiting for me to fall, holding their arms out for me, sincerely, gallantly. "No fucking way."

"It's all cool, it's all cool," the counselor said. Her hair was a shade of blond I'd seen only on *Playboy* covers, and she raised her hands as though backing away from a growling dog. "Sister," she said in an I'm-down-with-the-struggle voice, "you don't have to play this game. As a person of color, you shouldn't have to fit into any white, patriarchal system."

I said, "It's a bit too late for that."

In the next game, all I had to do was wait in a circle until it was my turn to say what inanimate object I wanted to be. One guy said he'd like to be a gadfly, like Socrates. "Stop me if I wax Platonic," he said. I didn't bother mentioning that gadflies weren't inanimate—it didn't seem to make a difference. The girl next to him was eating a rice cake. She wanted to be the Earth, she said. Earth with a capital E.

There was one other black person in the circle. He wore an Exeter T-shirt and his overly elastic expressions resembled a series of facial exercises. At the end of each person's turn, he smiled and bobbed his head with unfettered enthusiasm. "Oh, that was good," he said, as if the game were an experiment he'd set up and the results were turning out better than he'd expected. "Good, good, good!"

When it was my turn I said, "My name is Dina, and if I had to be any object, I guess I'd be a revolver."

Rather than openly declaring her identity, the narrator of Packer's story slips in clues to indicate who she is. As freshmen in college typically do, the narrator is engaged in the process of discerning her difference from the other students who have chosen to go to the same school. This school, Yale, calls up certain connotations of class, intellectual abilities, and educational background—and of course race. The narrator's response to the game of Trust indicates her wariness toward the other students. But the reference to Russian roulette also reveals more about her state of mind—not simply that she feels antagonism toward the other students but also perhaps that she might be depressed. The fact that the narrator uses the phrase *white boys* indicates that she is not white. It's not simply the fact that she regards them as Other; it's also that white people do not generally refer to other white people as "white people" unless race has already been placed on the table.

In contrast, once she finds herself at Yale, race is always on the table. The idea of falling into the arms of four white boys is not Dina's idea of a fun let's-get-acquainted game, and the blond—and white—counselor awkwardly tries to acknowledge this. Though the counselor is attempting to show empathy toward the narrator, the former's remark puts Dina in exactly the position the whole set of games is meant to alleviate. The purpose of the games is to encourage unity; "we" are all here as Yale students and thus can trust each other. But the racial divide between the narrator and the white boys precludes such trust. Similarly, the counselor's use of "Sister" would seem to say, "Well, we can at least bond as women," but her words have just the opposite effect on Dina. Her answer to the counselor's proposition to opt out of the "white patriarchal system" is witty—"It's a bit too late for that"—which references the fact that she has chosen to go to Yale, and so she's chosen to enter a white patriarchal institution. The deeper implication is that she can never escape the white patriarchal system; she was born into it. (But then so is the white counselor.)

Self-consciously, the narrator compares herself with the other member of her racial group in a white crowd. By the way that she notes his Exeter T-shirt, she reveals that she probably went to a public school. The other Black student's enthusiastic response to the games signals his desire to fit in; he seems comfortable with this crowd of white students in a way that the narrator does not. That she is quick to judge him indicates that perhaps she's also not prone to assume that she has a bond with him simply because they are both Black. When asked what inanimate object she'd be, the narrator picks up on her mention of Russian roulette and says, "I guess I'd be a revolver." She may be saying this as a joke, but it is a joke with a point: *I know I'm in danger here and in a site of racial antagonism, and no games of trust are going to change that.*

Eventually, Dina emerges as a singularly ironic, witty, and intelligent character, someone who rejects attempts by both Blacks and whites to connect with her. It's clear that there are reasons for Dina's anger and isolation beyond race. One major reason is that her mother has recently died, a loss that Dina tells no one about at college, even the white therapist she is assigned to after her revolver reply. Another reason for Dina's behavior stems from her sexual orientation. Early on she begins an ambiguous relationship with a white female student, Heidi, a relationship that ends in part because Heidi comes out as a lesbian and Dina wants nothing to do with such an identification. There are also a couple of small scenes of Dina's life back in Baltimore that indicate that she's grown up in a particularly impoverished Black neighborhood and feels shame about that. (She hides the exact location of her house—and the extent of her poverty—from a Black boy about her age that she meets.)

As the story progresses, issues of race seem to recede from the prominence they carry in these opening paragraphs. Of course, the poverty Dina grows up in cannot be separated from race, and Dina's general wariness and anger toward the world cannot be separated from her being a poor Black female either in Baltimore or at Yale. But Packer knows she doesn't have to emphasize this perspective once she's established it in the opening paragraphs.

What these paragraphs do, though, is instruct the reader on how to read Dina and her story through the lens of race. Once Packer has set this up, it is up to the reader to carry on this reading. The reader should understand that race informs Dina's reading of the world, despite the fact that she is loath to connect with other Black students simply on the basis of race. At the same time, this contradiction is part of what makes Dina such a fascinating and distinctive character. Because of Dina's personality, the presence of race is everywhere in the story and yet not articulated directly except in this opening. But how deeply the reader understands the racial context of this story depends, I would argue, on how deeply the reader understands the presence of race in American society.

I want to revisit Dina's choice of what she would be—a revolver. When I read this response, I immediately think of Afropessimism. Afropessimists argue that the ontology of slavery continues into the present. In this theory Whiteness is defined as human, Blackness as non-human. Whiteness is thus equated with being a citizen, part of a nation;

Blackness, for a slave, is always equated with being a noncitizen, part of no nation. As nonhuman and noncitizen, Blackness can be subjected to violence without the need of provocation or justification; violence upon the Black body requires no declaration of war or sanction by law. Further, Blackness is fungible; it can be bought and sold; Blacks are property.

In such a world—still shaped by the ontology of slavery—perhaps Dina's response here is not a sign of neurosis or mental problems but a reflection of the very real struggle she finds herself trapped in, a reflection of the forces arrayed against her. Dina is situated in an institution that has been and is historically and culturally white; she's interacting with fellow students and a therapist who have little idea of who she is, much less the ways their very existence challenges her own existence. As such, Dina understands that she is in mortal danger and that this danger is always present—if not bodily then certainly in terms of her psyche and soul. Answering "a revolver" goes to the heart of a division that clearly exists in our society—how power is structured racially.[3]

————

The larger implication is that the state of race in America is not simply determined by obvious political elements such as the justice system or economic racial disparities, or by overt and explicit conscious racism. No, our racial separations also take place within the world of the imagination, in fictional worlds white writers create and the rules through which they create those worlds. The St. Paul of Franzen's Berglunds can be seen as excluding their Black neighbors and the Black neighborhood just a few blocks away (as well as the nearby Southeast Asian population), and that

---

3. If readers question my connections between the legacy of slavery and Dina's view of her racial position in America, look at the video of Sandra Bland being stopped in 2015 by a policeman in Texas for supposedly making a wrong turn signal, a stop that resulted in Bland's arrest. Three days later, Bland allegedly committed suicide in her jail cell. If someone argues that Texas is not a liberal bastion like Yale, consider the following: in 2018, Lolade Siyonbola, a Black graduate student at Yale, fell asleep while studying in the common area of her dorm, and a white grad student, Sarah Braasch, found her and told Siyonbola she could not sleep there and called the campus police on her. When three officers arrived, they asked Siyonbola for her ID, saying, "You're in a Yale building, and we need to make sure you belong here." In a 2010 article in *The Humanist* circulated on Twitter, eight years prior to the Yale incident, Braasch asserted that some slaves may have wanted to be slaves: "Who are we to tell people that they can't be slaves if they want to be?"

is just fine, according to the aesthetics and practices of white writers.[4] But within the white space of Yale or the Black space of her Baltimore neighborhood, ZZ Packer's young Black narrator, Dina, understands that she is always in the presence of white power: in that presence her life is under constant threat of extinction.

Segregation of space, segregation of imagination, segregation of lives and deaths—these are all connected, and without seeing such connections we cannot make sense of America's racial landscape, as it is lived, as it is imagined. As Jess Row asks, "What would it mean to accept that America's great and impossible catastrophic failure is its failure to imagine what it means to live together?"

---

4. Similarly, while Philando Castile, a kitchen worker at a Montessori school in the Berglunds' neighborhood, might have served lunch to the Berglunds' children, his life and death at the hands of Officer Jeronimo Yanez cannot become part of the Berglunds' white world.

Psychotherapy and a
New National Narrative

THE WAYS WHITENESS TELLS STORIES OF ITSELF IN AMERICA IS OF course different from the ways Whiteness tells stories of itself in other countries, whether in Europe or in the former colonies of Europe. It can be illuminating at times for us to compare these perspectives on Whiteness, both what they share and how they differ.

White behavior in South Africa, for instance, has been viewed in recent American history as a particularly egregious example of racism and has functioned in this country's psyche as a comparison showing the United States in a favorable light. This is despite the fact that South Africa modeled its apartheid system after the example of Jim Crow South and found inspiration in the vehemence of its white supremacy. On a more contemporary level, as Michelle Alexander has pointed out in *The New Jim Crow*, the United States in the present imprisons a greater percentage of its Black population than South Africa did at the height of apartheid.

In a subtler comparison, the ways white American writers and white South African writers have dealt with the issues of race and identity have been decidedly different. While white American writers often have a difficult time identifying themselves or their characters as white, white South African novelists like J. M. Coetzee or Nadine Gordimer have not evaded or denied that identity in a similar fashion.[1] During racial recon-

---

1. I first encountered the work of these two writers years ago when I taught a course in postcolonial literature in English. We read such writers as Salman Rushdie, Bessie Head, Chinua Achebe, V. S. Naipaul, Jamaica Kincaid, and Derek Walcott, as well as Coetzee and Gordimer. What struck me at the time was that if I put Toni Morrison or Leslie Marmon Silko in that list, their work would make sense in that global context. But if I put, say, John Updike or Jay McInerney or Ann Beattie in that list, these white American writers, unlike Coetzee and Gordimer, would seem to come from a different world. Teaching that course made me question certain

ciliation in South Africa, the country heard testimony and stories from individuals of all races; it was understood that any true account of the nation's present required an acknowledgment of how racial identities had determined the past and how racial differences needed to be addressed to move toward a different future. America has not done this.

Coetzee's work has particularly intrigued me for its complex investigations into the identity of white South Africans and the ways that identity has distorted their psychological makeup, particularly the processing and avoidance of racial shame and guilt. Lately I have often been thinking about *The Good Story: Exchanges on Truth, Fiction and Psychotherapy*, a dialogue between Coetzee and the British psychologist Arabella Kurtz. Their dialogue examines the construction of individual narratives in psychotherapy through the interchange between patient and therapist. As the book progresses, Coetzee leads the discussion more and more into the issues of group psychology and national narratives, and how they can evade the truths of a nation's past.

––––––

At the beginning of *The Good Story*, Coetzee and Kurtz conduct a fascinating conversation on the nature and limits of psychotherapy. Coetzee starts out questioning the limits of psychotherapy in relationship to a conception of what constitutes "truth":

> As we are both aware, there are varieties of self-help therapy that pretty clearly see their goal as making the subject feel good about themselves, and that tend to be dismissive of the criterion of truth if the truth is too much to handle. We tend to look down on such therapies. We say that the cure they produce is only a seeming cure, that sooner or later the subject will again crash against reality. Yet what if, by some kind of social consensus, we agreed not to rock the boat but on the contrary to come together to affirm one another's fantasies, as happens in some therapeutic groups. Then there would be no reality to crash against.

––––––

assumptions about how we use the world *universal* in our conception of literary standards. When we speak of the *universal* in literature, whose universe are we talking about?

Kurtz replies that "a narrative about one's life that is too self-serving in the way you describe will have a frailty, a brittleness, a tendency to come undone on its own terms." The analyst therefore listens for inconsistencies, "aspects of a life-story [that] do not seem to hold." While therapy cannot stake a claim for historical or scientific or philosophical truth, it can offer an emotional truth; the need for this new emotional truth is not simply because one is unhappy but also "because something painful or difficult cannot be faced."

In their mutual investigating and unearthing of the past, the therapist helps the patient create a new narrative where the repressed can be accommodated and accepted—the painful or difficult, the traumatic or horrific events, the wound or the wounding, the abuse or the crime, the self-incriminating past misdeed. This incorporation allows the patient to address certain psychological difficulties they have been experiencing in their life rather than remain in a cycle of repetition and failure, of repression and denial:

> If one thinks about how, for example, a patient idealizes their mother in order to protect themselves from the full force of their disappointment in her, the key thing is to help the patient to explore the emotional logic of the situation and understand where it fits in their development, and how the resulting frame of mind obstructs forward movement. One might do this by in effect removing a distortion and revealing something that feels to the patient more real and more true in the external world. But as a psychotherapist one aims to operate by working to understand the internal world of the patient, taking away the need for distortion through an understanding of that need—rather than by too much presenting of external truth. . . .

While an individual is not a nation, I cannot help but see parallels here between idealizing one's mother and idealizing one's Founding Fathers. Sarah Palin's view of history—"our founding fathers worked tirelessly to end slavery"—may be a particularly ignorant and egregious example of the mythic lies blinding us to obvious truths. But if conservatives have a difficult time seeing the racism of the slave-holding George Washington or Thomas Jefferson or Robert E. Lee, liberals too have a difficult time incorporating the racism of Abraham Lincoln, with their admiration for the slave-emancipating Lincoln. In this way, the idealizing of father figures in our history is shared by white conservatives and white liberals.

————

Kurtz seems to be arguing that repression cannot ultimately succeed, and she says her belief rests "on faith in the justice of the universe." But aren't there examples, Coetzee asks, where repression does succeed? Aren't there people who have committed horrifying acts, torture, murder, and who then construct life stories where those acts have been removed, and who then go on to live in society undetected and seemingly normal, raising families, becoming respected members of a community. Kurtz keeps arguing that the unconscious will keep reappearing or asserting itself in different guises; she cites Dostoevsky's *Crime and Punishment* as an example of this.

Eventually, though, Coetzee reveals that his concern about "the ethical dimension of truth versus fiction" stems less from a consideration of individuals and the crimes of an individual and more from his national identity and his take on the stories nations tell themselves. Because Coetzee is mostly speaking about South Africa where he grew up and Australia where he now lives, an American reader might be more able to take in his larger point about confronting the "truth" of a nation's history:

> I am sure that my dogged concentration, here and in earlier exchanges between us, on the ethical dimension of truth versus fiction comes out of my experience of being a white South African who late in life became a white Australian and, in between, lived for years as a white in the United States, where whiteness as a social reality is more masked than in South Africa or Australia but is still there. That is to say, I have lived as a member of a conquering group which for a long while thought of itself in explicitly racial terms and believed that what it was achieving in settling ("civilising") a foreign land was something to be proud of, but which then, during my lifetime, for reasons of a world-historical nature, had to sharply revise its way of thinking about itself and its achievements, and therefore to revise the story it told itself about itself, that is, its history. . . .

In this better and truer history, white Australians today remain the heirs and beneficiaries of a great crime committed by their forebears, the sort of crime which enlightened people like themselves would never themselves commit but which their forebears, slaves to a false conception of themselves and their role in world history, could commit without crippling moral qualms.

If you tell the story of late twentieth-century historical revisionism in these terms, an ambivalence becomes visible which at the level of the individual psyche ought to split people apart and make any kind of easy, happy life impossible. My great-grandparents were criminals (the revised story goes), complicit in an evil project whose fruits I am at present enjoying. Yet at the same time my great-grandparents were courageous, upstanding people who suffered hardship so that their descendants could have a good life. . . .

I am speaking at a level of generality which makes for the crudest of arguments. Nevertheless, let me state my crude point: that the settler societies in question, the settler societies of today, ought to be riven with self-doubt but are not. They—or their more articulate members—say the following: (a) our forebears did bad things but they are not to be blamed because they were in the grip of false beliefs and a false understanding of their role in history; (b) we have more enlightened beliefs and a more enlightened understanding of our historical role; and (c) if, as history unfolds, we ourselves are revealed to have mistaken ourselves as deeply as our ancestors mistook themselves, there is nothing we can do about that, that is in the nature of history, which is just one story overtaking and supplanting another; therefore the best we can do is to get on with our lives without more fretting.

I don't want to push the therapeutic analogy recklessly, so let me simply ask the question: When a society (but for a few dissident members) decides that it does not feel troubled, how can healing even begin?

Note here that Coetzee pictures the citizens of the South African or Australian settler society as accepting that they are enjoying the fruits of an "evil project," something that in so many ways most white Americans still deny. In Australia or Canada, for instance, public ceremonies begin with an acknowledgment of the indigenous population and what was done to that population and how the land was taken from them.

That is not a common practice in the United States.

As a country, we Americans are far from such a widespread ritual and public confrontation with colonization; indeed, look how much effort must go into forcing only a tiny percentage of sports teams to give up their racist icons and names. Similarly, America has never gone through the truth and reconciliation public tribunals that took place in South Africa. We have no public ceremonies that acknowledge slavery or celebrate slaves. (Well, there's Black History Month.) We have far more monuments of Confederate generals and slave holders than we do of the slaves they exploited, abused, and tortured. Despite these differences, a larger question remains: can a nation continue to thrive while denying the crimes and evil acts of its past? Can those in the present merely sever their own identities and conceptions of themselves from that past and see themselves as having little connection to that past, claiming only what is deemed courageous, heroic, and righteous in their forebears?

Kurtz's answer is to the point:

> ... it is hard to imagine healing occurring at a social or an individual level when the prevailing discourse is one that cannot admit to disturbance. I would also suggest that the more determinedly a society feels the need to look upon itself as having risen above the past and as being free and distinct from it, the more likely it is that it will be in history's unconscious sway.
>
> The split awareness you describe in Australia, in which two largely unintegrated pictures of the early settlers coexist, sounds to me like a recipe for collective insecurity. ... In your account Australia's idea of itself as a civilized society seems to rest upon an idealized version of its past, a version in which cruelty and conflict are edited out. This does not sound like the basis for a happy, secure collective life, but an anxious one, in which any experience of well-being is fragile and can easily flip into a more troubled state when it comes up against memories and stories which do not fit with the idealized picture.

Further on, in explaining the way a patient breaks through repression and denial, Kurtz also provides a gloss on a nation's psyche. She explains that when repression occurs, experience is removed or evacuated from consciousness; the patient's conscious mind keeps trying to avoid "any sort of real encounter with unconscious experience." The conscious mind finds this experience too difficult or painful to accommodate. Eventually, though, the false or occluding narrative the patient has constructed no longer serves the patient but instead results in the patient making the same mistakes or repeating the same failures or destructive acts (against oneself or others) over and over. Again, therapy helps the patient to construct a new narrative. This new narrative will not be the complete truth, because the complete truth is ultimately not accessible, but what is possible is that the patient finally consciously acknowledges something that heretofore was denied, that was kept unconscious.

This repression often occurs because at an earlier age the patient could not have survived without such repression. When the repressed is finally allowed into consciousness, says Kurtz, it's as if the patient says to themselves: "Ah, now I see, this aspect of things was always there, I can see it now where I couldn't before. I have lived with it for so long but I have found ways of getting round it, or of simply not seeing it, or of pretending it was something else. But now I do see it, as clearly as that chair or table."

For America to move to a new story, that story must be able to allow facts that are now kept out of the national narrative, which remain in various ways unconscious in our national psyche. There are a myriad of such facts—from Jefferson's slaves and defense of slavery to Lincoln's racism to the genocide of Native Americans and stealing of their lands to the racial backlash of Reconstruction and the establishment of Jim Crow. A national psyche that ignores these facts will be, to use Kurtz's words, brittle, insecure, fragile, defensive. But it is not Black Americans or Indigenous Americans who cannot accept these facts; it is white America. And it is white America that cannot ask itself: in what ways is present-day America still connected with the slave owners' ontological assumptions about the difference between the White Owner and the Black Slave? That is the psychological work white America has yet to undertake in order to tell a true story of our mutual racial past.

As Kurtz observes, the inability or refusal to acknowledge the repressed can lead to failure after failure and fosters a psyche that is brittle, defensive, and unable to progress into a different future. So much energy is going to the repression of the past that movement toward a new course of action and set of goals cannot adequately take place. In terms of race, that is the psychological state white America continues to struggle to maintain—this despite mounting evidence that the national narrative we tell ourselves denies how we have arrived at the present state of racial relations.

———

Coetzee and Kurtz's examination of national narratives inevitably relates to the question of *who* constructs a nation's narrative. Certainly this question was addressed in South Africa's process of reconciliation where all different segments of the population came forth to tell their stories. One theme of my essays here has been that the story told by Whiteness and white America has until recently been deemed the sole, truthful, and official version of our past. Our national narratives have come to be filled with lies and myths and leave out the voices and stories of BIPOC Americans. In this way, BIPOC American stories have remained unconscious and nonexistent for many white Americans who exhibit great powers of repression in order to maintain a flattering portrait of themselves, a portrait which tells them they are the sole source of goodness and righteousness in the past and present. But the stories of Black Americans and what they tell of Whiteness and white people reveal the centrality of Blacks to what this country has been and is.

Take, for instance, the 2014 film *Selma,* directed by Ava DuVernay and written by Paul Webb. Perhaps not surprisingly, the African American DuVernay and the white British Webb had certain disagreements on the direction of the film. While Webb is listed as the sole screenwriter, DuVernay has been critical of his script, which she inherited from another director; she has stated that she rewrote the film and made substantial revisions. She did not get screenwriting credit because of Webb's original contract for the film. Thus the making of this film entailed a conflict between a white artist and a Black artist and their differing views and narrative constructions of our racial past. Webb's original script focused more on Lyndon B. Johnson and Martin Luther King Jr. and their interactions: history in the heroic mode. But DuVernay felt such a focus created too much of a white-savior slant; at the same time, she wanted to depict not just King but the African Americans around King: "I was very interested in enlongating our view of the Civil Rights Movement and not letting it rest only in Dr. King's hands, which is inaccurate," said DuVernay. In the final film, she was responsible for "everything outside of Johnson, King and the White House, whether it was the murder of Jimmie Lee Jackson, the murder of James Reeb, these things that enhanced the core story, which was the fight for voting rights." Where Webb wanted to tell a story where the powerful white president occupied center stage along with King, DuVernay conceives the story much more as the African American community's struggle for civil rights, in part because she sees that community as the moral center of that struggle and not Johnson.

The film focuses on the 1964 protests in Selma and the interactions among King, the Southern Christian Leadership Conference, the Student Nonviolent Coordinating Committee, and the residents of Selma. The story moves from the initial marches in Selma to Bloody Sunday, when six hundred Black marchers were violently beaten during their march across the Edmund Pettus Bridge, and then to the subsequent march from Selma to Montgomery, Alabama. In the film King at first interacts and clashes with individuals, organizations, and communities involved in these protests; there's a back-and-forth between those who wish to move faster than King desires, those who want him to take things more slowly, and those who support King's strategy wholeheartedly. We see his arguments with Malcolm X, who believes that his own rhetoric will move whites toward King; with John Lewis and the Student Nonviolent Coordinating Committee, who feel King is too conservative in his strategies.

As King engages with his Black community, he petitions President Johnson to enact legislation that would remove the ironclad restrictions against Blacks voting in the South. Johnson maintains that he cannot afford to spend political capital on this cause; he urges King to back his War on Poverty as a necessary alternative. But King is adamant: unless Johnson proposes and enacts the voting-rights legislation for Southern Blacks, he will continue with his protests.

Back in Selma, King and Black civil rights activists are blocked by a Bull Connor–like racist sheriff, James Gardner Clark Jr., and by Governor George Wallace, who stood at the University of Alabama and declared "segregation now, segregation tomorrow, segregation forever." Wallace sends state troopers to attack the marchers at Marion, Alabama, and they beat and shoot Jimmie Lee Jackson, who dies from his wounds; the threat of violence is everywhere for King and those in the civil rights movement, continuing a tradition of terrorism that has been a bedrock of the suppression of Blacks in the South. In 1964, a hundred years after the Emancipation Proclamation, Blacks in the South still could not vote because of restrictions like poll taxes, quizzes on the Constitution and the government, requiring a registered voter to vouch for the voter (impossible in counties where no Blacks were registered), fines for not voting in previous elections, and so forth.[2]

One hundred years and still no voting rights. When King spoke in 1963 at the march on Washington of the "fierce urgency of now," he was actually speaking of a hundred years of oppression—or really, of more than three hundred years of oppression and exclusion from America's democracy. Almost fifty years after the march on Selma, the film captured the fortitude, resilience, and spiritual strength of the nonviolent Black civil rights activists; their amazing courage in the face of death threats, murders, and state-sanctioned violence as well as from the Ku Klux Klan and private groups of white citizens. What the film and DuVernay make us see—if our eyes are open—is that the true spirit of American history, the history where we have strived for equality and justice, has always run through the Black community. They have always been the true moral compass of our nation on race, and their continuing fight for equality has improved this nation and made it a country closer to the ideals espoused in our Constitution.

Near the end of the film Wallace comes to the White House, and Lyndon Johnson tries to persuade him to allow the Blacks in his state to vote and thus end the protests, which are putting enormous political pressure on Johnson. Wallace refuses. Johnson invokes the future and how the year 1985 will look back at this time. But Wallace says he doesn't care

---

2. Black voters currently wait in line 45 percent longer and Latinx voters 46 percent longer than white voters to vote.

about that future, he cares about now and what the whites in his state want. Johnson then replies that he'll be damned if he's going down in history with the likes of Wallace. Instead, Johnson moves toward where King and protesting Blacks have been pushing him and other whites (though in the movie Johnson's emotions appear to be more motivated by his repugnance at Wallace than any admiration of King and the civil rights leaders). A short while later, Johnson makes a speech to Congress that starts the legislative process toward the Voting Rights Act of 1965. Johnson goes down on the right side of history by listening to King and his colleagues in the movement—not to Wallace, a choice that may seem obvious now but was not so obvious in 1965.[3]

Black Americans have always been on the right side of history in each instance of the racial struggle for equality. And yet always at first they have been opposed by the majority of white people. So why is it that whites in the present have never admitted this: *We got it wrong every time in our history, and you were correct—you were on the right side of history. Given how many times we got it wrong, perhaps we ought to listen to you and follow your lead now in the present.*

If white Americans were psychically able to make such a declaration, they would point themselves toward a different and indeed more liberating version of our history. We might actually be prepared psychologically and spiritually to address in a truthful way the original goal of America—freedom, equality, and democracy. We would recognize how the pursuit of racism, inequality, and the undemocratic repression of Black Americans historically has been a second (shadow) goal of America. Only when we truly acknowledge how this second goal has shaped our past and present can we be prepared psychically to abandon it. And only then can we begin to tell a new American story, where the Black struggle toward freedom, equality, and democracy tells an essential and central truth of who we are.

---

3. The Civil Rights Act of 1965 was struck down by the Supreme Court in 2013 with Chief Justice John Roberts falsely claiming there was no longer a need for it, that the racism that existed at the time of its passing was a thing of the past. Roberts's views were quickly proved wrong by measures all over the South and elsewhere to restrict the voting rights of Black Americans and other people of color, supported by the Trumpian surge in white nationalism and white hate groups.

PART III

WHERE DO WE
GO FROM HERE?

Questions of Identity

WHERE DO WE GO FROM HERE? I IMAGINE A READER ASKING AT THIS point in this book. These essays chart the historical reach and sources of American racism, examine white intransigence and regression on race, and explore the ways our historical and fictional narratives from the white perspective have distorted and lied about our past and our present. Certainly, we need a new national narrative that is both more complete and truthful, that incorporates the perspectives of our diverse population, that highlights how race has formed and deformed the goals of America and our search for a more perfect union.

The construction of such a narrative must take place on a variety of fronts, from our politics to our histories, from our artistic creations to the classroom. But perhaps the hardest to penetrate and change are the basic concepts—the ontology, the epistemology—of white identity and the psychic comforts and reassurances this false identity provides white people. At the same time, Black people, Indigenous people, people of color must work to create and affirm their own histories, their own knowledge, their own stories of America. Again, this struggle can take an outward form—in political activism, in artistic creation, in scholarship, in teaching—but this work also takes place in the psyches and souls of BIPOC America, a gathering of our power and a process of healing from the wounds and bias we struggle against daily in our lives.

James Baldwin observed that "the question of identity is a question involving the most profound panic—a terror as primary as the nightmare of the mortal fall." Identities are challenged and transformed when "the splendid" begin to fall or "the wretched" begin to rise or when a stranger enters the gates, "making you the stranger, less to the stranger, than to yourself." The story of America has always been one of strangers encountering strangers—from our first interracial encounters through slavery and colonialism to the continuing influx of immigrants from countries all over the globe. But in America today something else is happening, a growing awareness of a major shift in our demographics: sometime in the 2040s, we will no longer be a white-majority country; every racial group will be a minority.

In recent history, in South Africa we have seen a model where a white minority has tried to enforce white supremacy on a majority population of color. And a portion of white America is freaking out over the prospect of becoming a racial minority—as evidenced in the Trump presidency, the insurrection of January 6, 2021, and the recent rise in white supremacist organizations and activity. It is one thing to allow challenges to white supremacy if white people are the majority and feel secure in their power. But clearly a significant portion of white America no longer feels that security in the face of its coming loss of majority status. As evidenced by our history of racial regression, we can go backwards again. At the same time, this period of increasing white insecurity has been fueled not just by shifts in demographics but also in cultural influence of people of color, an influence showing itself in all areas of our society. The fiction of Nobel Prize author Toni Morrison, the films of Ava DuVernay, Michelle Alexander's book *The New Jim Crow*, the scholarship of MacArthur Fellow Saidiya V. Hartman, as well as obvious political shifts of Barack Hussein Obama's presidency are all part of this change.

We all are still engaged in that battle embodied in the Declaration of Independence's statement that "all men are created equal"—and the exclusion of women, Blacks, and Indigenous people from this statement, and the designation of Blacks as slaves and three-fifths of a person in our Constitution. This struggle continues outwardly in our politics in terms of gerrymandering; voting rights; police killings and bias; educational, economic, and health disparities; and a wide range of other issues. But it also continues inwardly, in our very souls.

———

Back in 1988, I wrote my first essay on race that focused on Black–white relations rather than on Asian American issues, "Strangers in the Village," which appeared in *The Graywolf Annual Five: Multi-Cultural Literacy*. The initial prompt for the essay was an article in the *Village Voice* depicting the tensions between white middle- and upper-class parents and the Black nannies employed to take care of their children, and how these tensions reveal a stark division in their understandings of race and racial positioning. One aspect of this division involves the white parents' desire for approval, warmth, and even friendship from their Black caregivers, and their dismay at the anger and resentment their Black employees sometimes express or perhaps guardedly allude to. The white parents want to be friends; they want to engage their Black employees simply on the plane of the individual, not confronting how racial (group) issues are inextricably bound up with the power difference between employer and employee. As the article observes, "As the nanny sits in the park watching a tow-haired child play, her own kids are coming home from school; they will do their homework alone and make dinner." Indeed, the white parents seem rather oblivious to this obvious discrepancy. Instead, they want to erase that difference; they seem to think they can do that by acting kindly toward their Black employee, giving gifts when they argue, such as when one nanny objects to the tone of voice her white employer uses. ("I'm not a child," says Bertha to her white employer. "I can talk to you any way I want. This is a free country.") The white parents seemingly want to be absolved of any sense of collective guilt or responsibility, and the Black employee senses that, resents that, and clearly views that as no part of the business contract between them:

> "Another reason we don't get along," Bertha continues, "is she always trying to figure me out. See, I'm a very complicated person. I'm a very moody person. . . . I'm independent. I figure I can deal with it myself. And we would sit there, I could just feel her eyes on me, and I'd have to get up and leave the room. . . . She just wants you to be satisfied all the time. . . . She wants me to tell her I love her. I just can't."

The white parents do not know what they do not know. In the end, they are not aware of—or want to be aware of—their lack of knowledge about the Black employee's life and their experiences outside the white environment of the parents' household, or how the forces of race have shaped the thinking and life of their employee.

Conversations between whites and Blacks with their accompanying gulf of understanding continue more than three decades later, and their persistence tells us how far we still have to go in addressing the problems of race. White parents in Manhattan still employ caregivers of color, and the manifestations of liberal guilt—and white fragility—still remain. Whites and Blacks in this country can certainly be friends, but that does not change the racial disparities and bias, the systemic racism that still exists in this country. Here I will reverse what I just said above: our country's racism cannot be solved solely on an individual level; the solution must also take place on a systemic, group level.

————

Beneath the *Village Voice* article, the deeper prompt for my essay was a critique of James Baldwin by the Black critic Stanley Crouch and my own defense of Baldwin: Crouch was arguing that Baldwin had become too political and strident in his rhetoric. In the Graywolf anthology I wrote:

> Certainly an argument can be made that King's appeal to a higher yet common morality was and will be more effective than Malcolm X's in changing the hearts and minds of whites in America, yet in his very approach to the problem, Crouch seems to put the burden for change upon the Black minority rather than on the white majority. There is something intellectually and morally dishonest about this. For whether one judges King's philosophy or Malcolm X's as correct depends in part on a reading of the hearts and minds of white Americans. If those hearts and minds are fiercely unchanging then Malcolm X's might seem the more logical stance. Either way, it is a judgment call and it involves a great deal of uncertainty, especially since that judgment involves actions in the future.

Looking back, I wonder what my thirty-six-year-old self would think of this present moment where the rise of Trump's Make America Great Again has captured the Republican Party, and the increasingly antidemocratic, authoritarian, xenophobic, and racist portions of America have become much more vocal and appear to be increasing in prominence. At the same moment, a more progressive portion of America has marched in support of Black Lives Matter, and so many corporations and institutions are trying to address their problems with racism and voice support of protests against police killings of unarmed Black men. We are still engaged in a battle over the soul of America regarding race, and how that battle will turn out is still an open question.

Baldwin continues to stand for me as our great diagnostician when it comes to race and the knots race has tied in our souls and psyches. What he understood about race in America went beyond our surface political and economic realities; he charted our internal racial geographies, within both white and Black psyches. And he contrasted the falseness of our rhetoric and political posturings on race with the truths of what happens in our souls when we give in to hate, when we let rage rule us, when we take power unjustly, or when we give power to those who should not have such power over us—and, most important, when we lie to ourselves. There are eternal human truths that we cannot escape, and all our obfuscations regarding race cannot erase these truths and their workings. Therefore, for Americans of any race or ethnicity, it is to Baldwin that we must first turn to discern where we may go from here. His is the map we should first study in order to find a new direction and a way out of this quagmire of racism and the destructions it causes.

James Baldwin

I Am Not Your Negro

The Burden of Racism and the Black Psyche

I

In his classic title essay "Notes of a Native Son," Baldwin yokes the death and funeral of his father with the riots that broke out in Harlem in 1943 around the same time. As a native of Harlem, Baldwin carefully charts the etiology of these riots, how they arose from the conditions imposed on the Blacks of Harlem by a racist society. Tellingly, he does not separate this etiology from the story of his father. Baldwin homes in on his father's hatred and bitterness over his own life, how his father blamed whites and their racism for the conditions of his life.

During his childhood, Baldwin was unaware that his father was not his biological father; all he knew was that this man treated him and his mother badly, in bouts of rage and criticism. (In *The Devil Finds Work*, Baldwin says his father called him the most ugly child he had ever seen.) His father's death and the Harlem riots form a framework for Baldwin's personal account of his early reckoning with race and the white world. This reckoning had in part been held off because Baldwin grew up in Harlem. Though he of course had encounters in Harlem with racist whites, especially police, overall he had not essentially been forced to directly confront the white world or how he might be received there.

Baldwin recalls the decline of his father's work as a preacher and his increasing bitterness as he drives through the debris of the riot to get to his father's burial:

We went from church to smaller and more improbable church, he found himself in less and less demand as a minister, and by the time he died none of his friends had come to see him for a long time. He had lived and died in an intolerable bitterness of spirit and it frightened me, as we drove him to the graveyard through those unquiet, ruined streets, to see how powerful and overflowing this bitterness could be and to realize that this bitterness now was mine.

When he died I had been away from home for a little over a year. In that year I had had time to become aware of the meaning of all my father's bitter warnings, had discovered the secret of his proudly pursed lips and rigid carriage: I had discovered the weight of white people in the world. I saw that this had been for my ancestors and now would be for me an awful thing to have to live with and that the bitterness which had helped to kill my father could also kill me.

Baldwin recognizes he cannot separate himself from his deceased father, and thus he knows that he too must confront the "weight of white people in the world." As a young Black man moving outside of the confines of Harlem, Baldwin apprehends how readily such weight can engender bitterness, rage, and despair. His father's life is a parable, which he the son must unravel; otherwise, the same bitterness will kill him—spiritually or literally.

Indeed, what follows is an account of how Baldwin almost gets himself killed. Growing up in Harlem, Baldwin had been aware of how Blacks were treated in the South, and how they were expected to behave in the face of such treatment, passively accepting it. However, in the Black community of Harlem, as a young man he had never believed that he might face the same treatment and be expected to respond in the same way. During World War II, in his late teens, he started working in a defense plant in New Jersey, and his first encounters with a more direct form of racism confounded him: "I simply did not know what was happening. I did not know what I had done, and I shortly began to wonder what anyone could possibly do, to bring about such unanimous, active, and unbearably vocal hostility. I knew about jim-crow but I had never experienced it." In New Jersey, Baldwin goes to a restaurant four times before he realizes that no one has taken his order and that Negroes are not served there; mistakenly he has picked up an order meant for a white patron. "Some dreadful scenes" follow his reaction to this discrimination, to the point that he is banned from the restaurant.

But instead of bowing to this de facto segregation, the young Baldwin instinctively fights it. He goes to other segregated restaurants where similar incidents occur, and he finds he is gaining a reputation in town—a reputation he must keep from reaching the plant where he works or else he might be dismissed from his job. Even then, he is fired three times and is unable to work at that plant:

> That year in New Jersey lives in my mind as though it were the year during which, having an unsuspected predilection for it, I first contracted some dread, chronic disease, the unfailing symptom of which is a kind of blind fever, a pounding in the skull and fire in the bowels. Once this disease is contracted one can never be really carefree again, for the fever, without an instant's warning, can recur at any moment. It can wreck more important things than race relations. There is not a Negro alive who does not have this rage in his blood—one has the choice, merely, of living with it consciously or surrendering to it. As for me, this fever has recurred in me, and does and will until the day I die.

While the metaphor of racism as a disease is common, less common is the idea that the effects of racism on Blacks is also a disease, a fever that can reappear over and over in a lifetime and that one is never rid of. The question is, How does one prevent this disease from taking over one's life and, more important to Baldwin, one's soul?

———

Baldwin then tells a story of his last night in New Jersey. He and a white friend go to the movies and then to an aptly named American Diner where the counterman refuses to serve Baldwin. Looking back, he is still not clear about what was going on with him that night; running from the diner, he rushes away from his white friend: "I wanted to do something to crush those white faces, which were crushing me. I walked for perhaps a block or two until I came to an enormous, glittering, and fashionable restaurant in which I knew not even the intercession of the Virgin could cause me to be served." Baldwin seats himself and waits. A white waitress comes up and tells him, "We don't serve Negroes here." Baldwin pretends not to hear so she will come closer, but she only leans in a little and repeats her declaration. Baldwin takes up a glass of water and throws it at the waitress, who ducks, and the glass shatters against the mirror behind the bar. The whole restaurant stops. Baldwin seems to come out of a trance and realizes what he has done, and he runs to the door. A heavy-set man grabs him and begins beating him, but Baldwin escapes his grasp and runs out; his white friend tells him to run and then misdirects the pursuers:

> I lived it over and over and over again, the way one relives an automobile accident after it has happened and one finds oneself alone and safe. I could not get over two facts, both equally difficult for the imagination to grasp, and one was that I could have been murdered. But the other was that I had been ready to commit murder. I saw nothing very clearly, but I did see this: that my life, my *real* life, was in danger, and not from anything other people might do but from the hatred I carried in my own heart.

Baldwin is asking himself a series of questions here. How do I rid myself of this hatred, this hatred that comes from the way this racist white world has treated me and will not stop? How do I rid myself of this disease—or, at the least, keep it from destroying my life? Yes, of course my life is dear to me, but what about that part of me that is even more dear, my soul? Baldwin is also asking: How do I escape the fate of my father, his bitterness and rage? And how do we as a people keep this rage from destroying us? How do we distinguish between our quest for justice and our desire for revenge?

In posing these questions, Baldwin holds himself to the principle he invokes over and over in his *Collected Essays*—one can face in others only what one has faced in oneself. The key to facing whites and their hatred of Blacks is facing the rage, bitterness, and hate growing in his own heart.

II

Lest certain readers protest that Baldwin is writing about a phenomenon of the 1940s and not today, I offer some contemporary examples of how the disease of racism engenders a version of Baldwin's self-described fever in today's America.

The first example is Erica Garner, the daughter of Eric Garner. On July 17, 2014, Eric Garner was strangled to death by New York City policeman Daniel Pantaleo, in a chokehold banned by the police department. Pantaleo and his fellow officers were arresting Garner for selling single cigarettes, "loosies," and they maintained Garner was resisting arrest. In a previous era, Eric Garner's death would never have made it to the news, and the police account of his death would never have been questioned. But as with recent infamous police encounters, a cell phone video was taken by a bystander, and in it Garner complains that the police are harassing him. When the police move to physically detain him, they and Garner wrestle; when Pantaleo starts applying the chokehold and Garner is tackled to the ground, Garner is heard repeatedly pleading, "I can't breathe, I can't breathe."

Pantaleo's employment by the NYPD was eventually terminated five years later, but he never faced criminal charges, as a Richmond County grand jury in December 2014 declined to indict him, and the U.S. Department of Justice declined to bring criminal charges against him.

On Christmas Eve of 2017, Erica Garner suffered a heart attack, fell into a coma, and died several days later. In an editorial titled "Erica Garner and How America Destroys Black Families," Kashana Cauley writes in the *New York Times*:

> One way to describe Erica Garner's last few years is to say she spent them fighting against police brutality. Another way is to say she fought against the forced separation and destruction of black families by the state. And that fight may have killed her, just as it might have killed the mother of Kalief Browder, a young man who had been unjustly accused of a minor crime and sent to Rikers Island, where he spent two horrific years in solitary confinement.
>
> "They do these things for you to give up," Erica Garner said in

an interview last month. "Look at Kalief Browder's mother. She died of a broken heart because she kept fighting for her son." She added, "I'm struggling right now, with the stress and everything."

"The system," she said, "beats you down to where you can't win."[1]

Erica Garner's words here are suffused more with weariness and grief than rage and hatred, and that is a tribute to the spirit of her soul. She had been devastated not just by her father's death but by the fact that the policeman who caused it never faced any charges, despite his use of the banned chokehold.

Garner channeled her reactions to her father's death and the failure of the justice system into activism; had nothing happened to her father, she would have lived a very different life. But there were aftereffects of his murder. Recent health research connects the presence of severe trauma in Black life, such as what Erica Garner experienced, with problems in psychological and physical health. Researchers and physicians like Dr. Rhea Boyd argue cogently that racism contributes to the disparity between life expectancy between whites and Blacks in obvious and not so obvious ways. If racism by the police doesn't kill you directly as it did Eric Garner, it can kill you slowly through the constant stress affecting the body at a cellular level, as perhaps occurred with Erica Garner. Beyond affecting the psyche of Blacks, racism stresses and degrades telomeres, the part of the chromosome that allows cells to reproduce and prevent aging.

If one takes Baldwin at his word, the same rage he struggled with also erupted in Erica Garner as she faced a system of racial injustice and the personal toll it took on her and her family. Kashana Cauley points to the ways various policies and practices in the justice system work deliberately to destroy Black families—through police killings, brutality, and

---

1. Kalief Browder's family was not allowed to post his bail because of a previous felony conviction. Browder maintained he was innocent and refused deals from prosecuting attorneys. Two years after his release when the charges against him were dismissed, Browder committed suicide, a result of the mental, physical, and sexual abuse he suffered in prison. Compare Browder's story with that of any number of convicted rich white men, and the starkly racist and classist discrimination of the American justice system is blatantly obvious.

racially disparate arrest rates, but also less overt aspects of these systems, for instance limiting phone calls between prisoners and families. Still, how such systems enact racial inequity is at least subject to critique bearing empirical data. What is not so easily measured is the psychic cost of such injustice on individual Black people and their families, the damage the system's blindness and indifference wreak on Black souls.

———

Such damage is far more extensive and exhausting than the majority of white people are even superficially aware of. In *Heavy: An American Memoir*, Kiese Laymon addresses his brilliant memoir to his mother and explores the deep and loving but also complicated and troubled relationship with the working-class Black woman who raised him as a single mother, obtained an advanced degree, and eventually taught college. As it follows him from childhood to college and young adulthood, the memoir depicts his problems with weight, a gambling compulsion he shared with his mother, his disapproval of her boyfriend, and his difficulties growing up as a Black boy in contemporary Mississippi. Unstinting in its honesty, the memoir includes frank accounts of the harsh physical punishment Laymon's mother metes out to him. She is determined that he will not become another Black crime statistic, that he will make something of himself; she is hyperaware of the dangers he faces as a young Black boy and the slim chances he has of making it beyond the boundaries of their Black working-class neighborhood—and the very real chances that he might be arrested, incarcerated, or killed by the police.

While the memoir is fashioned as a dialogue with his mother, Laymon never lets the reader forget that her actions, his actions, and their reactions to each other take place within the context of the racism of Mississippi, within the fears and trials that racism enacts upon Black people in America. Speaking of one of their frequent periods of quarreling, Laymon writes:

> Really, we're fighting because she raised me to never ever forget I was born on parole, which means no black hoodies in wrong neighborhoods, no jogging at night, hands in plain sight at all times in public, no intimate relationships with white women, never driving

over the speed limit or doing those rolling stops at stop signs, always speaking the King's English in the presence of white folks, never being outperformed in school or in public by white students, and most importantly, always remembering that no matter what, the worst of white folks will do anything to get you.

... There ain't no antidote to life, I tell her. How free can you be if you really accept that white folks are the traffic cops of your life? Mama tells me that she is not talking about freedom. She says that she is talking about survival.

In the title essay of his powerful collection *How to Slowly Kill Yourself and Others in America,* Laymon examines several incidents when people have pulled a gun on him—including a drunken racist white cop, a group of young Black men near his college, and his own contemplation of suicide. At one point he describes how his writings for his college's newspaper, mostly on race issues, engendered hostility from the administration and white students. In another incident he and a fellow Black woman student pass a group of white fraternity members, an encounter that quickly moves beyond stupid frat-boy racism (offensive costumes) to active racist harassment:

> As we walk out to the parking lot of my dorm, the Kappa Alpha and Kappa Sigma fraternities are in front of the dorm receiving their new members. They've been up drinking all night. Some of them have on black face and others have on Afro wigs and Confederate capes.
>
> We get close to Shonda's Saturn and one of the men says, "Kiese, write about this!" Then another voice calls me a "nigger" and Shonda a "nigger bitch." I think and feel a lot but mostly I feel that I can't do anything to make the boys feel like they've made us feel right there, so I go back to my dorm room to get something.
>
> On the way there, Shonda picks up a glass bottle out of the trash. I tell her to wait outside the room. I open the bottom drawer and look at the hoodies balled up on top of my gun. I pick up my gun and think about my grandma. I think not only about what she'd feel if I went out there with a gun. I think about how if Grandma walked out of that room with a gun in hand, she'd use it. No question.

I am her grandson.

I throw the gun back on top of the clothes, close the drawer, go in my closet and pick up a wooden T-ball bat.

When Laymon and Shonda go back to the parking lot, there's a confrontation but no one is seriously injured, and security breaks up the melee. Laymon and Shonda later make a call to the local news, and national publicity ensues. Eventually, the president of the college places Laymon and Shonda on disciplinary probation for using racially insensitive language while the fraternity members have their party privileges taken away. Commenting on the charge against him, Laymon writes, "If there was racially insensitive language Shonda and I could have used to make those boys feel like we felt, we would have never stepped to them in the first place."

In other words, in American society and in American English, there is no language, no words that could make the white frat boys feel as hurt, dismissed, or degraded as the white boys' insults. There is no white equivalent for the word *nigger*. The power of the white frat boys over Laymon is embedded in the very language they speak, the insults they hurl, their attitudes and emotions.

This hurtful power of language is something that exists outside of public policy or the consciousness of any one individual. It is a palpable force that the white frat boys know they possess and Laymon and Shonda do not. Of course, it is borne out in the fact that somehow the college president deems that what the whites did and what Laymon and Shonda did are equivalent and in the president's mind require similar punishment. But it is also borne out in the obliviousness of the frat boys and president to the power and advantages they wield. It is borne out in white persons' refusal to envision a world in which such power would not be available to them.[2]

White power isn't simply present in policies or the ways discipline is handed out—whether in an institution or the justice system. It is present in the ability to physically or emotionally hurt, detain, or imprison someone. And yet the white frat boys are unconscious of how such power is

---

2. Later, the president suspends Laymon for a year because he has taken *The Red Badge of Courage* out of the library without checking it out and then returned it the next day. Only by attending "therapy sessions for racial insensitivity" can he return to college.

achieved or where it comes from, though perhaps they do sense that it comes from the shared history of whites and Blacks in the South. It is the power to decide who is a legitimate member of society and who is not. The Master, the Slave. The innocent white citizen. The guilty Black criminal. The words here, in America's racist lexicon, are redundant. This ontology, this powerful set of tropes and readings of Blackness, remains a constant threat to Black Americans every single waking moment of their lives, conscious or not. That threat remains a constant presence— essentially, with any white person that the Black person encounters.

In a 2020 *Vanity Fair* piece titled "Mississippi: A Poem, in Days," Laymon references this incident and provides a chilling link between what happened and the political power dynamics of Mississippi and the current state of the Republican Party, for in that group of frat boys shouting racist epithets was the future governor of Mississippi, Tate Reeves. (Note: Laymon uses his partner's actual name rather than the pseudonym, Shonda, used in his first essay.)

> In college, my partner, Nzola, and I got into an altercation with two fraternities on Bid Day. Some fraternity members wore confederate capes, Afro wigs, and others blackened their faces. I've written about how they called us "niggers." . . .
>
> I have never written about the heartbreak of seeing the future governor of Mississippi in that group of white boys, proudly representing the Kappa Alpha fraternity and its confederate commitment to Black suffering. I have never admitted that after playing basketball against Tate all through high school, and knowing that he went to a public school called Florence, not a segregation academy, like so many other white boys we knew, it hurt my feelings to see Tate doing what white boys who pledged their identities to the Old South ideologies were supposed to do.
>
> When I saw Tate in that confederate cacophony of drunken white boyhood, doing what they did, I knew he could one day be governor of Mississippi and president of the United States.

What is revealing here is the hurt Laymon felt, and likely still feels, because he thought Reeves just might be different from the other white boys Laymon knew. At the heart of this Whiteness that buoys Reeves to this day is an arrogance, a sense of entitlement, a bully's pleasure in the power to hurt the less powerful. It is bolstered by the sure knowledge that whatever damage this white power wreaks, there will be no punishment or penalty; the existing systems of power—whether in their college or in the justice system or in the government—are designed to protect these white boys all through their lives from any consequence for their racism. Indeed, Laymon understands that the racism Reeves evinces as a young man does not disqualify him from becoming governor of the state. No, it's exactly the opposite: Reeves's racism actually marks him as someone who can and will become governor of the state.

But these questions seem to remain for Laymon and his fellow Blacks: What do I, Kiese, do with my awareness of this system that supports and promotes someone like Tate Reeves? How can I survive these insults? How do I maintain my sanity and psychological equilibrium in the face of such brutality and utter indifference to my humanity? How do I find a way not to seek revenge that will destroy me (for surely that is the lesson he learns in his encounter with the white president of the college). I, Kiese, will never be safe here, and yet how do I not let the system, which is designed to hurt me, go on to destroy my soul and my sanity?

In a 2020 *New York Times* op-ed, Black journalist Ernest Owens writes that the one positive for him during the Covid-19 quarantine has shown up in his therapy. Because he's been forced to stay at home, Owens has experienced what life might be like without encounters with white microaggressions, and the psychological stresses and existential threat that those microaggressions bring up; these are the costs of racism that most white people are unaware of and rarely see:

> I don't miss the panic I feel when I see a police car pass by me when I'm walking down the street alone. I don't miss the way my palms get sweaty as a cashier requests to see multiple forms of ID when I make a credit card purchase. I don't miss being asked questions about how I "got here" in a classroom of white students who weren't asked the same. I don't miss the way I can feel my whole face tense up when a white woman clutches her purse as we pass each other on the street. . . .

I think I'll be shopping less at grocery stores in person be-cause I've begun to recognize that a lot of the racist trauma I ex-perienced during my childhood took place while simply shopping for food with my family. I will be working from home more and less in co-working spaces and public areas, where I often feel sur-veilled by white people. I decided to pursue my master's degree in an online distance-learning program—I won't miss the questions about whether I'm lost on campus and the racist-themed parties that haunted my undergraduate experience. Are these significant changes? Yes, but no more significant than living with the angst that comes with navigating daily indignities.

The vast and throttling presence of Whiteness in the lives, psyches, and souls of Black Americans is not something that has disappeared into America's racist past; it is a constant in Black life. It is Whiteness and white people who have created and continue to create this constant an-imus, suspicion, and ostracism, not just in clearly racialized encounters with police or racist fraternity members, but in encounters with ordi-nary white people whose psyches and belief systems have been shaped by a history they remain ignorant of, a history that has dictated how they think of themselves and how they think of Black people.

———

Though Erica Gardner, Kiese Laymon, and Ernest Owens grew up a half-century after Baldwin, the basic dilemma created by America's rac-ism is the same. How do you deal with the powers of Whiteness, the ways it determines the circumstances of your life, the ways it constantly endangers your life? Do you express your desire for freedom and your hatred of racism openly, or do you repress it in order not to be destroyed by that racism? Do you give in to rage, a rage that can tear at you from the inside and make you even more vulnerable in the world? But how can you let go of the rage, when its causes never stop? How do you escape bit-terness, like the bitterness that ate up Baldwin's father, or the bitterness that caused the Harlem riots of 1943 or the demonstrations in Ferguson more than a half-century later? The bitterness of Erica Gardner or her father, both tired of and enraged by police harassment and injustice; the bitterness of Laymon and his mother, as they try to navigate the white supremacy of Mississippi? And what does all this tell us of how little race relations have changed since Baldwin's time?

Whiteness and white supremacy continue to ravage Black communities in America—through the justice system, through unemployment, through failures in the education system, through redlining and discriminatory lending practices, through political disempowerment, through disparities in health care and mortality, through the depictions of Whiteness and Blackness in the culture. In his time and in his essays, James Baldwin offers his version of this, and he is aware of this devastation not simply because he sees its evidence in his fellow Blacks—but also in himself. All his life, he worked to address the racism that constantly oppressed his community, but also to find his way out of his own debilitating reactions to that racism.

Baldwin's Spiritual Journey and Recovery

At the end of "Notes of a Native Son," which starts with the time of his late teens, Baldwin begins to articulate to himself the dilemma that white racism posed to the Black psyche, his own in particular. At the expensive New Jersey restaurant, he had found within himself a dangerous urge, an almost addictive compulsion to fling himself directly into the maw of white racism as if by doing so he could exert some control over it. He understands that such a tactic is not a viable solution, either on a practical level or on the level of his own psychic well-being. But what would constitute a different, more viable way of confronting the racism that surrounds him?

He relies on his own brilliant powers of analysis to state the dilemma, all the while knowing an easy solution is not readily available. In contemplating his youthful rage and bitterness, he comes to an understanding that giving in to hatred would entail a destruction of something inside himself—for hatred would involve a surrendering of his own intellect and awareness of the realities of the world, and that was something, as a writer, he could not afford to do; what's more, as a human being with a soul, he could not afford to do it. But at the same time, he recognized that forgoing hatred of whites was not the same as loving whites, something Martin Luther King Jr. urged his followers to do. Rather than simply endorsing King, Baldwin presents the paradoxical fate of American Blacks:

> In order to really hate white people, one has to blot so much out of mind—and the heart—that this hatred itself becomes an exhausting and self-destructive pose. But this does not mean, on the other hand, that love comes easily: the white world is too powerful, too complacent, too ready with gratuitous humiliation, and, above all, too ignorant and too innocent for that. One is absolutely forced to make perpetual qualifications and one's own reactions are always canceling each other out. It is this, really, which has driven so many people mad, both white and black. One is always in the position of having to decide between amputation and gangrene.

One was constantly turning from one impossible choice to the other: trying to live within a denigrating system that denied the rights as a human being on the one hand, and on the other, fighting against and refusing to give in to that system, thus endangering one's life and perhaps sanity:

> It began to seem that one would have to hold in the mind forever two ideas which seemed to be in opposition. The first idea was acceptance, the acceptance, totally without rancor, of life as it is, and men as they are; in the light of this idea, it goes without saying that injustice is a commonplace. But this did not mean that one could be complacent, for the second idea was of equal power: that one must never, in one's own life, accept these injustices as commonplace but must fight them with all one's strength.

Baldwin continued throughout his life to fight against what he regarded as America's original sin, a sin America had not yet come to terms with, choosing instead an insistence on amnesia, on its innocence, on its exceptional goodness. In various ways, as he lived and wrote further, he deepened the insights that conclude his most famous essay.

———

During the civil rights era, working as a journalist, Baldwin's travels in the South led him to a deeper understanding of what being Black in America meant. At one point, he meets a Black preacher and activist, part of the unsung legions who followed leaders and martyrs like King and Medgar Evers. He asks the preacher if he is afraid:

> There was no hint of defiance or bravado in his manner. Only, when I made my halting observation concerning his safety, a shade of sorrow crossed his face, deep, impatient, dark; then it was gone. It was the most impersonal anguish I had ever seen on a man's face. It was as though he were wrestling with the mighty fact that the danger in which he stood was as nothing compared to the spiritual horror which drove those who were trying to destroy him. They endangered him, but they doomed themselves.

This Black preacher isn't focused on his own sacrifice, nor does he approach himself and his work with a self-righteous tone. His is a spiritual, existential resolve, and one suspects his spiritual life and faith are essential to his work on race.

Later, while in the South, Baldwin finds himself confronted unexpectedly with the stark animus of segregation. He mistakenly goes in the front door of a segregated restaurant and is directed to the back to get his food. There he finds an older Black man eating. Rather than giving in to the feelings of rage of his more youthful self, the more worldly Baldwin focuses on the elder Black man's equanimity in the face of profound racism. He finds in that man a great strength, a strength he realizes must frighten the white Southerners who enforce his oppression:

> I watched the patient man as he ate, watched him with both wonder and respect. If he could do that, then the people on the other side of the mesh were right to be frightened—if he could do that, he could do anything and when he walked through the mesh there would be nothing to stop him. But I couldn't do it yet; my stomach was as tight as a black rubber ball. I took my hamburger and walked outside and dropped it into the weeds. The dark silence of the streets frightened me a little, and I walked back to my hotel.

In his travels in the South, Baldwin begins to see dialectically—that is, how the suffering and injustices wreaked upon American Blacks have forced them to find in themselves an enormous strength, a resilience to survive realities most whites cannot or refuse to imagine.

Baldwin starts to articulate how individual Southern Blacks must come to see the false premises on which whites build their world and psychology; they understand that while the white world will never acknowledge the Black world's sense of reality, their Black reality does exist. Thus, he sees how these Southern Blacks must hold contradictory racial conceptions in mind—the unreality of the white world and the very real fact of white power, and the reality of the Black world and the very real fact that Blacks are subject to the whims and hatred embodied in white power.

By charting the complexity of Black psychology, Baldwin describes the Black psyche in ways that contradict any white portrait of Black America—the liberal view of a suffering, downtrodden, pitiable, oppressed victim or the conservative view of the happy, contented Black living in a world free of racism or the less-than-human, criminal/welfare/Antifa Black. Suffering, he says, may not ennoble Black people, but it sure as hell has made them more knowing, more realistic, and stronger than white people. As he writes in *The Fire Next Time*:

> I do not mean to be sentimental about suffering—enough is certainly as good as a feast—but people who cannot suffer can never grow up, can never discover who they are. That man who is forced each day to snatch his manhood, his identity, out of the fire of human cruelty that rages to destroy it knows, if he survives his effort, and even if he does not survive it, something about himself and human life that no school on earth—and indeed, no church—can teach. He achieves his own authority, and that is unshakable. This is because, in order to save his life, he is forced to look beneath appearances, to take nothing for granted, to hear the meaning behind the words. If one is continually surviving the worst that life can bring, one eventually ceases to be controlled by a fear of what life can bring; whatever it brings must be borne. And at this level of experience one's bitterness begins to be palatable, and hatred becomes too heavy a sack to carry. The apprehension of life here so briefly and inadequately

sketched has been the experience of generations of Negroes, and it helps to explain how they have endured and how they have been able to produce children of kindergarten age who can walk through mobs to get to school. . . . It demands great spiritual resilience not to hate the hater whose foot is on your neck, and an even greater miracle of perception and charity not to teach your children to hate.

What emerges for Baldwin then is pride, which is not simply a slogan or a presumption, but is based on history, on the actual lives Black people have led, on what has allowed them to survive the Middle Passage, slavery, Jim Crow, segregation, police brutality, and all other manner of abuse and discrimination. With this sense of pride, the hatred and bitterness of the young Baldwin throwing a water glass in the face of white segregation becomes smaller and smaller. Though he understands the reasons for his father's bitterness, Baldwin sees there is another way, a way to escape from the fate his father seemed to bequeath to him, which the Harlem riots seemed to signal was his legacy:

> I am proud of these people not because of their color but because of their intelligence and their spiritual force and their beauty. The country should be proud of them, too, but, alas, not many people in this country even know of their existence. And the reason for this ignorance is that a knowledge of the role these people played—and play—in American life would reveal more about America to Americans than Americans wish to know.
>
> The American Negro has the great advantage of having never believed that collection of myths to which white Americans cling: that their ancestors were all freedom-loving heroes, that they were born in the greatest country the world has ever seen, or that Americans are invincible in battle and wise in peace, that Americans have always dealt honorably with Mexicans and Indians and all other neighbors or inferiors, that American men are the world's most direct and virile, that American women are pure. Negroes know far more about white Americans than that; it can almost be said, in fact, that they know about white Americans what parents—or anyway,

mothers—know about their children, and that they very often regard white Americans that way.

And here we come to the other side of Baldwin's road to spiritual recovery. For this recovery entailed not only seeing Black people more complexly: it involved seeing white people more clearly. As his own understanding of Black survival, the complexity of Black psychology, and the strength of Black spirituality grows, he sees more and more how whites cannot see, much less acknowledge, any of this. To do that, whites would have to face who they themselves are—people who have erected and lived on the privileges, power, wealth, and psychic self-satisfaction created by an unjust racist society.

II

At the same time he was reflecting on his encounters with Southern Blacks, Baldwin was also, through his reporting and his creative writing and his gay identity, making his way through the world of white people—liberals, conservatives, intellectuals, writers, politicians, lovers, young whites, parts of white society he never encountered growing up in Harlem. He came to see how ignorant they were of their country's own history, of the reality in which they lived, and of the lives—the experiential, the intellectual, the spiritual, the psychological, and the cultural—of Black people in America.

At first he attempts to explain to these whites the reality of Black America, and certainly his own writing is part of this enterprise. But gradually he comes to see that whites cannot face the whole truth of how deeply racism is embedded into American society and the American psyche. Baldwin knows that Black people have learned to constantly silence themselves before whites about the ways they view white people or the actual conditions of Black life. But he eventually sees that this Black silence and this white ignorance extend much deeper: whites prefer the myths they have made up of an honorable history, where slavery is so far in the past it never existed or is a minor mistake that was reversed entirely by the Civil War; where the Civil War is a noble cause of states' rights and defense of one's homeland; where the nostalgia for antebellum South is a harmless element of Southern culture—the myth of the Lost Cause. Similarly, the taking of Native American land and the genocide of Native Americans are not even worth mentioning, except to sing the praises of the brave and glorious whites who conquered ruthless savages. In short, says Baldwin, "What passes for identity in America is a series of myths about one's heroic ancestors."

Over and over in his essays he harpoons white myth after white myth: that there is a just way to control a ghetto ("the only way to police a ghetto is to be oppressive"); that historic pronouncements of equality are the same thing as the achievement of equality ("there was no point in dealing with white people in terms of their own moral professions, for they were not going to honor them"); that America is a Christian nation ("my father and my mother and my grandfather and my grandmother knew that Christians didn't act this way"); that white people are surely ready to give up the unjust power they wield over Blacks; that they will relinquish the rewards of that power if somehow Blacks just ask for change a little less loudly and angrily. Yet while white America continues to believe in these myths, Blacks (adults and children alike) surely know otherwise: "Every street boy—and I was a street boy, so I know—looking at the society which has produced him, looking at the standards of that society which are not honored by anybody, looking up at your churches and the government and the politicians, understands that this structure is operated for someone else's benefit—not for his. And there's no room in it for him."

An important extension of this: whites cannot bear the thought that Blacks make judgments of whites, much less that the Black judgment of white people bears any truth or accuracy:

White Americans find it as difficult as white people elsewhere do to divest themselves of the notion that they are in possession of some intrinsic value that black people need, or want. And this assumption—which, for example, makes the solution to the Negro problem depend on the speed with which Negroes accept and adopt white standards—is revealed in all kinds of striking ways, from Bobby Kennedy's assurance that a Negro can become President in forty years to the unfortunate tone of warm congratulations with which so many liberals address their Negro equals.[3] It is the Negro, of course, who is presumed to have become equal—an achievement that not only proves the comforting fact that perseverance has no color but also overwhelmingly corroborates the white man's sense of his own value. . . . Therefore, a vast amount of the energy that goes into what we call the Negro problem is produced by the white man's profound desire not to be judged by those who are not white, not to be seen as he is, and at the same time a vast amount of the white anguish is rooted in the white man's equally profound need to be seen as he is, to be released from the tyranny of his mirror.

Blacks cannot help but see whites as hypocrites and morally bankrupt—in light of white establishment and support of this racist society. The issues that white and Black America argue over may change over time—slavery, segregation, police brutality, unequal schools, systemic bias, microaggressions, kneeling NFL players—but what never changes is this: whatever Black Americans say about racial inequality, about the reality of their lives, about discrimination, or about white people, *Black truths can never be considered or accepted by the whites of their time as the ultimate truth*. Nothing that Black America says can make white people doubt this; white people must be the ultimate arbiters of reality. And this is the essence of white supremacy.[4]

Early in his writings, Baldwin makes this trenchant and somber observation on white innocence: "People who shut their eyes to reality simply invite their own destruction, and anyone who insists on remaining in a state of innocence long after that innocence is dead turns himself into a monster." But as his writings progress, another tone begins to emerge, one that depicts whites almost as children, or people who are too frail

---

3. Meeting with various Black intellectual and artistic leaders, Attorney General Kennedy thought he was allying himself with Baldwin when he predicted a future Black President. Yet Baldwin knew his people had been in America for more than three centuries while Kennedy's family arrived merely a generation ago. In the end, Kennedy dismissed Baldwin as crazy and ordered FBI director J. Edgar Hoover to step up surveillance on him.

4. Baldwin further says: "White America remains unable to believe that black America's grievances are real; they are unable to believe this because they cannot face what this fact says about themselves and their country; and the effect of this massive and hostile incomprehension is to increase the danger in which all black people live here, especially the young."

and fragile to deal with the realities they create. Yes, he says, white people can act monstrously, can wield power in enormously abusive ways, but what he's struck by is how weak they are:

> When a white man faces a black man, especially if the black man is helpless, terrible things are revealed. I know. I have been carried into precinct basements often enough, and I have seen and heard and endured the secrets of desperate white men and women, which they knew were safe with me, because even if I should speak, no one would believe me. And they would not believe me precisely because they would know what I said was true.

As these realizations take hold, Baldwin's tone is more often ironic. He sees that he understands white people better than they understand themselves, and thus he feels a certain pity or wry forbearance, despite the harm he knows they do. When addressing whites, he often takes up a position of sardonic distance or at times condescension, the way one would talk to a child who is too old to believe in Santa Claus yet still does, a child who refuses to become a grownup and acknowledge grownup realities.

This tone is evident in his answer to Norman Mailer's essays "The Talent in the Room" and "The White Negro"; in his own essay Baldwin explains why he and Mailer can never quite be friends, less because of their sense of rivalry as authors and more because Baldwin can never quite be honest with Mailer about how he is viewed by Baldwin and other Blacks:

> "Man," said a Negro musician to me once, talking about Norman, "the only trouble with that cat is that he's white." This does not mean exactly what it says—or, rather, it *does* mean exactly what it says, and not what it might be taken to mean—and it is a very shrewd observation. What my friend meant was that to become a Negro man, let alone a Negro artist, one had to make oneself up as one went along. This had to be done in the not-at-all-metaphorical teeth of the world's determination to destroy you. The world had prepared no place for you, and if the world had its way, no place would ever exist. Now, this is true for everyone, but, in the case of

a Negro, this truth is absolutely naked: if he deludes himself about it, he will die. This is not the way this truth presents itself to white men, who believe the world is theirs and who, albeit unconsciously, expect the world to help them in the achievement of their identity. But the world does not do this—for anyone; the world is not interested in anyone's identity. And, therefore, the anguish which can overtake a white man comes in the middle of his life, when he must make the almost inconceivable effort to divest himself of everything he has ever expected, or believed, when he must take himself apart and put himself together again, walking out of the world, into limbo, or into what certainly looks like limbo. This cannot yet happen to any Negro of Norman's age, for the reason that his delusions and defenses are either absolutely impenetrable by this time, or he has failed to survive them. "I want to know how power works," Norman once said to me, "how it really works, in detail." Well, I know how power works, it has worked on me, and if I didn't know how power worked, I would be dead. And it goes without saying, perhaps, that I have simply never been able to afford myself any illusions concerning the manipulation of that power.

We also see this biting and clear-eyed clarity in Baldwin's critique of Faulkner—of Faulkner's portraits of Blacks and his famous admonition to the North to "go slow":

Faulkner's portraits of Negroes, which lack a system of nuances that, perhaps, only a black writer can see in black life—for Faulkner could see Negroes only as they related to him, not as they related to each other—are nevertheless made vivid by the torment of their creator. He is seeking to exorcise a history which is also a curse. He wants the old order, which came into existence through unchecked greed and wanton murder, to redeem itself without further bloodshed—without, that is, any further menacing itself—and without coercion. This, old orders never do, less because they would not than because they cannot. They cannot because they have always existed in relation to a force which they have had to subdue. This subjugation is the key to their identity and the triumph and justification of their history, and it is also on this continued subjugation that their material well-being depends. One may see that the history, which is now indivisible from oneself, has been full of errors and excesses; but this is not the same thing as seeing that, for millions of people, this history—oneself—has been nothing but an intolerable yoke, a stinking prison, a shrieking grave.

In "No Name in the Street," Baldwin gives his take on hippies, the counterculture movement, and white political protests of the sixties. While he has some sympathy for these young people, he also sees that they do not know what they are up against, either from the forces that uphold society or from similar forces inside themselves, including an unspoken and unexamined loyalty to Whiteness:

> I remember one [white] boy who was already set to become an executive at one of the major airlines—for him, he joked, bleakly, the sky would be the limit. But he wondered if he could "hold on" to himself, if he could retain the respect of some of the people who respected him now. What he meant was that he hoped not to be programmed out of all meaningful human existence, and, clearly, he feared the worst. He, like many students, was being forced to choose between treason and irrelevance. Their moral obligations to the darker brother, if they were real, and if they were really to be acted on, placed them in conflict with all that they had loved and all that had given them an identity, rendered their present uncertain and their future still more so, and even jeopardized their means of staying alive. They were far from judging or repudiating the American state as oppressive or immoral—they were merely profoundly uneasy. . . . And what the white students had not expected to let themselves in for, when boarding the Freedom Train, was the realization that the black situation in America was but one aspect of the fraudulent nature of American life. They had not expected to be forced to judge their parents, their elders, and their antecedents, so harshly, and they had not realized how cheaply, after all, the rulers of the republic held their white lives to be. Coming to the defense of

the rejected and destitute, they were confronted with the extent of their own alienation, and the unimaginable dimensions of their own poverty. They were privileged and secure only so long as they did, in effect, what they were told: but they had been raised to believe they were free.

What these young white people end up confronting, then, are the rules for being white. Baldwin understands that for all their revolutionary rhetoric these young people, these hippies, still bear with them the weaknesses of such an identity, a childlike or adolescent inability to confront the realities of their existence and what has upheld their position in the world:

> White children, in the main, and whether they are rich or poor, grow up with a grasp of reality so feeble that they can very accurately be described as deluded—about themselves and the world they live in. White people have managed to get through entire lifetimes in this euphoric state, but black people have not been so lucky: a black man who sees the world the way John Wayne, for example, sees it would not be an eccentric patriot, but a raving maniac. The reason for this, at bottom, is that the doctrine of white supremacy, which still controls most white people, is itself a stupendous delusion: but to be born black in American is an immediate, a mortal challenge. People who cling to their delusions find it difficult, if not impossible, to learn anything worth learning: a people under the necessity of creating themselves must examine everything, and soak up learning the way the roots of a tree soak up water. A people still held in bondage must believe that *ye shall know the truth, and the truth shall make ye free.*

What neither Mailer nor Faulkner nor the hippies can do is relinquish their stake in Whiteness and in the society that upholds their status as whites. There is a political aspect to this, yes: they are clinging to a political and economic power they would have to let go of if the society were to make a true move toward equality. But this political and economic power is, at the level of the individual (depending on how powerful and rich that individual is), somewhat abstract. What is far less abstract is their stake as individual whites as part of white society: they cannot remain accepted by other whites if they go beyond the boundaries of what it is acceptable for whites to think and believe—on a political or social level.

This belonging to Whiteness is not simply the approval and acceptance of other whites; it entails the psychic comforts that come with such approval and acceptance. Such status and acceptance means that one is not isolated, not alone, not threatened by banishment or death. But beyond this, the deeper attachment to Whiteness is a protection against moral, spiritual, and psychological honesty, both from outside and in. The white person who truly abandons Whiteness must see that they are other than who they think they are. Without such a change, they will still remain embedded within the racial status quo, however much they might protest otherwise.[5]

———————

In other words, whites must change their identity, and this entails an abandonment of Whiteness as it has been defined and practiced throughout our history. And this, as Baldwin has observed, involves "a terror as primary as that of the nightmare of the mortal fall." In his view, Blacks who have struggled against the racial realities of the South have been forced to see and understand the limits of their power in the world, and thus the limits of those who hold power over them. In contrast, whites like Mailer or Faulkner or the white flower children can see none of that. It is not so much that they are invested in power on a political level, although they are so invested (the state of their lives is shaped and blessed by that power); it is that they are invested in their own conception of themselves. To let *that* go is extremely difficult. For such an undertaking would entail an abandonment and critique of the stories Whiteness tells about itself, the stories white people so love because they have grown up with them, have based their identities on them, have understood the world through them, have experienced a self-satisfying pleasure through them and a certainty about who they are as individuals and as a nation. White people read themselves into the stories of Whiteness; these

---

5. bell hooks observes that most white people "do not imagine the way whiteness makes its presence felt in black life, most often as terrorizing imposition, a power that wounds, hurts, tortures, is a reality that disrupts the fantasy of whiteness as representing goodness."

stories, of history and the present, nonfiction and fictional, are the flattering false reflections of themselves.

Why can't whites let all this go? Because of what such letting go requires: ultimately, whites must reduce their sense of self, their ego, in ways they cannot do presently, for that would require a humility they do not possess, a humility Blacks have been forced to acknowledge, often under the threat of and penalty of death.

This does not mean such a change on the part of whites is not possible or desirable, but its reward is far more of the soul than of this world. With such a transformation, a new strength emerges—the strength that comes from abandoning an illusion and all the burdens and blindness that illusion demands. The achievement of this strength is spiritual work, psychological work, rather than political work (though that too is obviously necessary). In the sixties, a certain portion of the young white population was willing to approach such a point, such a freedom, to question to some extent the basis of their society, but ultimately the price was too high for them, their fears too great, their attachment to Whiteness too deep.

In terms of race, political change cannot occur without moral and spiritual change, argues Baldwin, and this cannot occur without a psychological process whereby one loses one's old sense of identity and the comforts and certainties of that identity; one must enter the dangers and uncertainties of a new identity that more adequately expresses who one is, what one's relationship to the world is, and what the world actually is. For whites, this would entail giving up the dream of Whiteness and all the illusions and moral evasions that go with it:

> Any real change implies the break-up of the world as one has always known it, the loss of all that gave one an identity, the end of safety. And at such a moment . . . one clings to what one knew, or thought one knew. . . . Yet, it is only when a man is able, without bitterness or self-pity, to surrender a dream he has long cherished or a privilege long possessed that he is set free. . . . All men have gone through this, gone through it, each according to his degree, through their lives. It is one of the irreducible facts of life. And remembering this, especially since I am a Negro, affords me my only

means of understanding what is happening in the minds of white Southerners today.

Throughout Baldwin's *Collected Essays* we see someone who is willing to forgo safety and change his sense of his own identity, and he makes it clear, from that early great essay "Notes of a Native Son" onward, that he knows his own survival depends on this process. It is a lesson both Black and white readers can take on as their own, and it is essential to what makes Baldwin perhaps the most important American writer of the past century.

———

The last shall be first, the first last. This biblical premise, this promise of the New Testament, is fundamental to Black spirituality and to the spirituality of Baldwin, who was after all a child preacher. It is Baldwin's continuous project in the *Collected Essays* to understand not just the prophetic nature of this biblical pronouncement, but its spiritual and psychological truth. To explore that truth required him to examine how Black people have survived for centuries and continue to survive now; at the same time he came to understand deeply the ways whites have continued to exert their power over Black people and yet remained in denial as to how they have done so—and thus deluded as to who they as whites actually are.

With such understanding in his 1963 essay "A Talk to Teachers," Baldwin takes apart or "breaks down" the word *nigger*. Here in this essay I will cite below the oral version used in the recent film *I Am Not Your Negro*, which takes up Baldwin's later writings to explore his vision of America, proving his continued relevance to our current issues on race. In the oral version, Baldwin is telling other Black people and people of color that the key to our survival is in seeing whites and the white world accurately, seeing them not simply through the eyes of worldly power but in terms of the true measure of who whites are. For if whites are buoyed up and protected by an unjust, undemocratic, racist system of power, then the white assessment of their own achievements and who they are must be inflated in ways they are too afraid and too weak to acknowledge. And if this is true, when considered and evaluated in a spiritual, moral, and psychological context, whites are smaller, less knowing, less virtuous, less resilient, and weaker than they think they are. And their epistemology of racial superiority—their sense that their knowledge is not just superior but truly objective—is a trenchant and self-mystifying delusion.

Just as important, if the individual Black or person of color sees this true assessment of white people and Whiteness, the power of individual whites and Whiteness lessens. Thus the power of whatever insult or *microaggression*—to use the current term—whites might confront us with becomes much smaller. The ways the white world views us—however that white world affects our outer life—has less and less relevance to the ways we think of ourselves. We should not give in to their delusions, either about ourselves or themselves. We should make the white world and the thinking of whites smaller and smaller in our psyches. Their words cannot hurt us. We can step outside and beyond their racist epistemology. *We should not give psychic power to those who cannot see us.*

This is the one freedom people of color can wrest from a racist society, whatever our outward struggles to change that society. And it is the freedom that can sustain us in that work, for we then understand what our portion of that work is and what work only whites themselves can do. For Baldwin's pronouncement on the word *nigger* places the heart of our racial problem not in the psyche of Blacks and other people of color, but in the psyche of whites, including those whites who may not believe that they believe in the word *nigger,* even as our society continues to demonstrate that they do:

> What white people have to do is try and find out in their own hearts why it was necessary to have a "nigger" in the first place, because I'm not a nigger, I'm a man. But if you think I'm a nigger, it means you need him. The question that you've got to ask yourself, the white population of this country has to ask itself, North and South because it's one country and for a Negro there is no difference between the North and the South—it's just a difference in the way they castrate you, but the fact of the castration is the American fact. . . . If I'm not the nigger here and you invented him, you the white people have invented him, then you've got to find out why. And the future of the country depends on that, whether or not it is able to ask that question.

Here, Baldwin claims his innocence, a freedom from the warped judgments of Whiteness, a space of psychic peace. At the same time, he charges white America to take up the burden of its guilt, its responsibility for *what is,* and face both our past and our present in ways that actually might help us change our country and heal its troubled soul.

Abandoning Whiteness

The question of identity is a question involving the most profound panic—a terror as primary as the nightmare of the mortal fall. . . . An identity is questioned only when it is menaced, as when the mighty begin to fall, or when the wretched begin to rise, or when the stranger enters the gates, never, thereafter, to be a stranger: the stranger's presence making you the stranger, less to the stranger than to yourself. Identity would seem to be the garment with which one covers the nakedness of the self; in which case, it is best that the garment be loose, a little like the robes of the desert, through which robes one's nakedness can always be felt, and sometimes, discerned. This trust in one's nakedness is all that gives one the power to change one's robes.

—James Baldwin, *The Devil Finds Work*

FOR AN INDIVIDUAL WHITE PERSON TO UNDERGO A TRUE CHANGE ABOUT race, there are three main tasks, one involving knowledge and social interactions, one involving a spiritual journey, and one involving a political commitment.

The first is rather simple: you need to know more. In order to do that, you need to realize that you are more ignorant than you think you are. You must entertain the proposition that when it comes to race you do not know what you do not know.

To begin to gain this knowledge, one can read and study. In recent years, there have been advances in all areas in our understanding of racism—from the justice system to housing, history to philosophy, the medical system to the arts, political science to psychology. But knowledge of race and the problems of race in our society cannot come simply from books. It must also come from experiences that take the white person beyond the comfortable confines of the white world. In other words, if you as a white person live your social life almost entirely with other white people, you will never understand the nature of racism in our society: you will never know or understand people of color.

If you truly want to educate yourself about race, you will have to change the way you live, the way you socialize, the way you spend your time. Inevitably, this will mean that you will have to put yourself in social spaces where you are uncomfortable or where you are in a clear minority or perhaps even the only white person there. If you have enough of the latter experience, you will begin to understand something about the nature of race in American society that no other experience will tell you. Admittedly, there may be some spaces where you might be greeted with indifference or worse. And yes, you should be conscious that in certain spaces you are not wanted, and that it is the right of those there to feel that way, to view you as a white intruder—and you may have to leave. But all that will teach you something, too.

If you have no friends of color, there are reasons why you have no friends of color. If you have only one or two friends of color, there are reasons for that as well. You will have to look inside and ask yourself what those reasons are. This will involve internal changes in who *you are,* in how you understand your own identity and the identities of white people and people of color. But you will also have to change something inside yourself to expand your range of racial interactions. And you will have to do all this by trial and error: you will make mistakes; you may embarrass and mortify yourself; you will be greeted at times with anger—sometimes unjustified but more often justified and in ways you do not understand, in ways you may think are unfair. You will have to pull your defenses back then; you will have to listen or, even before that, learn to listen. And you should know that in your journey you will say things that are insensitive, things you did not realize were insensitive or ignorant or hurtful. You will make mistakes and have to own them. Such admission of fallibility makes this a spiritual journey. You will have to humble yourself. You will have to accept that perhaps you are not the person you think you are.

In various studies of student competency, researchers have found that students who know less about a subject, who do not have a full grasp of a subject, tend to overestimate how much they know. In contrast, students who know a lot about the subject, who have mastered the subject, are more accurate about the status of their knowledge; they may at times even underestimate their competence. When it comes to race, almost all whites are C students who think they are A students. If you have been getting As all your life, it is difficult to realize the true nature of your ignorance, your lack of competence. It is hard to see the reality of that C or D grade, and the fact that you have a long way to go, much longer than you think.

———

But learning—book learning or even social learning—is not enough. There is a second component to this process; it entails psychological and spiritual work. What you as an individual white person will have to undergo is a transformation of your identity. As James Baldwin told us, such questions, such changes involve "a terror as primary as the nightmare of the mortal fall"—as threatening as the knowledge of your own mortality. You will have to change the hierarchy in your mind concerning the way you see yourself in relationship to people of color. You will have to change the way you look at yourself in relationship to others, both whites and people of color; you will have to transform the way you look at institutions, society, history, and almost any field of endeavor you can name.

To envision this changed white person, it's useful to reiterate the way white America responds now to the critiques made by people of color. As almost every person of color knows that our critique of racial issues in an organization or a relationship will almost automatically be met with a response of denial or amelioration. *You're just playing the race card. You're being overly sensitive. I don't think so-and-so can be racist. This can't be possible. This can't be that bad. This institution/organization/individual isn't racist. I am not racist. I don't have a racist bone in my body.* If the person of color persists in their questioning, white people will generally begin to attack their critic, often in ad hominem fashion, so that the racial critique will be shunted aside for negative evaluations of the critic of color's character, personality, mode of critique or protest.

Rarely will the person of color's mention of a racial issue ever be met with an open-ended inquiry by their white audience, for example, with the white person asking, "Please tell me, why do you think that? Why do you feel the way you're feeling?" or "What is it I'm not seeing or understanding? What have I gotten wrong?"

In contrast, the white person's usual spoken or unspoken denial of any charge of racism can be reduced to something like this: "You [the person of color] don't understand the way I see things. Once you understand the way I see things, then you will agree with me, you'll see there really isn't much of a problem here, or even one at all." The white person isn't interested in truly listening to the person of color, much less truly entertaining the possibility that the person of color's experience may be so radically different from them that the person of color's assessment of their mutual reality could also be entirely different.

For the white person at this point isn't thinking about the person of color, much less what the person of color actually means by what they are saying; instead, the white person is responding to a sense of threat, a challenge to their sense of reality and their identity, to their sense of themselves; such a threat must be blocked and cannot be considered. In the mind of this white person, there is no possibility of a valid radical difference in the perception of reality, no possibility that the person of color might perceive something the white person has not: in the ideology of Whiteness, white knowledge is always positioned as superior and valid; it is the knowledge that validates all other knowledge. Black knowledge, the knowledge of people of color and Indigenous people, must always be suspect and subjective, must always wait for white approval for validity. That the white person in question doesn't see the racist premises of such a hierarchy of knowledge is part of the problem. (Again, the Black slave always knew the white master thought differently and why that was.)

At the same time, deeper in the white person's psyche, what's being provoked is a sense of shame, a threat of unworthiness. This shame is different from guilt, which results from and necessitates an acknowledgment of actual wrongs done or benefits received from wrongful actions of previous or other whites. When one actually accepts guilt and responsibility, a calm ensues, which is the acknowledgment of a reality long denied.

But when the white person feels shame—which is a form of denial and which threatens one's sense of self—their reaction is often intense anger, triggering fight, flight, or freeze: they view their shame as stemming from a hostile and unfair attack and attack back; or they retreat into silence and distance. Or there is a collapse of the white person's sense of self, which may entail weeping or self-flagellation or dramatic bouts of despair ("white fragility"). Perceiving itself under threat, the white person's present-day self must be defended at all costs; the self or imago is too weak, too invested in the old order, to entertain the possibility of change. If I enter into a new way of looking at the world and myself, the white person asks, who will I be? For the white person, the fear behind this question is felt as existential, though it doesn't have to be at all.

This in short is the crisis of white identity.[1]

———

What is the solution to this situation? As in the old Zen koan, the white person has to find a way to empty their mind—that is, to step aside from the racial assumptions and premises they've grown up with. They have to enter a new and different psychological and spiritual space; or, rather, they have to find or create that space in themselves. This space is generally one of unknowing, of a lack of certainty, of a willingness on the part to admit that *they might not know what they do not know.*

Let me make this clear, since certain conservative critics, including the African American linguist John McWhorter, have argued that the current racial rhetoric of the far left is engaged in shaming whites for their very existence: I don't think white shame or the inducing of white shame is useful. Indeed, as I've argued above, that shame comes from a misunderstanding of what is required on an individual level for a white person. But I am saying that white people do need to begin deconstructing the ways they have configured their white identity and what that identity

———

1. While whites charge people of color with a clinging to "identity politics," one could argue that it is actually white people who are far more tied to their particular racial identity, that is, to an identity where Whiteness is defined as the majority, the universal default, the center, and source of all validity. That is why more and more whites are freaked out by the possibility of losing the majority, while people of color are long used to such a status. Moreover, most people of color would readily entertain a vision of society where their racial identities actually and truly meant nothing—the so-called Star Trek vision of the future, which is far different from our present society in which racial identity of people of color has a marked effect on their lives and their reality even as they are constantly told that is not the case.

means to them and our society. Moreover, we know they will make mistakes on their journey toward a greater understanding of race in America, and that is part of their white privilege: those mistakes will not result in their death as Driving While Black can. A certain ignorance about race is built into white identity and the comforts it brings, but the mistakes they may make are also human and understandable. And if the white person keeps moving on their journey, they can and should be able to forgive their mistakes—and we people of color can also forgive their mistakes. No one in America knows everything about race; we all have pockets of ignorance and areas where we don't know what we don't know.

What I am saying is that there is a clear psychological and spiritual process whites must undergo if they are to let go of the lies and evasions of Whiteness and create a new white identity that allows for the truth of who we have been as a country and who we actually are now. In this psychological/spiritual journey, you the white person will go through what Elisabeth Kübler-Ross described in *On Death and Dying*: you will inevitably go through the five stages of grief: denial, anger, bargaining, grief, and acceptance. In order to birth a new self, your old self must be relinquished, must be allowed to be seen as fallible and mortal.

In the first stage you may be in complete denial about the extent of racism in American society or the way that it has affected and benefited you. You may want to relegate racism to the past and banish it from the present. You believe that racism cannot possibly exist to the extent that, say, those in Black Lives Matter maintain. You may even believe that now whites are more discriminated against than people of color because that is the way the world feels to you, and that is what whites around you are saying. Many whites remain in this state their whole lives. But sometimes something happens—like the murder of George Floyd—when your absolute certainty that racism against Black people has vanished cannot help but be challenged.

As your denial is challenged, you will feel angry. You will attack the messengers in order to discredit the message. *She is strident, has a chip on her shoulder, is overstating things, is too angry. You're making everything about race. Why is everything always blamed on white people? Surely, Blacks and other minorities are responsible for . . . ? Why do you keep bringing up the past? All Lives Matter.* Or you will play the victim: *White people are discriminated against too. It's whites who are now more discriminated against than people of color.*

After (if) your anger subsides, you will bargain: *It can't be that bad. . . . But not all white people are. . . . Other white people may be like that but I'm not. It's just a few rotten apples. . . .*

And then you grieve: *I didn't realize it was this bad. How do you stand it? I feel so sad. Is this really what America is? He was my hero. I looked up to her. They lied to me. I'm so ashamed. I feel so guilty.*

And then comes acceptance. Which is possible.

Once that happens, you can begin to construct a new identity, one that acknowledges truly what it has meant to be a white person historically in our country and what it means now.

Unfortunately, though, as an individual white person you will not be finished with your journey. There is a final task or stage: now you will have go out in the world and live and act from your new identity; you will have to challenge others, you will have to challenge those you love and those you work with; you will have to challenge the institutions you belong to.

If you do all this, what you will be faced with will be what you have just gone through: denial, anger, bargaining, grief, acceptance. You yourself will be attacked as the messenger. You yourself will be made the problem: *The problem is not racism. No, the problem is you, your character, your personality.* You will have to be willing to suffer the consequences for telling the truth, for challenging racism in individuals and institutions, in friends and in systems.

To do this requires character, requires spiritual strength, requires courage. You will be called on to persist and fight in ways that may seem beyond your capacities. But you will persist because you know it is right.

At the same time, if you do all this, you may very likely become someone you did not expect to be. Your world will be larger and more various; you will become stronger; you will bond with others who are different; you will lose the sense of shame that so many white people carry deep in their hearts, the shame that they would deny rather than confront.

For the individual white person here is what the journey of racial transformation entails:

1. Gather knowledge and educate yourself; interact and create relationships outside circles of white people.
2. Transform your identity; face the terror of correcting and losing your old self; go through the five stages of grief.
3. Develop the strength and character to fight for what you believe and endure the consequences.

———

This is not a simple list. Otherwise more white people would have accomplished it.

But if you do this, you and your world will grow and will grow stronger.

I know: once upon a time I thought myself white. And then I learned I wasn't.

You as a white person can also enter such a journey. And in doing so, you will discover that you are no longer white as white is defined by America, its racism, and the ideology of Whiteness.

As you set out to enter this journey, this shifting of your own identity, I leave you with this poem by Sufi mystic Rumi, translated by Coleman Barks:

> Keep walking though there's no place to get to.
> Don't try to see through the distances.
> That's not for human beings. Move within,
> but don't move the way fear makes you move.

"I Can't Breathe"

I

I wrote this final essay a week after George Floyd, a forty-six-year-old African American man, was murdered by Minneapolis policeman Derek Chauvin. Officer Chauvin kept his knee pressed on Floyd's neck for more than nine minutes while Floyd was handcuffed and on his stomach. Two other officers, J. Alexander Keung and Thomas K. Lane, were pressing their weight on Floyd's back and legs; a fourth officer, Tou Thao, stood by watching the bystanders and backing them away. Among them was seventeen-year-old African American Darnella Frazier, who used her cell phone to record Chavin continuing to press his knee on Floyd's neck. Several witnessing individuals protested for the police to let up as Floyd cried out, "Please," "Don't kill me," "Tell my kids I love them. I'm dead," "Mama," and repeatedly, "I can't breathe," until a point when Floyd was unresponsive for almost three minutes.

Only when an ambulance and paramedics arrived on the scene did Chauvin finally let his knee off of Floyd's neck. The paramedics, who reacted with remarkable complacency and slowness in attending to Floyd, found that he had no pulse, and no pulse returned after they tried electroshock to restart his heart. He was later officially declared dead at the hospital.

The police had been called because Floyd was suspected of using a counterfeit twenty-dollar bill at a local convenience store, Cup Foods. When Officer Lane comes to Floyd's car, Lane already has his gun drawn. (For a counterfeit twenty-dollar bill?) As if he knew he were fated to die, Floyd, who had been shot before by police, pleads, "Mr. Officer, please don't shoot me. Please, man," not knowing at that moment that his death by police would come not from a gun but from a knee on his neck. But Floyd was likely vividly aware that Philando Castile had been shot and killed by a police officer just four years before and five miles away, just as twenty-four-year-old Jamar Clark had been shot and killed five years before in North Minneapolis. Like Castile and Clark, George Floyd had experienced the same existential threat that the justice system posed throughout his life. That was why, even before he was thrown on the ground and choked to death by four police officers, he pleaded to them, "Don't shoot me." And the tragic irony of that plea is that they did not shoot him.

––––––––

Floyd's death sparked demonstrations in Minneapolis but also in cities across the country and world. In each of these, the demonstrators invoked not just his death but the myriad ways African Americans have been brutally treated by police departments in America, and the constant repetition of unarmed Black people being killed by police. Floyd's death came just two months after Breonna Taylor, a twenty-six-year-old African American emergency medical technician, was killed in her own bed in her own apartment when three Louisville, Kentucky, police in plainclothes busted down her door; they were serving a no-knock warrant upon suspicion that drugs were being stored there. (No drugs were found and at the time of the entry the suspect the police were looking for, Jamarcus Glover, had already been arrested miles away.) Taylor's African American boyfriend, Kenneth Walker, neighbors, and Taylor's family claim that the police did not announce who they were, even though Taylor was yelling multiple times, "Who is it?" A licensed handgun owner, Walker says he defended himself and opened fire and shot one of the police officers in the leg. The officers responded with twenty rounds, and Breonna Taylor was shot eight or more times and pronounced dead on the scene. For weeks Taylor's killing provoked little public reaction or response from city officials, and the case only received national attention after activist Shaun King posted about her murder.

Floyd's death occurred three months after Ahmaud Arbery, a twenty-five-year-old African American, was out jogging and was shot and killed near Brunswick in Glynn County, Georgia, by two local white residents, Travis McMichael and his father, Gregory. The McMichaels were both armed and started chasing Arbery in a pickup truck. They claimed that Arbery supposedly resembled a suspect in local robberies—this despite no police record of a string of robberies in the neighborhood. They also contended that Arbery had entered a house being built in the neighborhood (as had several other white passersby as recorded by a surveillance camera, none of whom the McMichaels chased). The Glynn County police said that the Brunswick district attorney's office told them on the day of the incident that no arrests should be made, and Brunswick Judicial Circuit Court Judge Jackie Johnson concurred.

After Johnson recused herself because of previous ties to the McMichael family, the case was assigned to District Attorney George Barnhill of neighboring Waycross. Barnhill later said that the killing of Arbery "was justifiable homicide" before recusing himself because of professional connections with the McMichaels. There was no national or much local outcry at this killing until ironically Gregory McMichael asked that a video recording of the incident be released. The recording was taken by a third white man, William Bryan, whom the McMichaels had called and who was following them in his car. It was only after the video became widely dispersed on the media that national attention focused on the case. Subsequently, both Gregory and Travis McMichael were arrested for felony murder and aggravated assault charges; Bryan was arrested for felony murder and attempt to commit false imprisonment charges.

Many critics claimed that the McMichaels' killing of Arbery was another instance where white people felt themselves absolutely justified in taking the law into their own hands in confronting a Black person, seeing themselves as proper extensions of law enforcement in the pursuit of Blacks—a belief and practice whose origins extend into slavery and the master's pursuit of the slave, as well as in the Black Codes laws after the Civil War. This legacy extends as well to the violence of the Ku Klux Klan and the general history of whites terrorizing Blacks, particularly in but not limited to the South.

———

The nationwide protests over the murder of George Floyd by the police invoked the killings of Breonna Taylor and Ahmaud Arbery. They invoked the killing of Eric Garner, who was strangled to death by New York police officer Daniel Pantaleo (using a chokehold, which had been banned from police practice). Pantaleo was eventually fired five years after the incident, but he was never charged with any crime. As Pantaleo continued to choke Garner after he was wrestled to the ground, Garner can be heard in a bystander video recording saying over and over, "I can't breathe, I can't breathe"—cries that George Floyd repeated.

These were not the only police killings that the protests invoked. Locally, in the Twin Cities where I live, there were the police killings of Philando Castile and Jamar Clark. Nationwide, there were other deaths of unarmed Black men by the police: the killing in Chicago of Laquan McDonald and the subsequent police coverup; the killing of Alton Sterling in Baton Rouge outside a convenience store as he was selling CDs and had reportedly threatened a man with a gun (the store owner said Sterling was "not the one causing trouble"); the killing of twelve-year-old Tamar Rice playing with a toy gun in a park in Cleveland; the killing of Walter Scott in North Charleston, South Carolina, who was shot in the back by a policeman who lied and said Scott had reached for his gun; the killing of seventeen-year-old Trayvon Martin by self-appointed vigilante George Zimmerman, as Martin walked from a convenience store to the apartment where he lived with his father in Sanford, Florida.

But the protests over George Floyd's killing also invoked for many another incident that did not involve police or armed white men, an incident that occurred in New York City's Central Park the same day Floyd was killed. A white woman, Amy Cooper, had let her dog run without a leash in the Ramble woodlands area of the park, where signs instruct that dogs be leashed because it's a protected area for bird-watching. One such bird-watcher, African American Christian Cooper (no relation), asked Amy Cooper to leash her dog. When she refused, Christian Cooper held out a dog treat—an action attracting dogs that he had used before to help get owners to leash their dog. At the same time, he started to record the confrontation with his phone. She threated to call the police on him and said she was going "to tell them there's an African American man threatening" her life. He told her to go ahead. She called the police, repeated those words, and emphasized that he was an "African American man."

In doing this, even though she was the one breaking the posted park rules, Amy Cooper called on the same white privilege the McMichaels and George Zimmerman invoked, the assumed white right for ordinary white citizens to police the actions of Black people. She did not worry that she was making a false accusation; she assumed that when the police arrived, they would side with her, a white woman, against the word of a Black man. She exercised her right to be considered innocent as a white woman, implying his guilt as a Black man. She demonstrated that *guilty* and *Black* are synonymous—for the police and for a professional white woman who has been a supporter of Democratic politicians such as John Kerry, Barack Obama, and Pete Buttigieg.

Though Amy Cooper later apologized for her actions, she was fired by her company, and she has complained that her "entire life is being destroyed right now." She clearly does not see herself in a long line of white women who have falsely accused Black men of crimes, accusations that have resulted in their deaths, lynchings, and other forms of racial violence: that bloody history includes Emmett Till, the Scottsboro Boys, and the 1921 Tulsa Race Massacre. She claims her actions were distorted by her fear of being confronted while alone in the Ramble, but her apology does not reference the deep racist roots of white people's fear of Black men. In her apology she claims she is not a racist; most likely she considers herself to be a liberal Democrat, not aligned with any conservative white vigilantes like the McMichaels or Zimmerman. Yet her actions indicate how white supremacy has been programmed deeply into the ways she sees the world around her, both consciously and unconsciously. At that moment, her racist programming snapped into place and revealed itself.

By the time the police arrived, both Amy Cooper and Christian Cooper were thankfully gone. But if they hadn't been, what she was calling down on him could easily have turned into what happened to George Floyd. If the Amy Coopers of America are programmed to act like this, why would we expect the mainly male, white-dominated, mostly conservative-leaning police forces of America to act any differently?

Of course, they do not.

Black people know they are not safe in America; they are not safe from police racial profiling, brutality, and murder; they are not safe from racist white vigilantes like the McMichaels or George Zimmerman; they are not safe from racist yet liberal-minded white women like Amy Cooper. They are not safe from Covid-19, from vast health disparities, fostered by racism and a medical system that fails them time again. Safety ought to be a basic human right in this country, but for a vast portion of Black and Brown people in America, this is not the case.

II

A couple of days ago, after coming back from a demonstration, I broke down in tears and sobbed in my son Nikko's arms. I began this book with an account of the killing of Philando Castile not more than two miles from our house in a near suburb of St. Paul, and now I am writing this essay just days after another local killing of a Black man by police in my hometown.

I live no more than three miles from where George Floyd was killed and even closer to the Third Precinct of the Minneapolis police, which was a center of demonstrations for the past week. Two of my adult children, Samantha and Nikko, work with young people from the area, Sam as the head of 826 Minneapolis, an organization that conducts creative writing classes and tutoring for underprivileged populations, and Nikko as a counselor and youth worker with the YMCA and Roosevelt High School. Both are angry and saddened by George Floyd's killing by the police; they are worried for the young people and students they work with and for the neighborhood in which we all live. One of Nikko's students, the brave seventeen-year-old Darnella Frazier, recorded the central video of Floyd's murder. Two of the other witnesses to Floyd's murder went to high school with my sons, Nikko and Tomo.

My children and I have participated in the local demonstrations, including my youngest, Tomo, who marched in Chicago. Nikko was almost hit twice by rubber bullets, one passing by his head and one missing him while he tried to help a fellow demonstrator who had been hit. He and his girlfriend, a Somali American, tried to talk some young people out of trashing a check cashing establishment and, for a moment, succeeded.

My three children went to a high school that is less than a mile from where Floyd was killed and a few blocks from the Third Precinct. It's a high school that is 20 percent Native American, 20 percent Black and East African (Somali, Ethiopian, Eritrean), 20 percent Latinx, 10 percent Asian, and 30 percent white. That same mix is what showed up at the demonstrations, a multiethnic, multiracial outpouring of anger, grief, outrage. Those demonstrators insisted that it is not just the police departments of this country that must change: we must do far, far, far more to erase the racism that exists as a system in all our institutions, in all areas of society, in so many of our everyday practices and beliefs, in a culture that has programmed the supporters of President Donald Trump and also the Amy Coopers who see themselves as opposed to them.

Much has been written about George Floyd, the police, and the political demonstrations that followed his death. I want to cite here a couple of items from my local paper, the *Star Tribune,* which provide some context for these events those elsewhere might not be aware of. The first is based on a Facebook post I put up around that time:

> For my friends across the country, here's a link to a local *Star Tribune* op-ed by a white resident of the neighborhood who witnessed an encounter involving Derek Chauvin, the officer who killed Floyd George by pressing a knee on George's neck. The writer describes three police cars closing in on three ten-year-old black boys and the pointlessly cruel way Chauvin treated the boys who were eventually let go—a treatment which gave chills to both the writer and another bystander. The white writer, David Leusser, chastises himself for not reporting or doing anything about the incident (see something, say something):
>
> > Now I am complicit. There's no other way to describe it. I should have done more, filed a report, said something out loud. It's my neighborhood, my city, my responsibility.
> >
> > I recognized two policemen in the video this week. The white one—the one with his knee on the man's neck—sent chills down my spine the last time I saw him. He patrols our block and the intersection of 38th and Chicago where, the other day, his partner stood in front of him unmoved. If you are white like me and you have not watched the video, you are complicit too.
> >
> > There was another incident last summer. I could see flashing lights from our front lawn. If you are reading this

from the suburbs or out state or from a corner of Minneapolis that seems far away and different let me describe our neighborhood.

It is mostly white. Many, many, young families push strollers and walk their dogs past our house every hour. There are black people too, they push strollers and walk dogs and are kind to us. My friend Tracey watches the church that's kitty-corner from our house and helps the kids at the local park collect money for church camp. He raked our lawn last fall when I couldn't get to it. He's black. I'm white. I'm embarrassed that I have to say that.

But I grew up in the suburbs and I spent my childhood visiting grandparents in southwest Minneapolis and I get it. The temptation to write off an area as "rough" or "bad" or "dangerous." Our neighborhood is none of those things. It used to get me off the hook, though, let me think there must have been a reason. The police were just doing their job.

And often the police are doing a good job. I am old and white and it is easy for me to trust the police—generally. But this guy was different.

So when I saw the flashing lights at the end of the block at Chicago Avenue near the corner of Phelps Park last summer, I remembered Philando Castile. I thought, I can be a witness if need be. So I walked the two blocks and stood, exactly two blocks from where a man died yesterday. There were three black boys around 10 years old. They looked a little confused. They were quiet. There were three police cars surrounding them and stopping traffic on Chicago Avenue. It was broad daylight.

I didn't get it. Four policemen were standing around cars. One was shielding a white policeman who was interrogating the boys. They were quiet and calm and didn't have much to say. A white woman was asking the cops what the boys had done. She was very respectful. The police ignored her.

By then I was within sight of the police and another white woman came out of her house and watched with me. There was something about this white policeman that scared me. He kept the boys for another five minutes or more without saying or doing anything. It was clear he was the powerful one, the one in charge. The other police clearly would do nothing without his cue.

Finally he let the boys go. There is no connection between him and the boys, no kindly, be-careful-out-there moment. Instead there is something chilling about his attitude and the subservience the other officers exhibit.

The two other white neighbors who have been witness share a look with me. One of them tells me there was evidently a call from the park building about the boys. What could they have done to elicit three police cars and six officers, we wondered.

Here's another item from that time. In the *Star Tribune,* Olivia Rodriguez wrote an op-ed from her perspective as a local teacher at a North Side school, which is predominantly Black. The Floyd encounter was in a part of South Minneapolis that is more racially mixed. She asked her all-Black sixth and seven graders to write a short piece called "My America":

Nearly 100% of my class wrote about their fear of police and police brutality. In seventh-grade words, they expressed unjust behaviors by authorities towards them. They are 12 and 13 years old. They do not need this weight on their shoulders right now. Their goals should be learning and being a kid. I sat down at my desk and sobbed thinking of what my students go through on a daily basis while they are walking, playing and talking while black. My students are funny, smart, worldly, wise, creative, loving, caring, generous, and independent young people. . . . Right now, they do not feel safe. As a young white child in St. Paul, I felt the police were there to protect me. My students have never felt that. This needs to change.

Let's not hurry past her first statement: nearly a hundred percent of her Black students describe America as a place where police brutality and injustice underline *their definition of this country*. What happened to George Floyd was not the exception but the rule, the inevitable outcome of a justice system that programmatically profiles and brutalizes African Americans and other people of color. What happened to George Floyd is an object lesson to so many Black children and their parents, a lesson that fills all of them with a waking terror that they can never be free of. If you are a Black parent, you not only have to be constantly worried about your own safety from the police, but you must also live with the knowledge that your children will grow up with the same fear and worry—and that nothing in your vast love for them can stop this.

In "Dear Editor," an essay he wrote shortly after the murder of George Floyd, my friend the African American poet Douglas Kearney says:

> As my wife and I explained to our ten-year-olds (who learned explicitly about a then-contemporaneous application of this constant, historic killing when St. Anthony police officer Jeronimo Yanez murdered Philando Castile): it isn't that law enforcement is simply disinterested in protecting Black people, but that US Culture/Law dictate that our very presence is the thing they are meant to protect against. . . .
>
> That White Supremacy put me in a position to make this a reasonable conversation to have with my then-six-year-olds is a violence I will never forgive. I will go to work carrying it. I will share social space carrying it. I will form friendships carrying it. Yet I will not forgive it.

Kearney's words here about his children, the students in Olivia Rodriguez's class: they haunt me, as they should every American.[1]

———

1. In their current attacks against Critical Race Theory and the teaching of America's racial history, conservatives cite the potential damage and hurt white children might experience learning about what actually occurred in our country's past. And yet these same conservatives are untroubled by the fact that Kearney and other Black parents must talk with their children about America's racially violent past because these parents and their children live in an America that perpetuates racial violence against Black people.

In 1992, nearly thirty years ago, my friend, the novelist and educator Alexs Pate, and I cowrote and acted in a performance piece *Secret Colors,* which began with the Rodney King video, one of the first recordings of police brutality that captured national attention. In the piece we examined the events that preceded and followed his beating: the sentence of no jail time for Korean store owner Soon Ja Du, who shot and killed fifteen-year-old Latasha Harlins over an argument about whether she was stealing a carton of orange juice; the acquittal of the police officers charged with the beating; the violence that followed the court's decision; the conflicts between Korean store owners and the Black and Latino communities; the Black community's outrage and anger that even with video proof of the brutality the police were still not held to account. (Few outside the community knew the Black community was also reacting to Du's lenient sentence for the killing of Latasha Harlins.)

During the time we were working on our performance piece, a policeman was shot at a Lake Street pizza parlor in Minneapolis. From witnesses, a sketch of the suspect, a Black man with dreadlocks, was created and then distributed throughout the city, and there was an understandable reaction of the police to capture the person who killed one of their own. But this sketch also had a profound effect on the Black community. When Pate went into a bar, the bartender would look at him and his dreads and then look at the sketch. When Pate went into a restaurant or a grocery store, the same thing would happen. After a couple of weeks of this constant surveillance, Pate was driving from St. Paul to Minneapolis on I-94, and there came over him an overwhelming feeling that he had killed someone. The feeling was so strong he had to pull over to the side of the road and say to himself, "You didn't kill anyone, you didn't kill anyone." He then wrote a poem, which went into our performance, called "The Outlaw Comes to Know Himself," about the constant placement of guilt on him and other Black men, about how that sense of guilt burdens their psyche but also comes to be seen as fate, as something that can't be avoided. Eventually he came to realize that his own psychological and spiritual recovery from America's racism would involve his recapturing a sense of innocence, which America's racist portraits of Blacks had taken away from him. (Richard Pryor used to comment, "I was a child until I was eight. Then I became a Negro.")

About eight years ago, Pate devised a program called the Innocent Classroom, which addresses the racial achievement gap by training teachers to improve their relationships with students of color. I've worked in the program both as a trainer and as director of training. One purpose of the program is to help teachers see and treat African American and other BIPOC students as individuals, not as embodiments or expressions of stereotypical depictions of young people of color.

At the beginning of training sessions, Pate has educators list the nouns and adjectives used by American society to describe Black and Brown children; the list always runs to forty or fifty words, almost all of them negative: criminal, angry, sassy, ugly, welfare, unwed mothers, gangs, violent, dangerous, stupid, dropout, less than, illegal, poor, promiscuous, alien, terrorist, absent fathers, threatening, thugs, drug uses/pushers, unemployed, absent, loud, unruly, disinterested, going nowhere—and so on. When the list is finished and displayed in front of the teachers, Pate talks about *stereotype threat,* a phenomenon that has been proven in academic research: the presence or knowledge of negative stereotypes has a detrimental effect on test taking and academic achievement. And of course, many young people of color come to feel that this list is not only descriptive, but it spells out their fate, what they will inevitably be.

Many conservatives, including some conservative Black thinkers, maintain that it is liberal pessimism about race that holds back Black children, since the assessed entrenchment of racism supposedly drains these children of initiative. But this list of negative stereotypes does not arrive from any liberal analysis of race, but from the pervasive racist way white Americans think of Black Americans and the ways white Americans continue to foster and dispense these stereotypes, consciously and unconsciously. Indeed, at an almost entirely Black Minneapolis grade school where I worked as a trainer in the Innocent Classroom, one fifth grade teacher asked his students for a list of terms for how American society views children of color, and the ten- and-eleven-year-old students came up with a list very similar to the one their teachers came up with.[2]

2. The Innocent Classroom doesn't instruct teachers to ask their students about the perception of children of color in American society; that's not part of the program. The teacher in this case decided on his own to ask his students about the ways they thought they were perceived.

None of these terms was derived from anything like Critical Race Theory (again an absurd notion), but simply the students' own perceptions of the society they live in and how that society views them. When the fifth grade class finished their list, they discussed among themselves the impact and significance of the terms and began to ask about an antidote to this list. One of the students said, "It's education," and another observed that when they misbehave they are messing with this antidote. Rather than hinder their belief in education, a clear assessment of the racism in American society led the students to a greater belief in their education.

The persistence of these negative stereotypes can be seen in the cultural depictions of Black people (which many are trying to change) and the ways they are portrayed in both liberal and conservative media and politics. But these stereotypes are reinforced every time a Black child enters a SuperAmerica or Target and is racially profiled, eyed with suspicion, and followed, in a real-life demonstration of the historic criminalization of Blackness. To think that these Black children don't know what many whites think of them is an insult to their intelligence, and again, their awareness of this has nothing to do with Critical Race Theory.

After the teachers create their list of negative stereotypes, Pate then tells them: *If you know this list, the children know this list. And many of them believe that you see them in exactly the same way.* So, Pate implies, why would such students be inclined to trust you? You cannot assume their trust or their belief in your good will; you will have to earn that, since your students live in a world that does not trust them or see their innocence as children.

But all children need to feel a sense of innocence, says Pate. A sense of their own innocence is what is required for them to believe in themselves and their future, for them to feel a sense of optimism, for them to believe that their education has a purpose and a promise. One key purpose of the Innocent Classroom is to nurture initiative in the students within a space of innocence, where negative stereotypes of a racist culture do not shape their thinking and their identities, where they are free from such clichés.

Since the Innocent Classroom focuses on education, what Pate doesn't add is the obvious: if many of the students believe some of their teachers see them like this, how can the students not believe the police see them like this? For, as in Olivia Rodriguez's class, her Black students *know* the police see them like this; the police treat them as if the stereotypes are not false projections of white supremacy but actual descriptions of Black and Brown children. CHILDREN.

Like so many others, I have been feeling a sense of anger and outrage at this senseless killing of George Floyd. But today I feel an immense sadness for the ways our country is failing another generation of young Black kids and kids of color. Their anger is palpable on the streets of Minneapolis and across the country and the world; it is present every day in the children my children work with. And part of this anger is that many have lost a sense of their own innocence.

This is what we are doing to Black children all across America—and yet we ask them to believe in a country and a police force that oppress them daily; an educational system that fails so many of them, so often racially profiling them in ways similar to the police (Black kindergarteners are four times more likely than white kindergarteners to be suspended); a housing system that still uses de facto redlining and other methods to maintain racial segregation; an industrial and government regulation system that pours pollution upon their neighborhoods and keeps it away from white neighborhoods; an economic system that ensures that Black unemployment will remain higher than white unemployment, and even more so in the time of Covid-19; a health system where Blacks suffer from Covid-19 deaths at a far higher rate than whites.

All of this is why Black people, Indigenous people, Asian people, Latinx people, Arab people, and white people are marching in my city, are marching on the streets of America even as I write this. For Black people, specifically, it is actually and surely a miracle, a testament to their humanity and patriotism that so many of them are marching and protesting peacefully, that so many do not want to destroy their neighborhoods or the property of their neighbors, but simply want to walk the streets and feel safe from the police; they want to breathe and to breathe the air of justice, an air that so many white Americans take for granted—that we as a country have denied Black Americans for four hundred years.

Coda

Daunte Wright

I FIRST ENDED THIS BOOK WITH THE PRECEDING ESSAY WHEN I SENT MY manuscript to the University of Minnesota Press in February 2021.

Then, on Easter Sunday, April 11, 2021, near the end of the trial of former police officer Derek Chauvin for the murder of George Floyd, another local Black man was killed by the police. In Brooklyn Center, Minnesota, just ten miles from where Chauvin was being tried, police stopped twenty-year-old Daunte Wright for expired license tags and for having an air freshener hanging from his rearview mirror. One officer tried to arrest and handcuff Daunte for an outstanding misdemeanor charge and for failure to show for a court date, but he wrested free and jumped back in the driver seat. As her fellow officer grabbed Daunte, Officer Kim Potter yelled, "Taser, taser, taser!" And then she shot Daunte not with her taser but with her Glock 17 handgun, and she killed him.

Given all that has happened in the Twin Cities with George Floyd's murder, given all the national publicity about that murder and the demonstrations that followed, given that the trial of ex-officer Chauvin was being covered daily by the national media, I would have thought the Brooklyn Center police who stopped Daunte would have been saying to themselves, "Just don't hurt this young man, just don't kill him, just don't repeat what happened to George Floyd."

Clearly, they were not thinking such thoughts. The officer who shot and killed Daunte, Officer Kim Potter, claims that she made a mistake; that it was not her intention to kill Daunte; that she thought she was holding her taser not her gun. I understand her belief in this explanation, and I believe it is in part true. But the question still remains: would she have made this same mistake if the driver of the car had been a teenage white girl or a middle-aged white woman or a white businessman in a suit or a working-class white man with a MAGA hat? Would she have seen these drivers the same way she saw Daunte? Would she have felt as threatened by them and thus as nervous and prone to make such a mistake? On another level, it is safe to say that very few of the Black residents of the area believe that if a young white man was stopped in the upscale suburb of Minnetonka under similar circumstances that young white man would have met the same fate as Daunte.

In so many ways, given our racial history, given how that history has structured white identity and psychology, these police couldn't see this twenty-year-old skinny young Black man—a kid, really. Daunte was someone my son had worked with a couple of years ago in a program at Edison High School in Minneapolis, someone his fellow students at Edison once voted class clown because, said his friend Emajay Driver, Daunte "loved to make people laugh." But when the police stopped Daunte, they treated him as a mortal threat—not just a criminal but a violent dangerous criminal who had to be stopped at all costs. And what was he stopped for? For having expired license tags? (Note: the state of Minnesota is behind in mailing these tags in proper time because of the Covid-19 pandemic.) For a dangling air freshener, which is banned in Minnesota? Yes, it appears that Daunte fled from the arresting police, and it is true that Daunte had failed to appear in court on a weapons charge for possessing a gun without a permit and had a petty misdemeanor charge for marijuana possession and disorderly conduct. But none of this should have ended with his execution.

And now Daunte is gone. Gone for his one-year-old son, Daunte Jr. Gone for his partner, Khaleda Rhaman, who was in the car and witnessed his murder. Gone for his mother, whom Daunte had called after he was stopped. Gone for his father and sister and aunt, whom I have seen this week crying out on television in anger and despair and bottomless grief for their loss. And my heart breaks for them, as it does for Philando and George and their loved ones. These men were members of my community, people I might have interacted with.

Why doesn't America value Black lives? Why didn't the police see the humanity of these men? Why does this keep happening over and over in

America? This book has been my attempt to answer these questions and to contribute to efforts to ensure that Black Lives Matter in America and will one day be valued just as much as white lives.

APPENDIX

A BRIEF GUIDE TO STRUCTURAL RACISM

White Assumptions

The Current Epistemology of White Supremacy

MOST WHITE CONSERVATIVES BELIEVE RACISM NO LONGER EXISTS IN America, or if it does, to a much lesser extent than Blacks and people of color maintain. The illusion of this postracial world is characterized by basic assumptions that hide and deny the actual practice of racial bias in any area—political, economic, social, cultural, legal, and others.

Here is a partial listing of some of these assumptions:

A racist is someone who does not believe in the equality of the races and performs acts of racial discrimination.

For a person to be deemed a racist, their acts of discrimination must entail the hurling of racial epithets, a professed belief in white supremacy, or threats or violent actions against people of color.

You cannot get anyone other than skinheads and neo-Nazis to say publicly, "I believe whites are superior, and I actively discriminate against people of color," and this proves racism is rare in today's America.

If a person professes to believe in equality and says they are not racially prejudiced, that person cannot be said to be racist or practice racial discrimination.

If a white person tells a personal or anecdotal story that illustrates that the welfare of people of color is not caused by racial discrimination but by their own actions (e.g., laziness, poor work habits, aversion to education, inferior intellect), that story is simply objective and true. Therefore, such a story cannot be said to be proof of any racism on the teller's part.

If a person professes to believe in equality and says they are not prejudiced, but they say something that might be deemed as racist (e.g., a racist joke); or if they act in a racially discriminatory manner (e.g., hiring, living with, or dating only whites)—we must believe what they profess publicly to believe, not whatever else they might say or do that contradicts their public stance.

––––––

On the basis of the above assumptions, there follows another set of assumptions that immediately cut off any possible debate about the continued existence of racism; these assumptions lay the blame for racial tensions on Blacks and others who bring up charges of racism and racial inequities:

Racism may have once been a major factor in American society, but that was in the distant past.

Racism is no longer a major factor in American society.

Those who bring up charges of racism therefore are living in the past or viewing current American society through the lens of the past.

Such people will not let the past go.

Their inability to let the past go is the source of the vast majority of racial tension that now exists in our country.

––––––

Discussions of the past inevitably bring up questions of white collective guilt and the assumptions used to neuter or block these questions:

Whites today are not responsible for the racist acts of whites in the past.

An individual white person should only be responsible for his or her actions; there is no such thing as collective guilt.

Whites today no longer benefit from the racist acts of whites in the past.

Any benefits from the past whites receive—such as Native American lands—came from actions too far in the past for us to deal with now; we can't keep dwelling in the past.

Given recent history with programs like affirmative action, whites are as likely or even more likely to have experienced racial discrimination than people of color.

———

Since racism no longer exists, additional assumptions address what is wrong with people of color who talk about race:

When people of color make a charge of racism, they are being too touchy or too sensitive. It is a misperception on their part; it may even be evidence of a fault in their character or psychological insecurity.

Any consideration of social practices that takes into account the practices of people grouped by race is inherently suspect, if not racist.

Consideration of racism is most likely a sign of racism—playing the race card.

Playing the race card is an attempt by people of color to gain an unfair advantage rhetorically, legally, economically, or politically through a false charge of racism; in practice, a false charge would be almost any charge of racism, since racism does not exist or is rare in today's America.

Every time people of color play the race card, it is further proof that in today's America it is whites who are unfairly disadvantaged or unfairly accused, and thus whites who are the real victims of racial prejudice.

———

Conversely, another assumption remains: there is a proper way to talk about race—don't.

Not talking about race (by whites or by people of color) is a sign that racism is no longer present.

Not talking about race is therefore the best way to solve any problems concerning race that might still exist.

Silence about race is proof that one is not a racist (e.g., "I don't even give a thought to considering the world in that way").

If no one talks about race, that proves racism doesn't exist.

———

A further set of assumptions addresses any evidence that might seem to argue that racism and racist practices still exist in today's America:

People should be judged as individuals and not as members of a group.

There is no need to consider any evidence of racial discrimination, since such information groups people by race.

If there is any evidence of racial bias in the practices of our society, such evidence is an exception and is more minor than it appears.

When seeming evidence of discriminatory practices is presented (e.g., lower incomes; higher rates of incarceration among Blacks and other people of color), the reason for these discrepancies is not racism.

These discrepancies are a result of individual choices (e.g., that individual didn't get an education, that individual committed a crime, that individual is lazy or stupid, that individual doesn't dress correctly).

Or these discrepancies are a result of the cultural practices of the members of the group.

Other nonracial factors—educational background, economic class, citizenship, demographics—may also be a cause of these discrepancies.

None of these nonracial factors has a racial component or cause.

No statistics can prove that racism exists in America because those statistics can be explained by any number of causes other than racism.

———

Another set of assumptions addresses the de facto continuation of racial segregation in America:

The separation of races that exists in America is not due to racial prejudice or discriminatory practices on the part of whites.

If there is proof that whites choose to live and socialize with whites, that is simply an illustration of the fact that those who are like each other live and socialize together.

The ways in which whites are like each other are not racially based but economic, cultural, religious—anything else but racial.

If whites choose to live in racially segregated areas, Blacks and other people of color do the same thing.

Blacks and other people of color self-segregate: they choose to be together because of their own racial preferences. (In such a worldview, redlining and discriminatory loan practices do not exist.)

Indeed, Blacks and other people of color are often more likely to self-segregate or racially group themselves than whites are.

––––––

Finally, any social, legal, or governmental programs that address the so-called problems of race are invalid for the following reasons:

Because of this general absence of racism, there is no significant need for programs or efforts to address the problem of racism.

Such programs merely encourage: (1) racial resentment; (2) an attachment to the past; (3) a disincentive for people of color to work harder and improve themselves and their lives.

Such programs therefore are inherently racist. They victimize people of color (by encouraging their victim psychology/psychopathology) and discriminate against whites.

––––––

While individual whites may not subscribe to all of the above assumptions, I would assert that these assumptions are fundamental to the ways most whites in today's America think and speak about race. They are fundamental to the ways in which whites on both sides of the political spectrum formulate their identities as whites; they are essential to the ideology of Whiteness.

Yet according to the above logic, as a person of color I am the racist for pointing out a basic difference between how most whites think about race and how many people of color and most Blacks think about race. Clearly, these assumptions are not premises most people of color would assent to as the basis of any discussion on race. That white interlocutors often force us to start with these assumptions underscores the power of whites as a group and the power of Whiteness as an ideology.

It's not just that the burden of proof for the existence of discrimination and other racist practices is placed almost solely on people of color—and a few renegade whites. Instead, given the above assumptions, such proof does not exist. There is no reason to argue the case—whether in the legal or political system, or in the arena of public debate. The decision has already been rendered and rendered final. Racism today either doesn't exist or is so minor and rare that no one needs to consider the subject.

Camouflaging and denial enable the practices of racial bias to continue. They are used not to hinder or prevent practices of racial bias but to defend such practices from ever being challenged. Thus they both represent and constitute the de facto and de jure continuation of racial bias in our society.

These assumptions that whites cite as proof of the absence of their racism, their racial bias, or racism in our society are deliberately used over and over again to enable racism to continue.

———

The only way for people of color to win is to refuse the premises that the majority of whites have set for the debate. But since our petitions to prove and redress racism must be made to white people, this refusal is impossible, except among ourselves.

Or so it would seem.

But if we do expose and delineate these premises, if we start the debate not on the level of proof but on the level of *how valid proof is defined,* then at least we have identified the weapons being used against us. They are the epistemological rules—the rules defining knowledge—used to enforce white supremacy. If we point out the illogical nature of these premises, if we point out their tautological characteristics, we have at least the possibility of changing the rules of the debate. At the very least, we can consciously declare our refusal to submit to these definitions and rules.

We can start instead with a declaration of our own premises: *a country that is not racist would not use and legalize a set of premises that would make it impossible to prove racism exists.* That is clearly not the country we live in.

To understand how race functions in our society, it's necessary for people to see themselves both as individuals and as members of a group.

Yet we live in a country whose culture privileges the individual over the group; our personal psychologies reflect this American tendency. In many ways, any social grouping goes against a dominant strain in American thought and culture—the emphasis on the individual.

Such cultural and historical tendency is not necessarily present in other countries and cultures. For instance, take the British novelist Doris Lessing, who was born in Iran and spent her childhood in Zimbabwe. As a female writer, Lessing's consciousness of gender roles is well known. What's perhaps less recognized was her acute awareness, in her particular racial environment, of how she was seen by others in a group setting: she was a white colonist living among African colonials.

> The fact is that we all live our lives in groups—the family, work groups, social, religious and political groups. Very few people indeed are happy as solitaries, and they tend to be seen by their neighbors as peculiar or selfish or worse. Most people cannot stand being alone for long. They are always seeking groups to belong to, and if one group dissolves, they look for another. We are group animals still, and there is nothing wrong with that. But what is dangerous is not belonging to a group, or groups, but not understanding the social laws that govern groups and govern us. When we're in a group, we tend to think as that group does: we may even have joined the group to find "like-minded" people. But we also find our thinking changing because we belong to a group. It is the hardest thing in the world to maintain an individual dissident opinion, as a member of a group.

Like many writers, I teach creative writing in poetry, memoir, and fiction. Sometimes when I work with students writing memoir, they have difficulty seeing themselves as a member of a group. This membership can involve any number of elements—gender, sexual orientation, ethnicity, race, religion, class, generation, culture, history, and so forth. This inability to recognize group membership is particularly prevalent when I deal with white students, especially with the question of their white identity. Many of these white students consciously and/or unconsciously assume either that they don't have a racial identity or that such an identity is not important to who they are or their life experiences.

To illustrate the difference in these two levels of consideration—individual and group—let me cite a study done in the 1990s concerning racial profiling. According to Michelle Alexander, in *The New Jim Crow*:

> In New Jersey the data showed that only 15 percent of all drivers on the New Jersey Turnpike were racial minorities, yet 42 percent of all stops and 73 percent of all arrests were of black motorists—despite the fact that blacks and whites violated traffic laws at almost exactly the same rate. While radar stops were relatively consistent with the percentage of minority violators, discretionary stops made by officers involved in drug interdiction resulted in double the number of stops of minorities.

It is worth noting that despite this racial discrepancy in stops by police, *whites were almost twice as likely to be found carrying illegal drugs or contraband as African Americans and five times more likely to be found with contraband than Latinos.*

These statistics represent the experience of all drivers, white and those of color, on the New Jersey Turnpike. They indicate that if you are white, you are less likely to be stopped by the police than if you are a person of color. If you are a person of color, your experience would be that you would more likely be stopped. Thus, the individual experience of whites and people of color reflects this difference. *But no one person can experience the entirety of this difference.* In other words, this phenomenon is not something that can be validated or invalidated through the lens of individual experience: this difference can only be experienced at the level of the grouping by race, which whites have been taught to suspect, challenge, or simply deny. Just as important, if you are white and you interpret our society solely on the basis of your individual experience, you must a priori discount statistics that group individual experience by race. Moreover, these statistics can never have the emotional and personal relevance to your view of the world that your own individual experience possesses. If you are white, you drove down this stretch of highway and were not stopped. That is your individual experience. At the same time, you did not generally see Black motorists stopped.

This does not mean that you as a white person do not think about the world on a group level. You do. You generalize from your own individual experience to all those who drive on that highway. If you insist on the primacy of individual experience, the statistics of what actually happens on that highway are basically irrelevant to you and your experience. When you are presented with these statistics, your individual experience has not equipped you to make the leap from your individual experiences to the level of a racial group different from your own.

But if you are a person of color, your individual experience of the highway is more likely to be that you have been stopped at some point while driving. Moreover, you are far more likely to have heard other individual accounts by people of color that affirm your own experience. When you are presented with the statistics concerning the sum total of experiences on this highway and those statistics demonstrate a racial bias, those numbers affirm your individual experience. It is therefore far easier for you as a person of color to make the leap from your own individual experience to that of your racial group and to see the experiences of those in your racial group as different from the experience of whites. Unlike most whites, you experience no logical contradiction between your experience as an individual and as a member of a group. At the same time, you can also readily acknowledge that the group experience of whites who rode down that road was different from the group experience of people of color: you don't generalize from your own experience and believe that white people experience the same reality as you do.

All this is simply one illustration of why white people have a hard time seeing themselves as members of a group, much less a group whose experiences are different from those of people of color as a group. What may be less clear is this: in any conversation about race, most whites start with the a priori suspicion (if not basic denial) of any description of experience grouped by race.

———

In a *New York Times* article from 2016 titled "A History of White Delusion," Nicholas Kristof examines the ways whites constantly underestimate the prevalence of racial bias in our society. Here is an excerpt from his piece:

In 1962, 85 percent of white Americans told Gallup that black children had as good a chance as white kids of getting a good education. The next year, in another Gallup survey, almost half of whites said that blacks had just as good a chance as whites of getting a job.

In retrospect, we can see that these white beliefs were delusional, and in other survey questions whites blithely acknowledged racist attitudes. In 1963, 45 percent said that they would object if a family member invited a black person home to dinner. . . .

Half of white Americans today say that discrimination against whites is as big a problem as discrimination against blacks. Really? That contradicts overwhelming research showing that blacks are more likely to be suspended from preschool, to be prosecuted for drug use, to receive longer sentences, to be discriminated against in housing, to be denied job interviews, to be rejected by doctors' offices, to suffer bias in almost every measurable sector of daily life.[1]

In certain cases, white delusion results from an ignorance of the facts and statistics. But this delusion is more extensive and deeper than simply ignorance. Even when presented with facts that contradict their stated beliefs, many whites continue to believe that racism is either over or less prevalent than others maintain; in some cases they even believe whites are more discriminated against than people of color.

This delusion is built into the rules of Whiteness—into the ways that white identity is constructed and into the rules of that identity concerning the nature of knowledge:

Ignore our racial history and assume that there is no connection between the past and the present—if the white person cannot see the connection, it must not exist.

Assume racism is always less extensive than Black people say it is.

Assume that Blacks and people of color are not credible witnesses to their own existence and lives.

_____

1.   http://www.nytimes.com/2016/07/14/opinion/a-history-of-white-delusion.html?action=click&pgtype=Homepage&clickSource=story-heading&module=opinion-c-col-left-region&region=opinion-c-col-left-region&WT.nav=opinion-c-col-left-region&_r=0.

Assume that only the white perspective and epistemology matters and gets to determine what is objective and what is the nature of reality.

The assumed primacy of the white view of reality over the Black view of reality—the basic premise of white epistemology—is what binds the racism of the past to the racism of the present.

Acknowledgments

I THANK CAROLYN HOLBROOK, MY FRIEND AND COEDITOR OF *WE ARE*
Meant to Rise: Voices for Justice from Minneapolis to the World, for suggesting I send the manuscript of this book to our editor Erik Anderson. Erik showed a keen understanding of what my book was about, and his criticism, support, and encouragement have been invaluable and restorative. I thank the staff at the University of Minnesota Press for their professionalism, enthusiasm, and hard work, including Jeff Moen, Heather Skinner, Maggie Sattler, Shelby Connelly, Emily Hamilton, and Rachel Moeller. Louisa Castner was particularly helpful as my copy editor and suggested excellent editorial advice. Agent Scott Edelstein provided valuable input in negotiating my contract and took me on even as he was retiring.

My friend Alexs Pate has been there for me for many years, as a friend and colleague. Through our work together, our dialogues, and his own work, he has shaped my thinking on race now for three decades. My friend and colleague Frank Wilderson and his work on Afropessimism have also been extremely influential. One day they'll write about how these two leading African American writers and theorists made their home for a time in Minneapolis.

I'd like to thank the many friends and writers who have supported me over the years: Garrett Hongo, my brother, another key influence on my thinking about race and key reader of my work and this book; Bao Phi, Ed Bok Lee, Sun Yung Shin, fellow community writers; Juliana Pegues, scholar and theorist; Elmaz Abinader, Diem Jones, Junot Díaz, M. Evelina Galang, Chris Abani, Maurice Carlos Ruffin, ZZ Packer, Suheir Hammad, Willie Perdomo, fellow VONA writers; Tim Seibles, with whom I have been talking about race since our MFA program; Alexis Paige and Lauren Alleyne, whose friendships and phone calls have sustained me; Sun Mee Chomet, for her constant encouragement and steadfast friendship.

Some of the thinking in this book started with my teaching a workshop, Writing on Race, for the Stonecoast MFA program, and I thank my fellow teacher in that course, Richard Hoffman, and the director, Annie Finch, for supporting that work. Lucille Clifton treated me as one of her poetic sons and welcomed me in a way that told me I belonged; Quincy Troupe and his stories instructed me on what it means to be an artist of color.

I thank my parents, Tom and Terry Mura, and my siblings, Susan, John, and Linda, for their love and support. Through their experiences and perspectives, my children, Samantha, Nikko, and Tomo, have taught me about the multiethnic, multiracial world they grew up in here in the Twin Cities. Finally, I owe countless and incalculable thanks to my wife, Dr. Susan Sencer, who has loved me and read my work since we first met in college. I would not be the writer or person I am without her.